# OLIVER FORD DAVIES

Oliver Ford Davies played his first Shakespeare leads, Othello and Falstaff, when a student at Oxford. He then became a history lecturer at Edinburgh University and a regional drama critic for the *Guardian* and the BBC. In 1967 he began as a professional actor at the Birmingham Rep and went on to leading parts in the regions and the West End in plays as diverse as *The School for Scandal*, *Tonight at 8.30*, *Hadrian VII* and *Long Day's Journey into Night*.

Since 1975 he has appeared in twenty-six productions for the Royal Shakespeare Company, including fifteen Shakespeares. His work at the National Theatre has ranged from *Hamlet* to the 1993 David Hare trilogy. For his role as Lionel Espy in Hare's *Racing Demon* he won the Olivier Award for Best Actor. Since 1997 he has played at the Almeida Theatre in *Ivanov* (the first British production of Chekhov to visit Moscow), Pirandello's *Naked* (with Juliette Binoche) and *Richard II* and *Coriolanus* (with Ralph Fiennes), which visited Tokyo and New York in 2000.

His films range from *Sense and Sensibility* to *Star Wars Episodes I* and *II*, and his many television appearances include five series as Head of Chambers in *Kavanagh QC*. He has also written plays for the theatre, television and the radio. *Playing Lear* is his first book.

# PLAYING LEAR

*Oliver Ford Davies*

London

# NICK HERN BOOKS

www.nickhernbooks.co.uk

A NICK HERN BOOK

*Playing Lear* first published in Great Britain in 2003
as a paperback original by Nick Hern Books Limited,
14 Larden Road, London W3 7ST

*Playing Lear* copyright © 2003 Oliver Ford Davies

Oliver Ford Davies has asserted his moral right
to be identified as the author of this work

British Library cataloguing data for this book
is available from the British Library

ISBN 1 85459 698 5

Cover design: Ned Hoste, 2H
Cover photo: Ivan Kyncl

Typeset by Country Setting, Kingsdown, Kent CT14 8ES
Printed and bound in Great Britain by Biddles, Guildford

FOR JENNY AND MIRANDA

# CONTENTS

# ILLUSTRATIONS

1. GONERIL: 'Sir, I do love you more than word can wield the matter.' Lear and Goneril (Oliver Ford Davies and Suzanne Burden), Act I, Scene i

2. THE FOOL: 'Can you make no use of nothing, nuncle?' The Fool (Anthony O'Donnell) and Lear, Act I, Scene iv

3. LEAR: 'O, Regan, will you take her by the hand?' Lear, the Fool, Regan (Lizzy McInnerny) and Goneril, Act II, Scene iv

4. LEAR: 'Blow winds and crack your cheeks!' The set, largely destroyed, Act III, Scene ii

5. KENT: 'Trouble him not; his wits are gone.' Gloucester (David Ryall), Kent (Paul Jesson), Lear, Edgar (Tom Hollander), Act III, Scene vi

6. LEAR: 'When we are born we cry that we are come to this great stage of fools.' Edgar, Gloucester and Lear, Act IV, Scene vi

7. CORDELIA: 'O my dear father, restoration hang thy medicine on my lips.' Cordelia (Nancy Carroll) and Lear, Act IV, Scene vii

8. LEAR: 'And my poor fool is hanged.' Cordelia and Lear, Act V, Scene iii

*All photos included by kind permission of Ivan Kyncl*

# ACKNOWLEDGEMENTS

I am hugely grateful to Jonathan Kent, artistic director of the Almeida Theatre, for asking me to play King Lear. His guidance, friendship and encouragement during rehearsal and performance have been incalculable. I also want to thank the Almeida staff for their support and extraordinary good humour. Nick Hern took a risk, on slim evidence, in agreeing to publish this book, and he and everyone at NHB have been ever-helpful. I am grateful to Ivan Kyncl both for his skill and his permission to use his photographs. I owe more than I can say to John Barton, who first cast me as a mad old man in John Ford's *Perkin Warbeck* nearly thirty years ago. His understanding of Shakespeare and his help over this book have been invaluable.

My daughter Miranda loves this play and has kindly given me numerous tutorials, mostly in Chinese restaurants.

I would especially like to thank my partner the actor Jenifer Armitage for our continuing dialogue about acting and the theatre.

# PLAYING LEAR

# *I*

# INTRODUCTION

In the spring of 1998 Jonathan Kent asked me to play Lear at the Almeida. 'Um . . . yes,' I replied. Actors don't say 'no' to Lear or Hamlet. The parts appear some sort of ultimate . . . but ultimate what? Test, accolade, exploration of the human condition? 'Better do it while you've still got the energy,' said Jonathan. There's no right age to play Lear. At fifty you have the energy, at seventy you have the empathy. I'm sixty – ideal compromise, or neither one thing or the other? I open the new Arden edition. '*King Lear* stands like a colossus at the centre of Shakespeare's achievement as the grandest effort of his imagination', writes Professor Foakes.[1] I feel the pressure mounting already.

David Hare, who directed Anthony Hopkins at the National Theatre, tries to cheer me. 'Look, there are eleven scenes, and no one can do them all. You're bound to be able to do some.' No actor can claim Lear lies within his range, it doesn't lie within anyone's range. Paul Scofield once suggested that the heights of the play must be reached by parachute rather than mountaineering. I think of Ralph Richardson's dictum that playing a large Shakespeare part is like lying on the floor with a machine gun firing at a ceiling covered with targets – you're bound to hit some bulls-eyes. A strange analogy, but comforting (mind you, Richardson avoided playing Lear all his life). Anyway it's just a part in a play (actors always say that when desperate – do violinists say 'it's only the Beethoven'?). And is the play really that good? Lamb said it couldn't be acted, Thackeray was bored by it, Bradley said it wasn't his best play, and Tolstoy found it riddled with

---

1 The best general introductions to *King Lear* are in R.A. Foakes's Arden edition (1997), and Stanley Wells's Oxford edition (2000). As the Oxford edition prints only the first quarto text, my scene and line references throughout are to the Arden edition (with the exception that I have divided the Arden 2.2. into 2.2, 2.3, and 2.4.). Whenever I quote Foakes and Wells without attribution it is from these introductions.

inconsistencies and poor motivations. I like the Howard Brenton plot summary – that you have a terrible family row and slam out of the house into the rain on Clapham Common: you shout at the rain for a bit, and then think – what am I going to do now? I tell Fiona Shaw, who's currently playing Medea, I'm determined not to see it as a test. 'No, no,' she replies, 'but of course it is.'

I was playing in Pirandello's *Naked* at the Almeida in 1998. It was my second production there with Jonathan Kent; the first had been Chekhov's early play *Ivanov* the previous year.[2] Acting in Chekhov with Jonathan, Ralph Fiennes, Harriet Walter, Bill Paterson, Diane Bull and Anthony O'Donnell, in a translation by David Hare, had proved one of the happiest times of my life. In April 1997 we'd played it at the Maly Theatre in Moscow, the first British production of a Chekhov to play in Russia. The Almeida has nothing if not cheek. Our extrovert style divided Russian critics, and apparently caused mayhem in the Stanislavsky-bound drama schools. *Naked* is another matter. If the British have a love affair with Chekhov, they have a hate affair with Pirandello. Too philosophical, too arid, too clever-clever. *Naked* is indeed a clever, teasing play. The entire action, till the closing minutes, is a dissection of what might or might not have happened in an incident months before. I played Ludovico Nota, a middle-aged writer, who invites back to his rooms a young woman, Ersilia, recovering from a suicide attempt. Does he want her as lover, housekeeper, daughter, specimen, muse? Perhaps all five? Jonathan, with typical bravura, had persuaded Juliette Binoche to play Ersilia. The play opened with a twenty-five minute duologue between Juliette and myself, which we rehearsed endlessly and with a great deal of laughter. The Almeida might only be paying £225 a week, but it does offer great compensations.

The Almeida has an extraordinary and chequered history. The building was completed in 1837 as the Islington Literary and Scientific Institute. This society was wound up in 1872 and the building became the Wellington Club Music Hall, where cockfights and wrestling matches were held: education and fighting, the two faces of Victoriana. Thirty years later it switched radically again and became a Salvation Army Citadel, and the auditorium was refashioned in its present format. From 1956 it was used as a 'carnival novelties

2  *Ivanov* was in a new version by David Hare (1997), and *Naked* in a new version by Nicholas Wright (1998).

manufactory and showroom' and eventually fell into dereliction, to
be rescued by Pierre Audi and his associates who opened it as a
theatre in 1981. In 1990 Ian McDiarmid and Jonathan Kent took it
over as a full-time producing theatre, and have presented a daring
mixture of classical and new plays, opera and new music. Through
its innovative work and tours at home and abroad, the Almeida has
gained a fanatical following and a huge international reputation.
Over it all hangs appropriately the whiff of lectures, wrestling, hot
gospelling and sulphur.

Ludovico Nota in *Naked* is one in a long line of father/uncle/sur-
rogate father figures that I have been playing all my life. Shakespeare
is rich in them. Right from the beginning of his career he examines
them in Capulet and Friar Laurence. I played both before I was 32.
Gaunt, Henry IV, Falstaff, the Banished Duke, Boyet, Camillo, Pan-
darus – they are all variations on a theme, and I've played them all.
Lear is another failed father. Perhaps that gave Jonathan the idea. To
get me in training he suggests I play in his millennium project,
*Richard II* and *Coriolanus*. Ralph Fiennes is playing both. I've already played Shabielsky, his uncle, in *Ivanov*, so why don't I play the
Duke of York and Menenius, two more of his uncle figures? I've done
both plays before, in different parts (Gaunt and Junius Brutus), and
I like the idea very much. It's ten years since I've done any Shakespeare – the last was Richard Eyre's *Hamlet* at the National, as Player
King (another surrogate father now I come to think of it). But before that Shakespeare had been my life for a decade. Between 1975
and 1986 I did fifteen of the plays at the RSC. But never *King Lear*.

Lear has been part of my mental landscape for most of my life. In
1955 my 'A' level set books were *Lear, The Winter's Tale*, Chaucer's
*Prologue* and *Knight's Tale*, and Tennyson's *In Memoriam* – serious
stuff. Some of the quotes I painstakingly learnt then have jangled
round in my mind ever since: 'as flies to wanton boys', 'nothing will
come of nothing', 'we two will sing like birds i' the cage'. I've used
them on random occasions, ironically, portentously, facetiously.
Now, forty-five years later, I face the text again. It's like standing in
the Louvre and staring again at the *Mona Lisa* after a lifetime of
seeing it at a distance in reproduction and mangled cartoon form.
This is it once more. What's so special about the real thing?

Of course I've seen productions of the play all my life. I can think
of ten, though there may be more. My father took me to see Donald
Wolfit at the King's Theatre, Hammersmith, when I was thirteen.

I remember that the set was a grey Stonehenge, that I believed Wolfit when he was being powerful and defiant but not when he was being weak and self-pitying. I later realized that Harold Pinter had been in the cast. I saw most of Michael Benthall's Shakespeares at the Old Vic in the 1950s, including Paul Rogers' strong Lear, Richard Burton as Coriolanus and Iago, John Neville as Hamlet and Othello.[3] Production values were not always lavish. There's a story that if an actor questioned Benthall about the meaning of a line, he used to reply: 'Well, if you don't understand it, the audience certainly won't, so we'll cut it.' It does speed up rehearsals.

The first Lear I remember clearly is Gielgud's, directed by George Devine in 1956. But again my memory is chiefly visual, as the designs were by Isamu Noguchi, and though intended to be timeless only succeeded in looking like outer space.[4] Kent in the stocks had one leg thrust through what appeared to be a Barbara Hepworth sculpture. It remained as a grim warning to me about futuristic settings. Gielgud, imprisoned in a huge horse-hair beard, seemed an archetype, a Merlin imbued with cosmic suffering and the wisdom of the ages. The verse speaking was consummate, and that is happily recaptured in a 1994 BBC/Renaissance audio cassette. There's something mandarin, perplexed, ironic about his Lear. It worked for him, but I think it's a dangerous model. In 1959 I went to Stratford with an Oxford University outdoor production of Jonson's *Bartholomew Fair*. Ken Loach and I were the comic villains, Knockem and Whit, and we made one entry by boat – rarely on cue, as I was rowing. In the Memorial Theatre it was the centenary season with Olivier as Coriolanus, Paul Robeson and Sam Wanamaker as Othello and Iago, Charles Laughton as Lear and Bottom, and a company including the young Albert Finney and Vanessa Redgrave. I stood at the back of the stalls to see *Lear*: those were the days when people camped out all night to get tickets. Laughton had been thinking about Lear for thirty years, but in the first half of the play he lacked, as Michael

3   I used to cycle from my home in Ealing to the Old Vic, and sit in the back row of the stalls at Saturday matinees for 2s 3d (11p; half-price to under-16s). The programme was 6d (2½p; only 1p in the Upper Circle). So the whole outing cost me 14p. Today it would be £10-15. Small wonder teenagers cannot afford to take themselves off to Shakespeare.

4   Gielgud recalled that Noguchi didn't usually do costumes, 'designed them very hastily, and left again before he had even seen the fittings'. Sheridan Morley, *John G: the Authorised Biography* (London: Hodder, 2001), p. 273.

Blakemore said, 'the machinery for the huge rhetorical passages'.[5] Bewilderment was the keynote. His reconciliation with Cordelia was heart-breaking: I shall never see it better played. It was also the first time I realized the second half of the play takes place in summer. Glen Byam Shaw, the director, had great sheaves of corn and bright sunlight, a startling contrast to the action.

Three years later, in 1962, I saw several times what has remained the benchmark production of my generation – the Peter Brook RSC production with Paul Scofield, a brooding, embattled dinosaur. It was a great performance, a great cast, a marvellous set, but Brook's interpretation was deeply troubling. Alec McCowen, who played the Fool, told me recently that he had prepared the part with great care, Brook had praised him after the read-through, and the next day had said 'So, Alec, what are we going to do with this part?' This starting from scratch, stripping bare, taking nothing for granted, is admirable. Brook, for example, insisted that Goneril and Regan's protestations of love for Lear, taken by themselves, sound perfectly sincere. But Brook cut two small but vital incidents, the comforting of Gloucester after his blinding by Cornwall's servants, and Edmund's deathbed attempt to save Lear and Cordelia. The common man and the villain were to have no redeeming features. The Brook *Lear* was unremittingly harsh, and his 1971 film goes even further down this road. Scofield, robbed of half his lines, seems entrapped within a character who barely changes and has no journey. It is hardly an accurate reflection of his stage performance. Much has been made of the influence of Jan Kott's essay, 'King Lear or Endgame', but I think the production came out of a more general 1960s apprehension of an existential, absurdist universe. There is a story that when someone complained that they hadn't been moved by his production, Brook asked: 'Where is it printed on your ticket that you should be moved by *King Lear*?' I was much impressed by this at the time, but since then I have become uneasy. Surely, at some level, we should find *The Comedy of Errors* funny, and *Titus Andronicus* shocking? However, no one who saw Scofield and McCowen sit side by side on a bench, while Lear quietly said 'O, let me not be mad', will ever forget it.

In 1971 I saw Timothy West play a strong Lear for the Prospect Theatre company. Tim was only thirty-seven, and capitalized on this

5 Simon Callow, *Charles Laughton* (London: Methuen, 1987), p. 263. For further discussion of this production see chap. 4.

by playing him very energetically at the start. In his search for a youngish Gloucester by way of balance, the director, Toby Robertson, interviewed me. I was only thirty-one, and he decided this was a step too far. It was however the first of a number of occasions when I have been shortlisted, or even offered, the part of Gloucester. It has never worked out, but it has left me with a feeling that I am seen as a natural Gloucester – and not a Lear. That's a useful piece of paranoia to take into rehearsals.

I then seem to have had a long break from seeing the play, mostly because I was with the RSC doing other Shakespeares. In the early 1990s there was a glut of Lears, and I saw most of them. First, Brian Cox, who was a crafty, wheel-chaired old devil, looking for humanity and humour at every turn. Deborah Warner, the director, turned the first scene into a wild Christmas party, where little sister wouldn't play and Santa Claus turned nasty. It was a bizarre solution, but it did emphasize the arbitrary way in which the wheel of fortune began to turn.[6] At the same time John Wood was doing it at Stratford for Nicholas Hytner – twentieth-century clothes, and a very conceptual and unhelpful set. Wood, looking like a retired gardener in old corduroys, was highly intelligent and fiercely neurotic. Three years later Tom Wilkinson did it at the Royal Court in Max Stafford-Clark's farewell production. Tom, who was particularly young for the part, played him, as he told me, like Colonel Blimp, which worked well for the earlier scenes but then seemed to limit the descent into madness. Can you do a 'character performance' as Lear, or should you play close to yourself? It's a problem I will have to solve.

Finally in 1994 I saw Robert Stephens at the RSC, who was already subdued through illness, but was very real and moving in the second half. The same could be said of Laurence Olivier in Michael Elliott's 1983 television film. I thought both were rather too keen to be liked. In Richard Eyre's 1997 film version of his National Theatre production, Ian Holm is rivetingly autocratic and splenetic, and plays the madness with great inward and idiosyncratic suffering.[7] There are two other film versions that greatly interested me. Akira Kurosawa's *Ran* is a reworking of the story, omitting the Gloucester plot and turning Lear's three children into men. It is very powerful,

6  Brian Cox gives an interesting, idiosyncratic account of this production in *The Lear Diaries* (London: Methuen, 1992).

7  The performances of Cox, Wood, Stephens and Holm are further discussed in chap. 4.

with terrific set pieces, but the cutting of most of Lear's demented speeches emasculates the part. Grigori Kozintsev's Russian film is also full of striking images and bold ideas, but his Lear is internal, tired, barely mad, making little contact with anyone except Cordelia.

I know that every Lear I have seen has influenced me in some way, whether it be in posing problems, choices, solutions, or more basely in providing ideas I can pinch. Clearly you can play Lear in many different ways, each of which will reveal different strands in the play. But you can't play every single variation – a 'Variorum' performance, as Tynan said of Michael Redgrave's final Hamlet ('at times he seems to be giving us three different interpretations of the same line *simultaneously*').[8] At some point I'm going to have to make up my mind – not too early, but let's hope not too late. At the same time I have to beware of tradition. I mustn't fall into the trap of thinking these are the only ways of playing Lear, or that certain things are immutable. I have to start from the text. I have to find my own Lear.

These thoughts were going through my mind as we did *Richard II* and *Coriolanus* in the summer of 2000. The setting was strange: an old power station, turned Gainsborough Film Studios, turned warehouse, in Shoreditch. Hitchcock had made many of his early films there, including *The Lady Vanishes*. It was, like Tate Modern in Southwark, a vast brick, secular cathedral, in our case partly ruinated. Paul Brown, who is to design *Lear*, imported for *Richard II* a floor of thick meadow grass, hummocks and all. The garden of England had invaded a ruined cathedral, a brilliant concept (use of space is one of Jonathan's many strengths). When, as Duke of York, I said:

> As in a theatre the eyes of men,
> After a well graced actor leaves the stage
> Are idly bent on him that enters next,
> Thinking his prattle to be tedious.

I knew that I was making the first mention of a 'theatre' in English drama, not half a mile from the original 'Theater' in Curtain St, where Shakespeare's early plays had been premiered. I liked that. During the run Jonathan tells me of firm plans for *Lear*. We are to do it early in 2002, in the Kings Cross bus garage the Almeida has

8  Kenneth Tynan, *Curtains* (London: Longman, 1961), p. 217.

taken over while rebuilding work is in progress. He hopes it will be an intimate space, seating no more than three hundred and fifty. *Lear* should do well in a 'found' space, with no theatrical trappings, and intimacy will suit many of the scenes. But eighteen months is a long time to wait. . .

I believe I first thought of becoming an actor when I was eleven. At school I played Richard II in a scene from Gordon Daviot's *Richard of Bordeaux*, a Gielgud triumph of the 1930s. The emotions in the scene – love for my wife, love but anger at my favourite Oxford, guilt and regret at dumping him – unleashed feelings in me I hardly knew I had. I was deep in, probably wallowing . . . it was wonderful. As best I can remember, I didn't so much want to project myself, as be someone totally different. I suspect it's the basis of my acting. Then when I was fifteen I played Mercutio in a school production of *Romeo and Juliet*. One of the staff, the philosopher John Wilson, reported to me that Clifford Williams, the director of the local rep, the Marlowe Theatre Canterbury, had seen the production and praised my performance. 'So are you going to become an actor?' John asked, as if it was the most normal thing in the world. I blushed deeply, and mumbled, 'I doubt it'. But the seed had been sown – someone professional had singled me out. Twenty-five years later I was rehearsing a play for the RSC, Solzhenitsyn's *The Love Girl and the Innocent*, directed by Clifford, and I told him the story of the indelible impression I had made on him. 'I'm sorry if I'm to blame for your becoming an actor,' said Clifford, 'but I have no memory of your performance at all.' We have remained friends.

At Oxford I was torn between theatre and history. Much was expected of me academically, as Merton College had given me a history scholarship when I was sixteen. I ran between the Bodleian and the rehearsal room. Oxford may not have been living through a golden age of actors (the McKellens and Jacobis were all at Cambridge), but it was a remarkable time for playwrights. Dennis Potter, John McGrath, Caryl Churchill, Julian Mitchell, Alan Bennett, John Wells and Terry Jones were all around. *Private Eye* was in embryo. The theatre and revue scene were buzzing. I managed to stay six years, because I started a D. Phil. thesis on the remote subject of the wealth and influence of the greater English aristocracy, 1688-1714 (I did get it eventually, but that's another story).[9] My original idea, 'Restoration

9   I was still writing it as an actor. I would arrive at a rep and, once the production was on, seek out the nearest university library and plod on.

Drama as a mirror of the social, economic, and political changes in society, 1660-1714', was firmly vetoed by Hugh Trevor-Roper: too theatre-based, too crossover. At the same time I became secretary, then president of the O.U.D.S, for whom I played Falstaff, Quince and Othello: I never seem to have played under forty in my life. However inadequate I was, I attracted the interest of agents, London critics and the RSC. But I decided to be an academic. Why? Love of history, parent and teacher expectation, security, fear of not being a good enough actor – perhaps all four? In 1964 I put in for academic jobs, and to my surprise was offered an Assistant Lectureship at Edinburgh University.

Edinburgh is a wonderful city, the university is world famous, the history department is excellent. I loved the teaching, lecturing came naturally, I was keen to finish my thesis. But after three weeks I knew it wasn't what I wanted to do with my life. I saw the next forty years as a lecturer unfolding before me, and knew I had to give theatre a chance. If I had had two lives, I would certainly have taught in one, but a choice had to be made. Fortunately my professor, Denys Hay, was very supportive. 'Go now,' he said, 'if you stay till you're thirty, and have a mortgage and babies, you won't risk it.' My colleagues divided between those who were amused or contemptuous at my rashness, and those who envied my daring.

In abandoning academia, I also gave up thoughts of becoming a critic. For four years I had written regional reviews for the *Guardian*, first at Oxford and then in Edinburgh. Most of my Scottish reviews had been of the newly formed Traverse Theatre under Jim Haynes, a heady mixture of C.P.Taylor, Pinter, Duras and Beckett. It left me with a healthy respect for the difficulties of drama criticism, difficulties which I think largely defeated me. I never felt certain whom I was writing for, or what level of knowledge I could assume in my readership. I found it very hard, after a bare hour's consideration, to say anything very penetrating in four hundred words, especially when the editor arbitrarily cut the final hundred. Of course it's possible to get by on describing the plot and the set, and listing likes and dislikes, but I wanted to be able to analyse what the author, director and actors were trying to do, whether these aims had been justifiable and illuminating, and how far they had succeeded. This is fiendishly difficult, particularly with new work. Music critics, I have noticed, are allowed to be much more circumspect. They often write that it will take several hearings by different players to evaluate what a composer has achieved. Drama critics are expected to blaze in, judge a play on one viewing, and sum up the precise contribution of writer, director and cast.

So at the age of twenty-six I started on the never-ending road of looking for work as an actor. As president of the O.U.D.S. I had entertained Peter Brook, Tyrone Guthrie, John Gielgud, George Devine and Peter Hall. I didn't have the courage to contact any of those. Fortunately I had been directed as Falstaff by Peter Dews, who had done all Shakespeare's history plays, *The Age of Kings*, for BBC television. He had recently taken over the Birmingham Rep, and he offered me smallish parts at £10 a week. My Edinburgh salary had been twice that, but I took the offer at once. 'I felt sure you'd turn it down, and not bother me again,' he later told me. The very young company included over the next two years Brian Cox, Michael Gambon, Anna Calder-Marshall and Timothy Dalton. I was practically the oldest there. The opening production was *Richard II*, and I was to play Salisbury, the Groom, and understudy Peter Dews as Gaunt. After ten days we had a run-through in which I stood in for Gaunt, and Peter gave me the part there and then. 'I'm not competing with that,' he said, 'but you've still got to play Salisbury and the Groom.' So I started my professional career as a twenty-seven-year-old John of Gaunt. 'As an actor you'll be alright when you're forty, and even better when you're fifty,' Peter prophesied. He was right, almost to the month. Such is the burden of physical type-casting.

I spent the next eight years largely in regional rep. There were odd forays into London: a year in Peter Luke's *Hadrian VII* at the Haymarket, Mia Farrow's father in Barrie's *Mary Rose* (I am four years older than Mia), and *Tonight at 8.30*, in front of Noël Coward himself, at the Fortune. But in the main it was Birmingham, Oxford, Leicester, Cambridge, Nottingham, with tours from Aberdeen to Aberystwyth. Occasionally I was allowed to play my own age, Don John in *Much Ado*, Aston in *The Caretaker*, Horatio in Ian Charleson's first *Hamlet*. But more often I was a grizzled elder, Mr Hardcastle in *She Stoops to Conquer*, James Tyrone in *Long Day's Journey into Night*, Sir Peter Teazle in *The School for Scandal*. In 1975 I went to the RSC to play Montjoy and 'anyone French with a message' in Alan Howard and Terry Hands' *Henry V.* I stayed ten years, and did fifteen Shakespeares, seven Greek plays for John Barton, and various others ranging from John Ford to John Whiting. Then from 1989 to 1993 I did six plays at the National Theatre, and started on a decade of new plays, many by David Hare and David Edgar. It's the kind of training almost unthinkable in today's gallop through the media. I've also done innumerable television and radio jobs, written plays for all the media, and appeared in films from *Sense and Sensibility* to *Star Wars*. And here I am, thirty-four years later, off to New York to do *Richard II* and *Coriolanus* at the Brooklyn Academy. Once the productions are on, I plan to have my first serious reading of *King Lear*.

# 2

# FIRST READING

I sit down and read the play in our hotel on West 57th St. It's a great location. Carnegie Hall and the Russian Tea Rooms are just opposite, Central Park is two blocks away. The hotel is a mystery at first: there is no coffee shop or bar, and there appears to be a church on the ground floor. Gradually we realize the Baptists built the hotel over their church, presumably as a source of income. The rooms are vast, but filled with large, unyielding furniture. The whole effect is dim, even sepulchral, a room inviting tragedy.

I try to read the play as if for the first time. I keep asking questions, and try not to come to any conclusions. When I finish I start making notes, though in truth this takes me several days. I make a little *précis* of the plot and give some scenes names.

**1.1**  *Lear divides his kingdom into three and sets his daughters a love test. Goneril and Regan flatter, but Cordelia refuses to play their game. Lear, outraged by her ingratitude, banishes her and his loyal friend Kent, who criticizes Lear's actions. The King of France proposes to the dowerless Cordelia, and she accepts him.*

I know this scene is a big problem, so I read it very carefully. In Kent and Gloucester's opening speeches there's immediately something I'd never realized. They seem to know that Lear is going to divide his kingdom, and divide it evenly between Albany and Cornwall – not, I note, between Goneril and Regan. They assume men are going to rule, and as Cordelia as yet has no husband she's presumably counted out in their eyes.

The actual division of the kingdom and the disinheriting of Cordelia is done in eighty-five lines. Shakespeare could hardly have managed it more briefly, and that must be intentional. But though brief and clear, it contains a lot of problems. Is Lear's announcement that he's dividing the kingdom into *three* a surprise, part of his 'darker purpose'? Since he seems keen that either France or Burgundy should marry Cordelia, did he envisage a Frenchman was going to rule a third (apparently the best third) of Britain? But then if

> I loved her most, and thought to set my rest
> On her kind nursery

did he intend to live with Cordelia in France, or hope she would stay in Britain as some sort of viceroy? If so, is his decision to spend a month each with Goneril and Regan made on the spur of the moment? Is

> only we shall retain
> The name, and all th'addition to a king

deliberately vague, or does Lear think everyone will understand what it covers? The abdication of British monarchs is a minefield to this day. There are no rules, few precedents. Is the 'love test' an improvisation, or an integral part of his plan? Though Lear says,

> That we our largest bounty may extend
> Where nature doth with merit challenge

he already seems to have decided which daughter gets what. Since, when he gets to Cordelia, he's already given away two portions, the third 'more opulent than your sisters' must have been intended for Cordelia all along. Why can't Cordelia heave her heart into her mouth? Is it in response to her sisters, or part of her relationship with Lear? What exactly does she mean by 'Love, and be silent'? 'This coronet part between you' is a problem. Lear presumably has a crown on. Have Albany and Cornwall already got coronets? Have Goneril and Regan? When Lear says, 'while we unburdened crawl towards death', is this formal rhetoric, a considered intention, or a self-abasing joke? Does 'crawl' prefigure a return to 'second childishness'? Is Lear's passage through the play a deliberate journey towards death?

There's plenty to puzzle over here, but all the while I have the nagging suspicion that Shakespeare would have had no answers. Precise motivations and intentions didn't seem to be important to him in this first scene. It's like a fairy story: the ugly sisters despise Cinderella, don't ask why. I think of *As You Like It*, which opens equally blatantly. Orlando tells Adam what Adam already knows, that his brother Oliver has brought him up meanly and his brother Jacques well. No reasons are given, that's just the plot. Orlandos down the ages have had sleepless nights about this opening speech, when the solution seems to be to play it broad and fast. The audience are not bothered, they understand the convention. Is *King Lear* similar? The audience all know the premise (or did in 1606), they're just keen to see how the dramatist develops it.

But this attitude is little comfort when you have to act it. Actors can't forget Freud and Stanislavsky. We have to invent and agree on what is now called the 'back story'. How long has Lear reigned? What sort of king has he been? Why does he decide to divide the kingdom? When did his wife die? Why do Goneril and Regan dislike their father? Why is Cordelia so different? I read the scene again. No solutions present themselves, just more queries. Cordelia says surprisingly little in the scene, even to her sisters. It offers a rare example of Shakespeare allowing women to comment at the end of a scene, though there could still have been a longer and more revealing argument. Lear behaves monstrously (I know I said I wouldn't come to any conclusions, but this seems inescapable). My challenge is how rash and unsympathetic to make him. But this can't be an arbitrary, isolated exercise. How you play the first scene decides Lear's past and affects everyone in his circle. So perhaps I shall only understand the first scene when I understand the whole play?

**1.4**    *Kent returns to Lear's service in disguise. Goneril argues with Lear about the size of his retinue, until he curses and disowns her, and leaves to stay with Regan.*

> By day and night he wrongs me. Every hour
> He flashes into one gross crime or other
> That sets us all at odds. I'll not endure it.
> His knights grow riotous and himself upbraids us
> On every trifle.

Do we believe Goneril? *Has* Lear flashed into one gross crime or other every hour? Does he upbraid her on every trifle? Has he done so for the last twenty odd years, or is this new? If Goneril is what the morality tradition would call a 'bad' character, she may be lying. Lear certainly denies it:

> My train are men of choice and rarest parts
> That all particulars of duty know.

Goneril's way of dealing with Lear is sly – 'put on what weary negligence you please', she says to Oswald – but perhaps she's learnt that's the only way of getting at her father? What are these 'authorities' he has given away – tyranny and unquestioning obedience? Lear's opening line, 'Let me not stay a jot for dinner: go, get it ready', suggests that he is peremptory and demanding, though nothing that the knights say indicates rowdiness. In speech they appear a pretty refined lot. Lear's arbitrary treatment of Oswald however indicates the kind of ruler he has been. It is also the first time for decades, or perhaps ever, that a subject has snubbed him. Then Lear says something unexpected, the first remark that humanizes him. His knight points out 'a great abatement of kindness' on Goneril and Albany's part, and Lear replies,

> Thou but rememberest me of mine own conception. I have
> perceived a most faint neglect of late, which I have rather
> blamed as mine own jealous curiosity than as a very pretence
> and purpose of unkindness.

So does he have self-doubt, self-criticisms? I'm interested in cracks in the authoritarian carapace.

The call for the Fool immediately raises the question of why he isn't in the first scene. Has he gone walkabout, like Feste, or should he be there, a mute witness? Would the Fool have dared to speak up in so formal a gathering – look what happened to Kent? Now he's under no such constraint and he pitches straight in. He's the first person, indeed the only person in the play, to criticize Lear for abdicating and dividing the kingdom. Why's this? Lear hears him out, seems to join in the fun, and threatens him with the whip. Is this the tempo of their relationship?

Lear and Goneril are very formal with one another. He calls her 'daughter', she calls him 'sir'. She takes the scene back into verse, and very ordered and highly wrought verse at that. Lear seems to puncture this with:

> LEAR   Does any here know me? Why, this is not Lear. Does
> Lear walk thus, speak thus? Where are his eyes? Either his

notion weakens, or his discernings are lethargied – Ha! sleeping
or waking? Sure, 'tis not so. Who is it that can tell me who
I am?

FOOL   Lear's shadow.

LEAR   I would learn that, for by the marks of sovereignty,
knowledge and reason, I should be false persuaded I had
daughters.

This is a very strange moment. Is Lear full of insight about his abdicated authority, or is it merely incredulous sarcasm? Does he hear
the Fool's reply (in the Quarto the line is Lear's)? It makes better
sense that he doesn't, but that could be a missed opportunity for
learning about himself. 'Sovereignty, knowledge and reason' seem to
be all the things that the sane Lear is clinging on to, and that he is
about to lose. When Lear asks Goneril, 'Your name, fair gentle-
woman?' she dismisses it as 'your new pranks' and launches into her
second denunciation of his knights, with the final threat,

> Be then desired,
> By her that else will take the thing she begs,
> A little to disquantity your train.

I had never noticed before that she intends to cut down his retinue
whether he agrees or not: a pity the line is a little obscure. Lear's response, 'Darkness and devils', seems pure irrational anger. We
quickly get to 'Ingratitude', one of the great Shakespearian fixations.
And then suddenly a second flash of insight:

> O most small fault,
> How ugly didst thou in Cordelia show,
> Which like an engine wrenched my frame of nature
> From the fixed place, drew from my heart all love
> And added to the gall. O Lear, Lear, Lear!
> Beat at this gate that let thy folly in
> And thy dear judgement out.

How soon has Lear come to regret his treatment of Cordelia? I need
to chart very carefully both his feeling about Cordelia, and his fear
of madness. Lear could have stopped there, but in fact he moves up
a gear in his cursing of Goneril:

> Suspend thy purpose if thou didst intend
> To make this creature fruitful.
> Into her womb convey sterility,
> Dry up in her the organs of increase,
> And from her derogate body never spring
> A babe to honour her.

This is clearly excessive, but how unbalanced is it? The language remains quite ordered.

> Let it stamp wrinkles in her brow of youth,
> With cadent tears fret channels in her cheeks

could be lines from an early sonnet. Lear exits, but returns almost immediately. Why? He's crying by now, and becomes more rambling: 'Yea, is't come to this? Ha? Let it be so.' His parting shot is a rather oblique reference to taking back the crown. So how much is he disintegrating? Why is he talking about plucking out his eyes, when she's only threatened to cut down his train? Is Goneril's behaviour a complete shock, or does he deep down anticipate it? Where does his extreme anger come from? Alan Howard, who recently played Lear for Peter Hall, has already warned me that he found this one of the most difficult problems. It's certainly going to be a challenge for me, who rarely allow myself to lose my temper at anything.

**1.5**    *Lear confides in the Fool that he did Cordelia wrong and that he fears madness.*

I'd forgotten this was a separate scene. It's clearly the same day, but Lear has had time to write letters. Why does he want them sent to Gloucester: the town or the earl? He's aiming to visit Cornwall and Regan. How does he know they're staying at Gloucester's? Does it matter? The language is in total contrast to the previous scene. It's very prosey, terse, in fact Lear is almost monosyllabic. He tries to do his bit in the double act, but is he listening to the Fool at all? What must be on his mind is first

> I did her wrong.

and then,

> To take't again perforce – monster ingratitude!

How seriously is he thinking of taking back the crown? What is unexpected is,

> O let me not be mad, not mad, sweet heaven!
> Keep me in temper, I would not be mad.

Is this as a result of something specific – the rejection and cursing of Goneril? Or has he felt for some time that his mind is not operating normally? He refers to himself as 'so kind a father'. Does he really think this? It would explain 'monster ingratitude'. The scene feels like a soliloquy: interesting that Shakespeare didn't write it as such (as he would have done with, say, Hamlet or Falstaff). I'm already feeling the insistent repetition of key words – father, daughter, nature, eyes/seeing, nothing, old, folly.

Lear now gets a three hundred and twenty-line rest. I've noticed watching the play how well spaced out most of the part is. That's a relief.

**2.4**   *Lear is outraged that Kent has been put in the stocks. Regan*
*pleads with him to return to Goneril. Goneril arrives, and the*
*two daughters urge him to dismiss his followers. Insulted and*
*maddened, Lear rushes out into the stormy night.*

This seems to be two days later, at Gloucester's (see 2.2.28). Has Lear travelled from London via Cornwall? Whatever state he's in, he's knocked off balance by seeing Kent in the stocks, and his language immediately becomes intemperate – 'tis worse than murder'. And then we get,

> O, how this mother swells up towards my heart!
> Hysterica passio, down, thou climbing sorrow,
> Thy element's below.

Did Shakespeare have any idea what he was saying medically? It can't literally be a swelling up from the womb, though it could be argued that Lear is now father and mother to his children. Is it just a choking in the throat? It brings me up against a key question. Did Shakespeare know much about breakdowns and madness? Or is he simply reproducing what he's observed? How far should I go in investigating what sort of breakdown Shakespeare had in mind?

The 'fiery duke' speech to Gloucester shows marvellously Lear grappling to keep his temper and sanity. He nearly controls himself, and then the sight of Kent sets him off again. But first he says,

> We are not ourselves
> When Nature, being oppress'd, commands the mind
> To suffer with the body.

More insight. The scene with Regan is fascinating. Two daughters have already betrayed him, although he already sees how 'small was Cordelia's fault'. Regan is his last chance, and he is apparently very loving towards her. Is this policy, desperation, or has he always preferred her to Goneril? When Regan says she is glad to see him, Lear replies,

> If thou shouldst not be glad,
> I would divorce me from thy mother's tomb,
> Sepulchring an adultress.

So at least we know that Lear had a wife, and that she's dead. But this is the sole reference to her, and it seems cold and unloving. Did Shakespeare intend that? When Regan urges him to return to Goneril, Lear goes into a parody act of humility,

> Dear daughter, I confess that I am old;
> Age is unnecessary. On my knees I beg
> That you'll vouchsafe me raiment, bed and food.

Sarcasm, rather than irony, seems one of Lear's main weapons. How far should I take this? The direction 'Kneels' suggests quite far. When Regan protests at his renewed cursing of Goneril, Lear replies,

> No, Regan, thou shalt never have my curse.
> Thy tender-hafted nature shall not give

> Thee o'er to harshness. Her eyes are fierce, but thine
> Do comfort and not burn.

Does Lear really think this, or is he so desperate for Regan's love? Goneril arrives and Regan takes her hand. Is this the moment Lear knows he's going to crack. His rage at Goneril, his anger over Kent, his fear of madness seem all muddled up. Which is uppermost?

> I prithee, daughter, do not make me mad:
> I will not trouble thee, my child. Farewell:
> We'll no more meet, no more see one another.

Is he terrified of Goneril, trying to make amends, or straining to keep his sanity? When Regan plucks up courage to suggest he cut his retinue to twenty-five rather than fifty, Lear vows he'll return to Goneril,

> Thy fifty yet doth double five and twenty,
> And thou art twice her love.

Is this ironic, even comic? Or is it serious, an indication that Lear thinks love can be measured and quantified? Is Lear incapable of real, intimate relationships? Is it an indication that the numbers are just a surface quarrel, masking deep underlying doubts, insecurities, antipathies in the family? Goneril and Regan press their advantage, and ask why he needs any knights at all. Lear bursts out,

> O, reason not the need! Our basest beggars
> Are in the poorest thing superfluous;
> Allow not nature more than nature needs,
> Man's life is cheap as beast's.

Where does such a response come from? It shows an awareness of the human condition, a philosophy that we haven't seen in Lear before – or have we? He very soon breaks down and begins to wallow in self-pity. And then comes this extraordinary moment. He loses it. For the first time (in his life?) he doesn't know what he's going to do.

> I will have such revenges on you both
> That all the world shall – I will do such things –

> What they are yet I know not, but they shall be
> The terrors of the earth!

This must be a key moment. The writing is brilliant. In another context it would be very funny, it's actually a very basic gag. How far is he breaking down? The last line is 'O fool, I shall go mad'. Is that a sign that he's still sane? He stumbles off into the storm, has he any idea where he's going? The contradictions in this scene are enormous.

I'm exhausted already, just reading the play, and I know I have the heath still to come. I don't know how long I'm going to be able to play this part . . .

**3.2**    *Lear rages at the storm. Kent finds him and leads him away to a nearby hovel.*

Only a seventy line gap before the storm; less if the Kent-Gentleman scene is cut down. I'm full of half-remembered ideas about the storm being in Lear's mind, Lear summoning up the storm. So is there a storm? Well, the Folio puts in stage directions about the storm, the Fool says it's raining, and Kent refers to 'sheets of fire, such bursts of horrid thunder, such groans of roaring wind and rain' – so I think we can safely say in Shakespeare's mind there was a real storm. How the director decides to do it (taped sound, percussion, thunder sheets etc.) is another matter. Is no audible storm an option?

What exactly is Lear saying? He's urging the storm to storm, to singe his head, to destroy the world. He's on his old tack of telling Nature what to do. He says he won't call the storm unkind as the storm owes him nothing, unlike his daughters. But then he does accuse the storm of being in league with his daughters. Is he demented, or just furious with Nature because he can't control her, can't read her intentions? When he calls himself 'poor, infirm, weak and despised' he seems to be sane, if full of self-pity. After Kent's entrance, his argument turns quite dramatically. He starts talking about the gods finding out criminals. Where does that come from? How blinkered is 'I am a man more sinned against than sinning'? Is he beginning to see mankind as more wicked than he is? 'My wits begin to turn' – how does he know his mind's going? How much is Shakespeare signposting the audience? He is suddenly concerned for the Fool's welfare.

> Come on, my boy. How dost my boy? Art cold?
> I am cold myself.

Why, and how real is this?


**3.4**    *Lear refuses to go into the hovel, meets and becomes fixated on
Edgar as Poor Tom, and is finally led away by Gloucester to
proper shelter.*

Why does Shakespeare break up the three scenes on the heath? Was
it to remind the audience other plots are afoot, provide some relief
from the heath's extremities, give Burbage a breather – all three?
Lear gives a clear analysis of what's going on in his mind. He thinks
dwelling on his daughters' ingratitude will turn him mad. Is he right
to think this is the reason? For the first time he starts to think of
others' comfort when he begs Kent and the Fool to take their ease
in the hovel. This is a prelude to

> Poor, naked wretches, wheresoe'er you are,
> That bide the pelting of this pitiless storm,
> How shall your houseless heads and unfed sides,
> Your looped and windowed raggedness, defend you
> From seasons such as these? O, I have ta'en
> Too little care of this. Take physic, pomp,
> Expose thyself to feel what wretches feel,
> That thou mayst shake the superflux to them
> And show the heavens more just.

This must be a thematic turning point. But where does it come
from? Is it simply being forced (so he thinks) out into a storm with
no shelter, something he has never experienced before? Are there
other reasons he starts identifying with the dispossessed? Because
he's lost his kingdom, his sovereignty? Because he's going mad?
Because he thinks he's been a bad ruler (a theme that obsessed
Shakespeare: look at the Duke in *Measure for Measure*)?

When Poor Tom enters, Lear immediately says 'Didst thou give
all to thy two daughters?' Is this the moment when Lear finally goes
mad? Or is it savage, but sane, irony? His obsession with the idea
does suggest madness. He's also struck by Tom's near nakedness
(I say 'near' because the Fool says he's 'reserved a blanket').

Is man no more than this? Consider him well. Thou ow'st the worm no silk, the beast no hide, the sheep no wool, the cat no perfume. Ha? Here's three on's us are sophisticated; thou art the thing itself. Unaccommodated man is no more but such a poor, bare, forked animal as thou art. Off, off, you lendings: come, unbutton here.

What is Lear's attitude to 'unaccommodated man'? Does he admire, condemn, or accept it as a fact of the human condition? Is he jealous of a man who hasn't had to endure the burden of kingship? He ends the speech by starting to strip, which for an eighty-year-old in a storm is a demented act. To bare or not to bare? In production Poor Tom usually has a loin-cloth. Should Lear go down to that, or in his madness all the way? Stripping naked is a very potent image (I've done it on stage before – it certainly rivets the audience's attention, though not, alas, to the words). But it takes time to get all your clothes off, even in an 844 BC robe, and would Kent and the Fool let him ('else we had all been shamed')? The Fool's next line, 'Prithee, nuncle, be contented; 'tis a naughty night to swim in', suggests that he does stop Lear. However, just because the Jacobeans were prudish, doesn't mean that Shakespeare wouldn't have liked his Lear to strip entirely. We shall doubtless experiment.

Gloucester enters, and Lear doesn't acknowledge him, he's so obsessed by Tom. That does suggest madness. It's also apparent that from the moment Tom enters, Lear takes no notice of what the Fool says. The supposed real fool has supplanted the professional Fool. Is this a major clue to Lear's madness?

**3.6**     *Lear enters Gloucester's shelter, stages a trial of Goneril and Regan, and finally falls asleep. Gloucester urges Kent and the Fool to take Lear to Dover.*

Are we in some room, or outhouse, in Gloucester's mansion? In many productions Lear enters Tom's 'hovel', but this is contrary to the text. Folio cuts the 'mock trial' of Goneril and Regan, ll. 17-55. There are length reasons to cut it (I'm reminded of those musicals where the director cuts the star's favourite number because it doesn't forward the action), but no director of *Lear* does because it's such good theatre.

> The little dogs and all,
> Trey, Blanch and Sweetheart, see, they bark at me.

In Lear's mind all three daughters have now combined to bark at him, even though Cordelia is characterized as 'sweetheart'. Edgar defends him, and calls them all 'curs'. What is going on here? Why does Lear suddenly go to sleep? Is he satisfied, or just exhausted? In the theatre I have found these two 'hovel' scenes long drawn out, but mainly I think because it's so difficult to relate to Poor Tom's ravings. Lear hasn't discarded the Fool, he's talking to him again, but I'm very aware the Fool is about to vanish. The Quarto doesn't even give him the last line: 'And I'll go to bed at noon'. This is another famous problem. Does the Fool slip away, mutely appear later, or help Lear towards Dover and get lost (hanged?) on the way? If the part was doubled with Cordelia, is it to give him/her time to change back? Adrian Noble had Michael Gambon's Lear inadvertently kill Antony Sher's Fool, but this seems a desperate solution.

Lear now gets a long break – four to five hundred lines plus presumably the interval, so that must be at least forty-five minutes. I like the thought of that *very much*.

**4.6**    DOVER BEACH. *The demented Lear encounters Edgar and the blind Gloucester in the countryside near Dover. Cordelia's servants try to subdue him, but Lear runs away.*

The Quarto has 'Enter Lear mad', though Folio intriguingly cuts the 'mad'. Why? Did Shakespeare want to cut down on the impression of Lear's madness? Perhaps it's a printer's error. I like the idea that scholars have poured over some anomaly simply because the printer wanted his lunch and made a mistake. The first Quarto of *Romeo and Juliet* gives the Queen Mab speech to Benvolio – supposing the printer was right?

Lear enters after Gloucester has thrown himself (as he thinks) off Dover Cliffs, the most 'absurd' scene in Shakespeare. So we're in strange territory. It appears to be some months later and high summer, to judge by the flowers Lear has collected, but Shakespeare makes no direct mention of this. Edgar and Gloucester could easily have walked to Dover in a fortnight. I doubt if the audience sense that more than a few weeks have passed. However, a change of costume, and hopefully some light on the stage at last. Lear's opening speeches are in that wonderfully disjointed prose that Shakespeare excelled in – they remind me of Falstaff and Shallow (perhaps my favourite scenes in Shakespeare). I must find reasons to be specific, why he passes from one image to another. There are many problems. How lucid or how ironic is 'Ay, every inch a king'? When Lear engages with Gloucester he goes into verse for a while, then back into prose – why? Lear launches into sex, adultery, copulation, and it leads to the great 'sulphurous pit' speech.

> Down from the waist they are centaurs, though women all
> above. But to the girdle do the gods inherit, beneath is all the
> fiend's: there's hell, there's darkness, there is the sulphurous
> pit, burning, scalding, stench, consumption!

Where does this loathing of women/sex come from? Is it about Goneril and Regan? Is it about Lear's wife/wives? Is it about syphilis, and if so is this a Lear or a Shakespeare obsession (think of *Troilus and Cressida*, and sonnet 129)?

> I remember thine eyes well enough. Dost thou squiny at me?

How intentionally cruel is his handling of Gloucester's eyes? For a moment he's back on the justice theme, and 'the great image of authority: a dog's obeyed in office'. Then back (in verse) to sex and the hotly lusting beadle, and on to politicians and 'furred gowns' hiding great vices. Justice, politics, sex – these are the themes that madness has released (or which Shakespeare wants to handle under the cloak of a character's madness).

> Through tattered clothes great vices do appear;
> Robes and furred gowns hide all. Plate sin with gold,
> And the strong lance of justice hurtless breaks;
> Arm it in rags, a pigmy's straw does pierce it.
> None does offend, none, I say none.

Quarto has 'small vices', which makes better sense, but is a less rolling line – better try both. Has Lear always known this about his society, or is it a revelation? What has triggered it? Is he still siding with the dispossessed, is it anger at man's hypocrisy, or the ironic reflections of a statesman who's seen it all? If 'none does offend', is he now an anarchist? Some decisions here seem vital. Lear then reveals that he has recognized Gloucester. Is he passing in and out of madness? Is he feigning madness?

> When we are born, we cry that we are come
> To this great stage of fools.

Is Lear at his most profound and observant when mad? What is Shakespeare saying here – that madness unlocks our deepest thoughts? It's a wonderful scene. I look forward to it, with trepidation.

**4.7**    THE RECOGNITION. *Lear is brought asleep to Cordelia and Kent. He wakes, eventually recognizes his daughter, and a reconciliation takes place.*

The great rage has gone, but then so has the profundity of thought. Lear seems literally a different person (as people in hospital after a breakdown sometimes are).

> You do me wrong to take me out o' the grave.
> Thou art a soul in bliss, but I am bound
> Upon a wheel of fire, that mine own tears
> Do scald like molten lead.

Is he really angry that he's been taken out of the grave? Is he still on a 'wheel of fire'? How perceptive is he about his past state of mind? How happy is he to recognize Cordelia; he seems full of guilt and regret?

> If you have poison for me, I will drink it.
> I know you do not love me.

He asks Cordelia to 'forget and forgive', but she doesn't reply. The silences of Shakespeare's women are often riddling (viz. Isabella at the end of *Measure for Measure*). Or did the Jacobeans just assume that young women would defer to older men? Perhaps the only good thing that happens to Lear in the play is that he is reunited with, and achieves a deeper understanding of, Cordelia? But how deep is this

understanding – Cordelia says so little? Who *does* Lear relate to in
the play? At the moment it seems to me only the Fool, Cordelia,
Kent/Caius and, in his madness, Poor Tom. I must work on this. The
scene looks as if it plays itself, but there may be traps. I'm scared
that it looks too simple.

**5.3**    THE PRISON. *Cordelia's French army has been defeated. Lear
and Cordelia are now prisoners of Edmund, who sends them off
to prison. Lear is happy simply to be with his daughter.*

Lear has just 19 lines, and again they seem simple. Lear is so happy
that he still has Cordelia, that nothing else matters.

> Come, let's away to prison;
> We two alone will sing like birds i' the cage.
> When thou dost ask me blessing I'll kneel down
> And ask of thee forgiveness. So we'll live
> And pray, and sing, and tell old tales, and laugh
> At gilded butterflies, and hear poor rogues
> Talk of court news.

Lear's vision of prison is clearly unrealistic. How unbalanced is he
still? The lack of dynamic in the scene is worrying. It's so unlike the
other tragedies, where Hamlet, Othello, Macbeth, Coriolanus are
rushing about trying to resolve things. Lear seems to want to hide
himself away. The action has passed him by. Shakespeare has to
cram a vast amount of plot into the last act – the battle, the duel, the
deaths of Goneril, Regan, Gloucester and Edmund – and Lear is
hardly affecting it. I'm conscious that all previous versions of the
story had Cordelia win the battle and put Lear back on the throne.
Shakespeare has deliberately changed that, but as a victim Lear has
little to do. What is Shakespeare up to?

**5.3**    LEAR'S DEATH. *Lear carries in Cordelia, hanged in prison,
attempts to revive her, and dies himself.*

In the theatre I always find Lear's last entrance unexpected, even
though the Edmund-Edgar-Albany exchange prepares us for it. It's

as though we've forgotten that Lear is still part of the story. The fact that Cordelia is dead is very surprising, and shocking. Does Lear know that she is dead? Is he playing with the idea she might revive? How unbalanced is he? Lear's death is the last big problem, compounded by the fact that quarto and folio are so different. Quarto goes:

> LEAR   Pray you undo this button. Thank you, sir. O,o,o,o.
>
> KENT   He faints: my lord, my lord.
>
> LEAR   Break heart, I prithee break.

So the quarto Lear appears intent on dying, with no redeeming thoughts: clear and bleak. Folio has:

> LEAR   Pray you undo this button. Thank you, sir. Do
> you see this? Look on her: look, her lips, look there, look
> there! [*He dies.*]

What does he see, if anything? Is it possible that Lear dies happy in the thought that Cordelia lives? If we accept that Shakespeare wrote both these versions, it shows how uncertain he was about how to end the play. Is the change crucial? Hardly anyone reverts to the bleak quarto ending, but it's a challenge. I must investigate how different the quarto is from folio. It may answer a lot of questions, or it may pose a lot more.

The last minor problem is the undoing of the button. A great naturalistic touch certainly, but why? And is it Lear or Cordelia's button? Is Lear choking, or does he want to take his clothes off? This last idea is appealing, particularly as the word 'unbutton' ties in with 3.4.107. Lear dies naked?

## WHAT DO THE OTHER CHARACTERS SAY ABOUT HIM?

I was taught long ago to note down what the other characters in the play have to say about my character, and it's a practice I've always followed. Sometimes it tells you more about the speaker than their subject, but more often it gives you clues to the author's intentions. Anyway, it's vital to take into account what information the audience are being fed about you, particularly when you're not on stage.

Goneril has most to say about Lear. In scene one she thinks he has 'poor judgement', is 'rash even at his best and soundest of times', and concludes 'we must look from his age to receive not alone the imperfections of long-engrafted condition, but therewithal the unruly waywardness that infirm and choleric years bring with them.' After Lear has stayed with her, she complains that 'every hour he flashes into one gross crime or other . . . himself upbraids us on every trifle', and talks of his whims, his 'every dream, buzz, fancy, complaint, dislike.' But what she really concentrates on is his childish 'dotage' – a word she uses three times. She calls him 'idle old man', 'old fools are babes again', 'as you are old and reverend should be wise', and refers to his 'other new pranks'.

Regan calls him 'rash, wilful, weak, unconstant.' Three times she calls him 'old', and adds 'nature in you stands on the very verge of her confine.' She is less venomous than Goneril, but perhaps shrewder. ''Tis the infirmity of his age, yet he hath ever but slenderly known himself' is an interesting analysis. And it's Regan, when Lear says 'I gave you all', who tartly replies, 'And in good time you gave it'.

The Fool's remarks about Lear concentrate almost entirely on his folly in dividing his kingdom and turning away Cordelia – 'If I gave them [Goneril and Regan] all my living, I'd keep my coxcombs myself', 'all thy other titles thou hast given away, that [the title of Fool] thou wast born with', 'thou hadst little wit in thy bald crown when thou gav'st thy golden one away', 'I'd have thee beaten for being old before thy time . . . thou shouldst not have been old till thou hadst been wise'.

Kent is the only other character who comments much on Lear. In scene one he addresses him as 'Royal Lear, whom I have ever honoured as my king, loved as my father, as my master followed, as my great patron thought on in my prayers.' When disguised as Caius he says that Lear has 'authority' in his countenance. Is all this conventional courtier blarney, or an honest summary of his views? We are encouraged to think that Kent is the blunt truth-teller. In the stocks he calls him 'good king'. He also calls Lear 'old', 'mad', notes how 'majesty falls to folly', and refers to his 'hideous rashness'.

Cordelia twice calls him 'dear father', talks of 'our aged father's right', and has a speech over his sleeping body showing how much she pities and loves him. Gloucester risks his own life to get Lear to safety, insisting 'the king my old master must be relieved.' Edgar too wishes, 'Safe scape the king'. Albany always refers to him with respect:

> A father, and a gracious aged man
> Whose reverence even the head-lugged bear would lick
> Most barbarous, most degenerate, have you madded. (4.2.42-4)

The 'good' characters in the play therefore all show concern and respect for Lear, though it's not clear how much this is deference to his age and majesty, or how much an admiration of his qualities. The 'bad' characters, Edmund, Cornwall and Oswald, hardly refer to him. No one talks about positive qualities; what a good father and what a good ruler he has been, how strong and contented the nation has been under him. But conversely no one suggests that he has been cruel, tyrannical or unsuccessful. This is both a plus and a minus for the actor and director. It will enable us to make up what back story we like, but will prevent us from playing characteristics that will mystify the audience. The words that stick with me from all this are 'old', 'rash', and 'folly'.

# 3

## SECOND READINGS

With the first reading completed, I settle down to enjoy New York. We are playing at BAM Harvey, an abandoned musical comedy theatre rescued by Harvey Lichtenstein, former head of the nearby Brooklyn Academy. They've carved a new auditorium out of the circle and balcony and, at the suggestion of Peter Brook, left it in a partly distressed state. It's a great space to play. The audiences are exciting too, more responsive than in London, particularly to *Coriolanus*. It's September 2000, and we are less than two months from the presidential election. What are George W. Bush and Al Gore but American aristocrats putting on the gown of 'regular guy' to seek the common voice? We are sold out, with queues down the street. I do all the usual tourist things, visit the galleries from Cloisters to the Frick, and even swim at Brighton Beach and take the train to P'keepsie.

Tokyo in October is another matter. Our producers were particularly keen to have *Coriolanus*. Perhaps the Japanese identify the play with the samurai warrior and the peasantry? Kurosawa certainly made the story a superb warrior epic in his film *Ran*. We feel we have to prove ourselves, in a new theatre that resembles an Ikea warehouse. The audience is totally silent, either out of respect for Shakespeare or because they are glued to the simultaneous translation. But when your characters have most of the comedy in both plays, as mine do, and have been getting (some) laughs for six months, it's very unnerving. Word of mouth is good, or maybe the Japanese fall for Ralph Fiennes and Linus Roache, and the last ten days are a sell-out. Europe seems to be in town – the Berlin Phil, the Vienna Phil, Ashkenazy, Sting. John Barton's version of ten Greek plays, which I did at the Aldwych in 1980, has just finished in a Japanese production. Culture, along with technology, are the big travellers these days. At weekends I manage to escape to the mountains, which are in autumn leaf and extraordinarily beautiful. Mount Fuji, of course, remains obstinately in cloud. Fifteen floors up in my hotel room in trendy Shibuya I keep reading *King Lear*.

I return home, deep in debt and determined to make enough money in the next year to finance my doing Lear for six months on Almeida money. To this end I turn down various very attractive theatre jobs, and stick doggedly to television and films. These range from playing the Archbishop of Canterbury at the time of Edward VIII's abdication, to Lord Hailsham at the time of Northern Ireland's Bloody Sunday, and from *Star Wars* to Trollope. We do my *Star Wars: Part 2* scene at Ealing Studios, past which I used to cycle in my childhood when Alec Guinness was filming *Kind Hearts and Coronets*. The rest of my scene with Natalie Portman was filmed nine months ago in Italy. They now film me playing my lines to a drama student, off camera, and then they'll insert me electronically into the picture. This is movie-world 2001. The Trollope for BBC television is *The Way We Live Now*, a very interesting late novel, too radical for the 1870s readership. A mid-European financier creates a share fortune out of a mythical railroad from Utah to Mexico, and the impoverished English aristocracy batten on to him in the hope of saving their crumbling estates. My character, Longestaffe, is a self-important family tyrant, with a terrible relationship with his daughter . . .

I can't get Lear out of my head, and I decide to start reading up about the play. I think it's much better to get this done well in advance. When rehearsals start in December, I want to be focused on the text. The books wholly or partly about *Lear* must run into thousands, so I decide to start with those I already have at home. My daughter, Miranda, has recently finished reading English at Oxford, and *Lear* is her favourite play, so she lends me several more, and we discuss endlessly. I spend a few days in the British Library. I also keep reading the play. After a hundred readings some sense of the character, and hopefully the lines themselves, should have 'osmosed' into my subconscious.[1] I start taking notes on what seem to me to be the key areas.

---

1 Anthony Hopkins prescribes reading the script a hundred times. By that time you know it well enough for film – you may only be doing two minutes of text a day – but not alas for theatre.

## THE TEXT

The actor is normally only concerned with a Shakespeare text where cutting or interpreting disputed words are in question. But *Lear* is different – far more than I had imagined. The first recorded performance took place in front of James I on 26 December 1606, but various references suggest that the play was written in 1605, or even 1604. We have three versions: the first quarto of 1608 (Q), the second quarto of 1619 (Q2), and the folio of 1623 (F), the last two published after Shakespeare's death. Q is particularly badly printed and full of mistakes, some of which are corrected by Q2, on which F seems to be partly based. The differences are not marginal. F cuts some three hundred lines that appear in Q, and adds a further hundred lines. This is remarkable. Do we have here an example of Shakespeare in action, as director, writer and editor? Did he perhaps revise the play in 1609-10, for the opening of the indoor Blackfriars' Theatre? Why the cuts? Some lines would seem to be superfluous or hold up the action. Others seem to have been politically dangerous; for example the Fool's remark about monopolies, and the mock trial (a satire on the absolutist Chancery commission). The added lines generally make things clearer (further explanation of Lear's abdication for example), but also alter the character of certain protagonists and their balance in the play. F also adds a number of stage directions, which clearly indicate stage practice (viz. marking the continuation of the storm).

Once Nahum Tate's 1681 'happy-end' version was abandoned after 1838, it was assumed that F was an improvement on Q, if sometimes drastic in its cutting. Texts were published as 'conflations', or including all four hundred disputed lines. In the last thirty years, however, it has been argued that Q and F are essentially two different versions, neither superior to the other, and their integrity should be honoured. You should act one or the other, not mix and match. In fact this is seldom done, since it would mean cutting some of the most potent moments in the play. Most directors pick and choose, conflate and prepare their own version, and I imagine this is what we shall do. I can already see that I would like to do this with the part of Lear (more anon). There are perils in this. I worked several times at the RSC with John Barton, who loves a spot of conflation. In his 1960s version of the history plays, *The Wars of the Roses*, he actually wrote in about a thousand lines of his own. I acted in John's 1984 production of H. Granville-Barker's *Waste*, a play which exists in a 1906

version and a 1926 rewrite. John tended to pick out the 'best' lines
from each version, and this caused problems, since the Edwardian
period and sensibility is quite different from the 1920s. I'm on my
guard. Is the F Lear different from the Q original *on purpose*?

Fortunately for me, the parts that are most in question are the
Fool, Edgar and Albany. The Fool loses many of his rhymes in F,
and becomes more of a choric commentator. Michael Williams, who
played the Fool twice for the RSC (with Eric Porter and Donald
Sinden), found that when he came to play a pure folio text in the
Gielgud radio version he lost a good deal of his comedy, and had to
compensate by making his Fool less harsh. The part that is most enhanced is Edgar, usually at the expense of Albany. Goneril becomes
less intransigent in F, while Cordelia is made more of a war leader.
Lear's part is only really affected at the beginning and end, but there
are small but significant changes elsewhere. For example, at 1.4.203
when Lear asks 'Who is it that can tell me who I am', Q gives the
reply 'Lear's shadow' to Lear, F to the Fool. In scene one, Q has 'The
map there', F 'Give me the map there.' Conversely at 1.5.17 Q has
'Why, what canst thou tell, my boy?', F 'What canst tell, boy?' The
variations may seem slight, but taken collectively they are important
indications of character. Do I play a blunt, staccato Lear, or a more
polite, measured king? Generally, Q seems to me a tough, harsh first
version, F a mellower, more polished reworking. Why? Did Shakespeare think he'd gone too far with Lear, the Fool, Goneril and Poor
Tom? Was he reacting to court or public disapproval? Did actors'
'improvements' somehow get into the F draft? Did someone else
think the verse needed tidying into neat iambic pentameters?

The 'two play' advocates argue that a play about foreign war and
familial struggle in Q becomes one about civil disturbance and
personal struggle in F. Lear's part in F becomes larger and more intensely tragic. The opposite view is that F is hardly a major revision,
there are no long speeches added, and that many of the changes are
no more than scribes' or printers' errors, actors' additions, or are
prompted by the need for cutting. Audiences viewing the two plays
would actually notice little difference.[2]

2   There is already a large bibliography on the 'Two-text Controversy'. The
best place to start might be Gary Taylor and Michael Warren (eds), *The Division
of the Kingdoms: Shakespeare's two versions of King Lear* (New York and London:
Oxford UP, 1983), and articles collected by Jay L. Halio (ed), *Critical Essays on
Shakespeare's King Lear* (New York: Simon and Schuster, 1996).

## THE SOURCES

Studying the source material may also seem a purely academic exercise, but I find it very revealing. Where does Shakespeare simply flesh out his sources (as he sometimes did with Holinshed and Plutarch), and where does he invent? Playing a largely invented character, like Mercutio, Falstaff, Menenius, or any of the clown figures, you can feel the freedom of the writing, and this encourages the actor to be free. Look at the vastly different ways the Fool has been played in the last twenty years.

The Lear story is a mixture of elements derived from myth, legend and history. The story of the father setting his three daughters a love test, which the youngest fails through her honesty, is a universal folk-tale. The Lear version first appears in Geoffrey of Monmouth's twelfth-century *History of Britain*. Lear was the tenth king after Brute, great-grandson of Aeneas and legendary founder of Britain. The story essentially is that Lear divides his kingdom, banishes Cordelia, falls out with Goneril and Regan, and is reconciled in France to Cordelia. The French king raises an army and puts him back on the throne. He dies three years later, and is succeeded by Cordelia. Holinshed's version, which Shakespeare usually read, is that Lear handed over only half the kingdom to Cornwall and Albany and retained the other half, which the two dukes later seized from him (a more probable story I think). Later sixteenth-century versions of the story, as in Spenser's *Fairie Queene*, have Cordelia kill herself after a revolt by her nephews. So, the first two acts of Shakespeare's play follow the legend in outline, Acts Three and Four are largely invented, and Act Five is radically reworked. There is also the fascinating contemporary example of Sir Brian Annesley, who left the bulk of his estate to his youngest daughter, Cordell (named with extraordinary prescience?). When Sir Brian became senile in 1603 his eldest daughter, Grace, tried to prove that he had been insane when he made his will, but Cordell successfully protected him. Finally we have the play that had been doing the rounds for twelve years before 1606, the anonymous *True Chronicle History of King Leir, and his three daughters*. This is a huge bonus. I'm convinced that some of the problems in *Hamlet* would be clearer if we had Kyd's lost play. The first third of the *Leir* play, seven scenes in all, is devoted to the love test, the marrying off of all the daughters and the division of the kingdom. Reasons are supplied for each of Leir's actions (a rationalization which Tolstoy so preferred), and the play proceeds, part comically, to a happy ending. Shakespeare clearly lifted a number of ideas and lines from the *Leir* play, but the changes he made are far more significant than the similarities.

Shakespeare radically shortened the opening of the play, and left it something of a conundrum. He removed nearly all the Christian references, and made his universe pagan. He made Lear go mad. He killed off both Lear and Cordelia at the end. And, as if the plot was not complicated enough already, he took the Gloucester plot from Sidney's *Arcadia*, and interwove it with the main action. These are enormous changes. Did Shakespeare have this new structure clearly in mind when he started to write, or did he alter the legend as he went along because he found it didn't serve his emerging purpose? I have often felt playing Shakespeare that by Acts Three and Four he was inventing randomly and intuitively, his only anchor being the need to wrap things up tidily in Act Five. Whether planned or not, I'm convinced the changes provide the key to what Shakespeare was trying to do in *King Lear*.

## THE SETTING

The setting of the play is usually up to the director and the designer. While the director tries to keep as many options open as possible, the designer is obliged to have detailed plans at the workshop and wardrobe months ahead. Unless director and designer are in full accord, rehearsals can start with the cast presented with a set model and costumes designs which may not reflect the way the production evolves. The Globe had no such problems . . .

Nearly all Shakespeare plays can happily belong to one of three periods: the age they are set in (usually pre-1550), the year they were written in, or the age they are being performed in. *Julius Caesar* can work well set in 42 BC Rome, 1605 Gunpowder Plot England, or, for instance, contemporary South America. *King Lear* has furnished many possibilities. It has been set in 844 BC, Anglo-Saxon, medieval, Jacobean, any subsequent period up to 1914 (the last date it's argued that kingdoms were still being divided up), contemporary or futuristic. Its location is so vague (various undescribed interiors and then the open air) that it can work set in a room or on a bare stage, a madhouse or an old people's home. Jan Kott sees the second half of the play as 'four beggars wandering in a wilderness'. 844 BC, futuristic or abstract give the play cosmic scope, but no sense of a specific social order. Jacobean, nineteenth century or modern provide the detailed society, but limit the universality. Peter Brook said that 'all periods are inappropriate', and the lack of background to the play seems to me to release it from history. The play is at once ancient and modern, so that we're not troubled by possible anachronisms. Setting Shakespeare too specifically out of his time can create as many problems as it solves. I've been in a *Much Ado* set in 1914. The 'cucumber sandwiches on the lawn' atmosphere worked well, but the background war is not one of mass slaughter in the trenches. It's always tempting to set *Coriolanus* in the French Revolution, only to find that Shakespeare's mob and aristocracy don't have 1789 attitudes.

I am therefore keen to know what period and setting we're going to use, as it will feed my imagination as I work on the play. I don't want to start thinking Stonehenge, if we're doing it Bismarck Prussian. It's far more than just appearance. Alan Howard, who played it recently, told me that by doing it Jacobean, and in a large theatre (the Old Vic), it made them accentuate 'the King'. In a smaller space, with less formal costuming, he thought you would naturally veer towards what he called 'Mister'. In the current production at the replica Globe Theatre, Julian Glover plays him as a very virile, public figure, which that theatre seems to demand. Perhaps Burbage played it differently when the play was presented at Court? Ian Holm, in the small Cottesloe theatre in 1997, played him very much as a domestic tyrant. Jonathan Kent has so far told me that the set will be a room, the audience only three hundred plus, and the period twentieth-century. I like the feeling of intimacy and immediacy that should result – and my voice might survive seven shows a week.

## THE LANGUAGE

This is the actor's secret weapon. However badly I'm playing the scene, Shakespeare's language is still doing much of the work for me. The rhythm, the sound, the structure, the meaning is carrying me along. My job isn't to analyze too closely, it's to respond with every sense I have to what the language is doing for me. As Granville-Barker says, in the storm scene the actor has to incarnate the poetry in himself, to surrender to it, to forget himself in it. Harold Bloom writes: 'Lear is not one of Shakespeare's overwhelming intellects. . . but Lear's imagination, and the language it engenders, is both the largest and the most normative in all Shakespeare'.[3] The patterning of language and image is extraordinarily rich. In this sense, Wells says, 'the play is pure poetry, but poetry in which language, action, stage effect, and even silence are inextricably interwoven'.

*King Lear* isn't an easy play to read, not just because it's so bleak and multi-layered, but because the language is at times so complicated. I can't believe contemporary audiences, particularly at the Globe, found it easy. Some ideas are so cryptic as to be incomprehensible, syntax is strained to the point of contortion. What are we to make of Lear's 'The good years shall devour them, flesh and fell,/ ere they shall make us weep'; Cordelia's 'To watch, poor perdu,/ was this thin helm'; Goneril's 'May all the building in my fancy pluck/ upon my hateful life'? 'Beautiful' verse is kept to a minimum. In fact the one obvious purple passage, the Gentleman's 'sunshine and rain' speech in 4.3, is cut in F. Lear has some striking, regular verse early on, especially when cursing his children, but what humanizes him are the simple, domestic, personal lines, mostly in prose, which take over as madness descends. As Jonathan Bate says, 'Shakespeare is most Shakespeare not when some character is philosophizing or moralizing or talking politics, but when Lear says 'Pray you undo this button'. It is the art of immediacy which memorably impresses that sense upon our sensibilities.'[4] In the part of Lear I can feel Shakespeare experimenting with how jagged he can make thought and word. One result is to make Lear the least quotable of tragic heroes. For which relief much thanks.

Words are key. The repetition of 'see', 'eyes', 'speak', 'fool/folly', 'nature', 'old', 'nothing', 'justice', insistently bore into the mind. In *Dover Beach* Lear talks of 'authority', 'justice', 'nature', 'clothes', 'lust', 'eyesight', 'nothingness'. Images of the suffering body are everywhere. Animals are constantly referred to – sixty-four in all. The word 'look' occurs four times in Lear's last ten words. But the more the words recur, the more open to dispute they become. As Ted Hughes says, 'it is no accident that Shakespeare's most terrific drama revolves around the failure and falsity of words'. Goneril says she loves her father 'dearer than eyesight'. The play puts this to the test in innumerable ways. Lear acts as if he can read nature's mind and orders her about accordingly. His journey will involve a meeting in a natural

3   Harold Bloom, *Shakespeare* (London: Fourth Estate, 1999), p. 512.

4   Jonathan Bate, *The Genius of Shakespeare* (London: Picador, 1997), p. 152.

storm with a 'natural' man, who is in fact counterfeiting, but which helps him to discover something about his own true nature. My task is to be aware of this interplay, but not to underline the word. Nature may be a leitmotif in the play, but it's lecturing, not acting, to give it a capital 'N'. Verbal and character analysis are always interrelated. Words are at the service of character, and vice versa.

Terry Eagleton has written interestingly in post-structuralist vein on the 'value' of language. The play starts with Goneril and Regan's 'severe linguistic inflation', which reveals her 'more than all' to be nothing. Since 'all' means nothing, Cordelia's 'nothing' is the 'only sound currency', and 'only by a fundamental inversion and undercutting of this whole lunatic language game can the ground be cleared for a modest "something" to begin gradually to emerge'. The more Lear insists that words and love can be weighed and valued, the more the paradoxes abound. Cordelia is 'most rich, being poor'. Lear learns on the heath that 'to regain touch with the harsh materiality of things, to discover that one is nothing in comparison with all one had imagined, is in that very act to become something'. After Lear's death Edgar implores everyone 'to speak what we feel, not what we ought to say'. This had been Cordelia's credo, and she has died for it. The paradoxes and contradictions in language lie at the centre of the play.[5]

## KING V. OLD MAN

There are two extreme ways of interpreting Lear. He's a powerful king, who gives away his power prematurely, arrogantly thinks that his authority will not be affected by his loss of power, is brought low by his predatory successors, but remains a king even into madness. In the eighteenth century, Lear wandered the heath still in crown and ermine. At the other extreme, Lear is an ailing old man, possibly suffering from senile dementia, who makes a series of unbalanced decisions, and destroys himself in the process. As Hughes grandiloquently puts it, if Lear can't be a 'Jehovan Goddess-killing tyrant', he can be 'an infantile, frail, brain-washed idiot savant, the child of his daughter'.[6] The text has material to support either interpretation. What you can't do is play both at the same time.

5   Terry Eagleton, 'Language and Value in King Lear', reprinted in Kiernan Ryan (ed.), *King Lear: New Casebook* (Houndsmill: Macmillan, 1993), pp. 84-91.

6   Ted Hughes, *Shakespeare and the Goddess of Complete Being* (London: Faber and Faber, 1992), p. 261.

In between these two extremes lie an infinite number of variations, which most productions explore. But I think that any performance falls, however marginally, into one category or the other. The kingship aspect cannot be ignored. It's obviously central to the first scene, and to the examination of power and authority that runs right through the play. Lear is referred to by almost everyone as 'the King', and Albany proposes to Edgar at the very end of the play that they should resign their 'absolute power' to 'this old majesty'. Lear may give his power away, but he cannot stop being king. Kingship, however, is not an issue that seems either relevant or sympathetic to the 21st-century. The Jacobean audience's instinctive response to the importance of maintaining the royal line is not one we can share. I'm also aware, having just done *Richard II*, that Shakespeare has dealt with the issues of kingship very thoroughly elsewhere, and that it was no longer a subject primarily on his mind in 1606. However, the problem of the ageing, all-powerful ruler still has a very modern ring – Stalin, Tito, de Gaulle, Churchill, Castro, Reagan, Mobuto. But what also seems relevant today are Kott's 'beggars wandering in a wilderness' as symbols of displacement, homelessness, and lack of regard for the old and mad. The familial aspects of the play are crucial. Like *Hamlet, King Lear* is a play about the destruction of two dysfunctional families. From the moment that Goneril starts to complain about Lear's 'gross crimes' in 1.3, we are plunged into a play about fractured relationships, in which 'old fools are babes again'.

R.A. Foakes makes an interesting distinction between 'King' being primarily a play about what Lear does, 'Old Man' a play about what is done to him.[7] The movement of the play seems to be from one to the other. Lear divides his kingdom and rejects Cordelia entirely of his own volition. He may or may not provoke Goneril and Regan's wrath, but he chooses to go out into the storm and stay there. From this moment he stops driving the action. Things are done to him. Unlike Shakespeare's other tragic heroes, Lear brings disaster upon himself, but then is incapable of doing anything to avert it. An alternative view is that Lear does remain active to the end. He kills Cordelia's hangman, and spend his last minutes trying to revive her. My daughter argues that 'Old Man' is about what happens within Lear, that Shakespeare's purpose is to show the dispossessed Lear

7   R.A. Foakes, Arden introduction, pp. 29-30.

making discoveries about the human condition. Whether these discoveries 'change' Lear is another question. The play, I feel, works
best if equal weight is given to the suffering old man and the king
corrupted by absolute power. Can we achieve that balance, or is it
impossible?

## SCENE ONE

There is no easing one's way into the part of Lear. He's no Hamlet,
standing among the courtiers, making rebellious asides. He's the
king, at the height of his authority, making two shocking demands –
that Britain accepts that it is no longer to be a unity, and that his
daughters have to compete for their dowries. The scene is on the
face of it terse and formal. It's the necessary premise of the legend.
In the terms of an old morality play, it's the vision of sacred unity
which is about to be shattered. Shakespeare seems unconcerned
with how long Lear has reigned, what sort of king he has been, why
he divides his kingdom. Q explains as little as possible. It's interesting that Shakespeare found it necessary in F to add a few explan-
atory lines; viz. 'while we unburdened crawl toward death', 'that
future strife may be prevented now', 'we will divest us both of rule,/
interest of territory, cares of state'. But there are still questions that
won't go away. Has Lear reigned for sixty years (forty years in Holinshed) and just lost his wife, as in *Leir*? Or did his wife die giving birth
to Cordelia, and the two eldest have never forgiven the baby, who
was brought up Daddy's pet? Has Lear united Britain himself, as
Edward I did in the thirteenth century? Does he deliberately break
up his greatest achievement because he thinks no one person –
certainly not Albany or Cornwall – can replace him? Is it the manic
act of a dying dictator? Did Shakespeare choose the name 'Edgar'
because he was the king who finally united England?

There's a lot going on in the scene that must have been important
to Jacobean audiences. Queen Elizabeth's lack of children had meant
that for decades England had feared at her death some struggle for
power, some break-up of the kingdom. James I, who was also James
VI of Scotland, was very aware that the two countries were newly
united in his blood. He saw himself as a second Brutus, the legendary founder of Britain, re-establishing the iconic nature of the
king's body. Lear's determination to dismantle the kingdom, James
would have seen as a terrible warning. Conflict and civil war could

only ensue, kingship and patriarchy could only be undermined. As Leonard Tennenhouse writes: 'When the will of the king is to divest monarchy of power, the carnage that ensues implies that it is a primal law of nature that has been violated'.[8] Persuasive as this argument is, it is curious that no one in the play, apart from the Fool, berates Lear for his action. Scene One presents an apparently secure state, a solid hierarchy, where the king's authority is total. Scene Two immediately undermines this. Gloucester speaks of how disorderly the state is: 'in cities, mutinies; in countries, discord; in palaces, treason, and the bond cracked 'twixt son and father'. Are we to infer that this has happened as a result of Lear's action, has the state been in turmoil for years, is Shakespeare commenting on the state of Jacobean England, or is it merely Gloucester's reading of the late eclipses? However we interpret it, the image of a nation in chaos has been implanted.

The love test also has both a contemporary and a folk-tale resonance. In the latter the youngest daughter often says she loves her father as 'meat loves salt'. When the two are finally reconciled, Lear is made to eat meat without salt, to experience how unsavoury it is. In Tudor England the deference that children, especially daughters, were supposed to show their fathers was enormous. Goneril and Regan's speeches are not by the standards of the time excessive. In 1613 Princess Elizabeth wrote to her father James I, on her marriage to Prince Frederick of Bohemia, that her eyes wept at 'their privation of the sight of the most precious object, which they could have beheld in this world.' But contemporaries felt that this deference was breaking down, that young people were becoming ruthlessly ambitious and had to be kept in check. Daughters rebelling against their fathers, as Celia does in *As You Like It*, were becoming a favourite dramatic device. Shakespeare adds lines in F to underline this. Gloucester laments the antagonism between child and father: 'We have seen the best of our time. Machinations, hollowness, treachery and all ruinous disorders follow us disquietly to our graves.' The love test then was not necessarily a crazy whim, nor a way of dividing the kingdom – since the three shares had clearly been allotted. In the absence of any formal bond, it was Lear's way of ensuring that his now all-powerful daughters would still show him deference. A

8   Leonard Tennenhouse, 'The Theatre of Punishment', *New Casebook*, op. cit., p.63.

different reading is that Lear is trading power for love. Stanley Cavell argues that he wants what a bribe can buy – a public expression of love, however false. He wants to look like a loved man, but doesn't want to return it in kind. Cordelia understands this, and it renders her speechless because she can only offer the real thing. Or, as Foakes puts it, Cordelia 'exposes the gap between what Lear thinks he is doing, generously donating his land and power to loving and grateful children, and what he is actually doing, giving away everything to daughters he doesn't know except as ceremonial figures, trappings of his former power.'[9] A modern audience, however, relating the play to their own experience, will see the aged head of the family business dividing the firm among his three children, hoping they will keep him in the state to which he is accustomed. Everyone will know of cases where the children have promptly packed the parent off to a retirement home, and stripped him of his three Jags. This modern scenario is always jangling in my mind. How far should we go to accommodate it?

Where does this leave Lear? Scene One gives no clear indication of his state of mind or body. Granville-Barker notes that Lear the 'man' doesn't emerge till his next scene, 1.4. Germaine Greer berates scholars for not admitting Lear's senility. She finds him 'confused, paranoid, arbitrary'; his behaviour is 'typical of sufferers from atherosclerosis of the brain, grown old without ever being wise'.[10] Goneril is somewhat more moderate: she accuses him of 'the unruly waywardness that infirm and choleric years bring with them'. 'Wayward' and 'choleric' seem undeniable, but how 'infirm' is Lear? Should he enter attended by doctors, or leaning on Cordelia as Olivier did? Is he confused? His opening speeches are very lucid and well ordered. His treatment of Cordelia is perhaps paranoid and arbitrary, but then her response must have seemed to him extremely confusing. Tyrannical he may be, but there is nothing in Scene One to suggest that he is not in full possession of his faculties. Nevertheless Goneril's accusations may be pertinent. Lear is unpredictable and angry. The scene is not easy to interpret, and is therefore a field day for director and actor.

9   Stanley Cavell, 'The Avoidance of Love', reprinted in Frank Kermode (ed.), *King Lear: Casebook* (Basingstoke: Macmillan, 1992), pp. 235-6. R.A. Foakes, *Hamlet versus Lear* (Cambridge: Cambridge UP, 1993), p. 184.

10   Germaine Greer, *Shakespeare* (Oxford: Oxford Paperbacks, 1986), pp. 88-9.

## LEAR AND HIS DAUGHTERS

The relationship between Lear and his daughters is the crucial factor in the action of the main plot. One feminist view of the play is that it's about patriarchal misogyny. Kathleen McLuskie argues that patriarchy is seen as the only thing that keeps chaos at bay. 'Feminist criticism must also assert the power of resistance, subverting rather than co-opting the domination of the patriarchal Bard.' Women are represented as the source of the primal sin of lust, and Lear expresses in his madness his violent loathing of the female sex. Cordelia initially threatens the family through her insubordination. Goneril and Regan's subsequent actions are represented as fundamental violations of human nature.[11] Cordelia may love Lear, but she becomes as much a sanctified stereotype as her sisters' demonised ones.

A quite different reading of the play is that it's about the contemporary shifting power relations between men and women. Both Lear and Gloucester head families without mothers and clearly suffering from a lack of love. It's interesting that though Lear can be accused of acting like a patriarch in 1.1, all the witnesses see his action as a shocking deviation from the patriarchal norm. As Coppelia Kahn argues, Lear wants both absolute control over his daughters, and to be absolutely dependent on them. As Freud says, Lear is 'his majesty the baby'. Both Lear and Gloucester run from love, because they see it as a demeaning dependency. Lear cannot bear to be seen crying, as it is 'womanish'. He refers to his madness as 'this mother' and 'hysterica passio', a disease arising from the womb. Cordelia is a kind of daughter-wife to Lear in scene one, but her renunciation awakens a deep emotional need in Lear for Cordelia as daughter-mother.[12] It is with Cordelia that Lear finally comes to a mature acceptance of his human dependency. Janet Adelman agrees that there is a hidden mother in Lear's inner world, and that his infantile fantasies are real enough, but she adds that women can be deeply moved by the play, because they too are complicit in the fear of separation from the mother.

Are the daughters stereotypes? Greer thinks Shakespeare maintains a balance. Goneril and Regan's conduct is vile but comprehensible, Cordelia is just but cruel. If Goneril is speaking the truth, her

11    Kathleen McLuskie, 'The Patriarchal Bard', *New Casebook*, op. cit., pp. 48-57.

12    Coppelia Kahn, 'The Absent Mother in King Lear', *New Casebook*, ibid., pp. 92-108.

objections to the hundred riotous knights seem reasonable. Goneril, who could have expected to be Lear's sole heir, also has reason to feel slighted at the division of the kingdom. Regan's decision to ally herself with her sister, particularly as Lear threatens to be a permanent guest, is understandable. They both declare they'll receive him gladly if he'll dispense with his followers, though this may be self-justifying. It seems significant that Goneril's lines about Lear being an 'idle old man' and an 'old fool' were cut in F. I don't think, given the legend, Shakespeare set out to demonize Goneril and Regan, but to make them as reasonable as possible in the first two acts. But I also feel that Lear is closer to 'our dearest Regan' than he is to Goneril, 'our eldest born'. I sense that he and Goneril are old adversaries, while Regan has always played her cards more carefully, or perhaps she simply follows and elaborates any clear lead that is presented to her, whether of love or cruelty. 2.4. certainly works better if Lear genuinely expects her support. The daughters' actions thereafter are harder to defend, but it's arguable that the threat of civil war and a French invasion, added to their desire to maintain their new-found status in a very masculine world, drive them to unbalanced extremes.

Cordelia is harder to fathom. Hughes had wanted to call his vast book about Shakespeare *The Silence of Cordelia*. 'Love and be silent' is indeed both the mainspring of the plot and an enigma. Shakespeare always understood just how much, and how little, to make a character say at moments of crisis; witness Iago's final two lines. Cordelia, as queen and leader of an army, may very well be a different character from the first scene, but throughout the play she finds only brief, succinct words to say to both her father and her sisters, though elsewhere, before Lear wakes in the *Recognition* for example, she is eloquent. When he does wake she treats him more as a monarch than a father, and wants to give him back what he no longer seems to desire – power and status. In the last scenes she is everything to Lear, and he is at his happiest when being led away with her to prison, but her response to him is strangely truncated. As the father of a daughter myself, I think Shakespeare, father of Susanna and Judith, understood something very profound about a daughter's difficulty in communicating with her father, and this we will have to resolve. All three daughters are clearly their father's children. Perhaps the course of the play is that they turn into men, as Lear turns into a woman? I foresee heavy discussions ahead.

## LEAR AND THE FOOL

If Lear's most important relationship is with his daughters, his clos-
est friend and confidant is the Fool. The way they play together –
both as characters and actors – must be crucial. No part has been
more variously interpreted in the last forty years, whether male,
female, clown, music-hall comedian, puppet, half-wit, or aged cynic.
His age is a mystery. Lear and he call one another 'boy' and 'nuncle',
but this tells us little. If they've been together forty years, this could
refer to the start of their relationship. Playing him young or female
never seems to me to work well. The text suggests to me an experienced man who's seen it all. I think it much more likely that the part
was written for the 'quick, dwarfish, and charmingly ugly' Robert
Armin, the regular 'clown' in Shakespeare's later company, than for
a boy who doubled it with Cordelia.[13]

In the first two acts Lear's actions are largely unsympathetic. The
one thing that seems to humanize him is his relationship with the
Fool. The Fool acts as a link with the audience, since he makes the sort
of judgements – about Lear's division of the kingdom, Cordelia's
banishment, and Goneril and Regan's hypocrisy – which we the audience are making. These judgements also act as a choric commen-
tary, since no other character on stage could get away with them –
witness Lear's treatment of Kent. When the Fool first enters he
offers first Kent, and then Lear, his coxcomb. As Enid Welsford
writes, he seems to ask, 'What am I? What is madness? The world
being what it is, do I necessarily insult a man by investing him with
motley?'[14] Lear takes on this motley during the storm, and that is
both his burden, but also his passage into understanding. Was it a
price worth paying? The audience accept the Fool as commentator,
voice of cynical truth, even voice of the author, in the same way as
they do Feste and Touchstone. It was a very difficult balance for
Shakespeare to maintain, as his folio rewritings of the Fool show.
Shakespeare also found it hard to know what to do with his fools,
once the plot thickened. Touchstone is hived off into his relationship
with Audrey, Feste is replaced by Fabian in the baiting of Malvolio,
and Lear's Fool simply vanishes, supplanted as feed to Lear by first
Poor Tom and then Gloucester. How can you be fool to a madman?

13   Park Honan, *Shakespeare: A Life* (Oxford: Oxford Paperbacks, 1999), p. 335
14   Enid Welsford, *The Fool in King Lear* (1935), *Casebook*, op. cit., p. 123.

Or, as Greer puts it, the holy fool of Erasmus is supplanted by a pretend religious maniac – Shakespeare at his most dazzling.

What is hard to determine is how much Lear listens to the Fool, what he hears, what he disregards. In 1.4. they are quite intimate and Lear seems to play his part in the cross-talk. Lear tries to continue this in 1.5, but his mind is really on confessing that he has done Cordelia wrong and that he fears madness. In 2.4. Lear seems to pay little attention to what the Fool says, and in the second part of the scene the Fool is silent. Once out on the heath Lear becomes very protective towards the Fool, but listens to him less and less. Once Lear is mad, the Fool's role is gone. Does he realize this – is this the meaning of his last line added in F, 'And I'll go to bed at noon'? Is it because his love for Lear is so great that his failure to keep him sane makes him abandon his master in despair? Wells argues that Lear 'subsumes the Fool's role within himself, directing against others and against society . . . the kind of satire that the Fool has directed against him'. This is particularly evident in *Dover Beach*, where Lear takes over both the Fool's 'simple' humour and his attacking satire. As Edgar observes, 'matter and impertinency mixed'.


## THE HUNDRED KNIGHTS

Lear's successive rows with Goneril and Regan centre on their threats and attempts to reduce his retinue. Modern audiences may have difficulty sympathizing with Lear's intransigence. Jacobean audiences would not. When Lear talks about 'all th'addition to a king', I think he has the size of his retinue primarily in mind. This was a very live issue in 1606. In the 1570s the second Earl of Southampton, father of Shakespeare's patron, was attended by a hundred gentlemen with gold chains round their necks. The Earl of Oxford had a hundred and fifty servants in livery, Derby a staff of one hundred and eighteen. Partly through an economic downturn and partly through Elizabeth's determination to humble the 'over mighty subject', by 1600 most households were down to fifty. As Raleigh said, with his usual exaggeration, 'there were many earls could bring into the field a thousand barbed horses, whereas now

15   Lawrence Stone, *The Crisis of the Aristocracy* (Oxford: Clarendon Press, 1965), pp. 208-17.

very few of them can furnish twenty to serve the king'.[15] It is significant that Shakespeare increases the sixty knights mentioned in his sources to a hundred (plus, presumably, further servants).

Elizabeth I and James I, however, were determined not to see a similar reduction in the royal household. Elizabeth had spent every summer on royal progress right up until 1602. As a boy Shakespeare may have witnessed her 1575 visit to Kenilworth and the pageant of the Lady of the Lake. The queen would set off with a huge entourage of courtiers, privy counsellors, chamber officers, gentlemen pensioners, a hundred and thirty yeomen of the guard, horses, dogs and bears. Six hundred carts would carry their equipment. Burghley objected to the £2000 p.a. this cost her, but her expenses were nothing to the way it bankrupted her hosts. Lord Keeper Egerton spent £1260 on her four-day stay at Harefield. Banquets could include three hundred dishes, expensive gifts to the queen were obligatory.[16] When Regan says she is not 'provided for your fit welcome', she is thinking in terms of hundreds of pigs, chickens, herrings and barrels of ale. James I gathered to himself a vast retinue when he travelled south in 1603. He described his first year as king as a 'Christmas time' for all the presents he received and gave. In 1604 he spent £47,000 on jewels, and by 1608 he was £600,000 in debt, when his basic income was no more than £125,000. As Kishlansky says, 'Even the dullest Lord Treasurer realized that the King had the financial acumen of a child in a sweetshop'.[17] James would certainly have been alive to the horrors of a cut in the royal retinue.

## LEAR AND GLOUCESTER

Shakespeare's introduction of a complex parallel plot is a bold risk, unique in his tragedies. I've always found that the amount of tying up this involves in Act Five is the weakest thing about the play; but until then it's all gain. The purpose seems to be that Gloucester should both contrast and mirror Lear. The play opens with two scenes showing the duplicity of their children, but while Gloucester is tricked by a son bent on his destruction, Lear essentially fools

16   Zillah Dovey, *An Elizabethan Progress* (Gloucester: Sutton, 1996), *passim*. Carolly Erickson, *The First Elizabeth* (New York: Summit Books, 1983), pp. 284-94.

17   M. Kishlansky, *A Monarchy Transformed: Britain 1603-1714* (London: Penguin, 1996), pp. 82-3, 86.

himself into banishing Cordelia. Lear is like Leontes, not Othello. Gloucester scene follows Lear scene throughout the play, Gloucester nearly always being shown in a more passive, conventional role. Robert B. Heilman argues, 'Lear, without questioning his own rightness, imposes his will upon others; Gloucester accepts the will of others, without effectually questioning their rightness.'[18] I always feel Gloucester is a typical Jacobean aristocrat, Lear a ruler almost impossible to date. Howard Felperin argues that the Gloucester story is a morality plot (with Edmund a morality villain), whereas the Lear story develops in quite unexpected, 'unmorality' directions.[19] Lear, like Hamlet, reveals constantly shifting attitudes to role and self, and to form and experience. Gloucester does at times mirror Lear. In 4.1. for example Gloucester discovers that man is 'superfluous and lust dieted', and sees the need for 'distribution' to 'undo excess', and 'each man have enough': a discovery Lear has already made in 'poor naked wretches'. Foakes observes that 'Gloucester's passage through a kind of death and restoration to life may be seen as a parallel to Lear's obliviousness in the loss of his wits and subsequent return to sanity'. In the tragedy where Shakespeare most clearly divides his characters into 'good' and 'bad', Lear and Gloucester are alike in ambiguity. Although they may be foolish and bring about their own destruction, they also invite our sympathy. The double plot therefore makes the discussion of suffering more complex and ambivalent, but paradoxically clarifies the play.

I'm wary of digging too deep into the parallel plots, because I keep remembering that Lear knows very little of all this. He knows that Edgar has betrayed his father and he reveals in *Dover Beach* that he knows Gloucester is blind, but Shakespeare seems determined that until this scene they shall not fully relate. He needs to keep them apart. In 2.4, for example, when Lear complains of Goneril's unkindness in Gloucester's presence, Gloucester does not take the opportunity to speak of Edgar's treachery. When they do finally meet in *Dover Beach*, Lear's cruelty is hard to interpret. Is it to test whether Gloucester is really blind, to downplay physical suffering, or to ward off mutual sympathy and love? Whatever the reason, he does eventually confide in Gloucester in an intimacy unimaginable at the start of the play.

18   Robert B. Heilman, 'The Unity of King Lear', *Casebook*, op. cit., p. 154.
19   Howard Felperin, 'Plays Within Plays', *New Casebook*, op. cit., pp. 31-44.

## THE HEATH

Nowhere in Q or F is the word 'heath' mentioned. It seems to be a Nahum Tate invention, and has an obvious source in the 'blasted heath' of *Macbeth*. But whatever the nature of the terrain, something remarkable happens there: Lear discovers an understanding of his realm's underclass, and he goes mad. In Shakespeare the countryside is usually a barren and unkind place – as the lovers in *A Midsummer's Night Dream* find. The Banished Duke in *As You Like It* is a kind of prototype Lear, cast out into the 'icy fang and churlish chiding of the winter's wind', which he too turns into an asset. Michael Ignatieff makes the point that the Jacobeans understood the heath as a very real place, where the poor, the mad and the outcast went. In its place we now have prisons and psychiatric hospitals.[20]

The storm is also a metaphor for so many things. Lear has lost the security of 'indoors', his realm is heading towards war and disintegration, his family have turned against him, and his mind is in torment. Brian Cox thinks Lear creates the storm, he conducts it, encourages it and then it turns against him.[21] Hughes thinks Lear is reborn by the storm. He doesn't have the strength to fight Goneril and Regan, so he retreats and runs away. Although he begins on a familiar note by rebuking the storm for uniting his daughters against him, he breaks new ground by calling on the storm to expose those sinners who've hidden their crimes, and finally addresses a prayer to help fugitive outcasts. With Poor Tom his new self finally emerges – and his twin preoccupations, the cruelty of family and the injustice of those who wield power. This may be too schematic, but it must be important that even as Lear loses his reason, he begins to see that if human life has value, it does not lie in the 'marks of sovereignty, knowledge and reason' but in the weak, the poor and the imbecile. In the Kozintsev film the hovel is full of other naked wretches, and this makes a strong statement of the vast underclass that Lear has never attended to. As Lear's mind disintegrates, he begins to treat those around him with courteous humility. A sea-change has occurred.

I have no idea how to play this. I feel daunted by a preconception that Lear should be a Titan on the heath, Coleridge's 'La Terribilita',

20    Michael Ignatieff, *The Needs of Strangers* (1984), quoted in an RSC programme (1990).

21    Brian Cox, *The Lear Diaries* (1992), op. cit., p.44.

'a picture more terrific than any a Michelangelo inspired by a Dante could have conceived' (mind you, Samuel T. did get carried away when lecturing). Somehow Lear has to be at one with the storm. Granville-Barker says the actor has to incarnate the poetry in himself, and I feel that must be the right track.[22] Lear is liberated by the storm, whether he thinks he has created it or not – liberated into new understandings and into madness.

## LEAR'S MADNESS

Madness thrives in Shakespeare's plays. Love, lust, jealousy, ambition, betrayal, remorse unbalance his characters – comedically with Malvolio and Ford, tragically with Hamlet, Othello and Lady Macbeth. But no one, with the exception of Ophelia, tips as far into the abyss as Lear. It may be that he is in the early stages of dementia when the play opens. It may be that he only becomes demented at the very end of Act Three, and even then he continues to have moments of lucidity. The cause of his madness given in the text is his treatment by his daughters. As Wilson Knight says,

'Lear has trained himself to think he cannot be wrong: he finds he is wrong. He has fed his heart on sentimental knowledge of his children's love: he finds their love is not sentimental. There is now a gaping dualism in his mind . . . and he endures madness.'[23]

I don't know that we can pin down its clinical nature. It may be a form of manic depression, or as F.D. Hoeniger says the Renaissance idea of 'acute hypochondriacal melancholy developing into mania'.[24] Regan's 'he hath ever but slenderly known himself' seems a key. His rash, ungovernable temper must be another. Shakespeare charts Lear's fear of madness and outbursts of anger with great precision. From 'Let me not be mad' (1.5.43), through 'O fool, I shall go mad' (2.2.475), to 'my wits begin to turn' (3.2.67), both actor and audience are signposted. Alongside this Lear feels some apoplexy welling up inside him: 'O how this mother swells up toward my heart' (2.2.246), 'O me, my heart! My rising heart! But down' (2.2.310), 'O sides, you are too tough! Will you yet hold' (2.2.386-7).

22   H. Granville-Barker, *Prefaces to Shakespeare, vol. 1* (1930), op. cit., p. 268.

23   G. Wilson Knight, 'King Lear and the Comedy of the Grotesque', *Casebook*, op. cit., p. 109.

24   Quoted in Foakes, Arden intro. p. 59.

It has become modish to link Lear with Alzheimer's disease, but this has loss of memory as a primary symptom and is a progressive illness, neither of which fits Shakespeare's play. Jonathan Miller, who has directed the play five times and is himself a doctor, told me that he feels Shakespeare is non-specific, that Lear becomes demented through an extreme sense of dislocation. John Barton suggested to me that the reason Shakespeare may have cut the mock trial in F is that he did not want Lear to appear mad in Act 3, merely confused and delusional.

The 'mad' make frequent appearances in Jacobean plays, usually as a form of theatrical spectacle (viz. *The Changeling* and *The Duchess of Malfi*). On the frontispiece of the two *Lear* quartos great prominence is given to Edgar's 'sullen and assumed humor of TOM of Bedlam'. It was plainly a major selling point. Lear however is not a conventional mad performer; Shakespeare confronts his distress more directly and sympathetically, though he continues to use the word indiscriminately. We have become much more circumspect about the gradations of 'unbalanced', 'delusional', 'demented', 'mentally ill', 'lunatic' and 'insane'. But since the word 'mad' is so central to the play, I shall often use it when one of the above terms might be more appropriate. The Jacobeans in fact often used the words 'mad' and 'angry' interchangeably, and anger is Lear's chief characteristic in the opening scenes. Wrath is the second of the seven deadly sins. It consumes Lear, just as envy seizes Iago and then Othello, pride Coriolanus, avarice Shylock, and lust Antony and Cleopatra. The prime candidate for gluttony and sloth must be Falstaff. Lear has some understanding of his angry nature. He tells Kent not to come between 'the dragon and his wrath'. As my daughter pointed out to me, Lear sees himself not as, say, a graceful lordly lion, but as a reptilian, fiery, destructive monster, whose essence is anger. The exiled and embittered Coriolanus also calls himself a 'lonely dragon'. When in 2.4. Lear finally turns on his daughters he implores the gods to 'touch me with noble anger'. For Lear anger is not only the proper response to ingratitude, it has a nobility about it. But soon after, in the storm, when Lear inveighs against his daughters, he recognizes that wrath will be his undoing:

> O, that way madness lies, let me shun that;
> No more of that.

In *Dover Beach* Lear is still at times convulsed with anger, and it is not until the *Recognition* that the doctor confirms that 'the great rage you see is killed in him'. Richard Burton in his *Anatomy of Melancholy*, published in 1621, wrote:

> Kings, princes, monarchs and magistrates seem to be most happy, but look into their estate, you shall find them to be most encumbered with cares in perpetual fear, agony, suspicion, jealousy . . . Sovereignty is a tempest of the soul; Sylla-like, they have brave titles, but terrible fits . . . Anger is a cruel tempest of the mind, making his eyes sparkle fire and stare, teeth gnash in his head, his tongue flutter, his face pale, or red, and what more filthy imitation can be made of a mad man . . .[25]

Anger is closely correlated to melancholy (depression), and therefore to manic depression (or bipolar disorder), but it can be a symptom of many other illnesses, including senile dementia, Alzheimer's and even syphilis. But whatever the medical diagnosis, Shakespeare made Lear go mad for a purpose. One is his gain in perception. Just as Gloucester stumbled when he saw, so Lear was blinkered when sane. Before the classical age of reason set in and madness became a scandal and a shame to be shut away, the Renaissance saw madness as the 'truth' of knowledge, the sane man's knowledge and learning an absurd folly. The Fool, in his wise idiocy, already knew this. Cavell claims that Lear 'has a powerful, raging mind; and its eclipse into madness only confirms its intelligence . . . because the nature of his madness . . . is the sign, in fact and in Renaissance thought, of genius; an option open only to minds of the highest reach.' When mad he has a single-minded vision of a corrupt world where vice and guilt do not exist, social forms and human nature do not correspond. Felperin argues that his madness is the opposite pole to morality, 'a vision of undifferentiated anarchy as opposed to a wholly mapped out order'. Bloom thinks Lear 'is mad only as William Blake was mad: prophetically, against both nature and society'.[26] Frank Kermode thinks *Dover Beach* is the cruellest and most beautiful scene in Shakespeare. The dreadful emphasis on blindness is the prime

25   Richard Burton, *The Anatomy of Melancholy* (1676 ed.), pp. 63,67.
26   Harold Bloom, *Shakespeare*, op. cit., p. 515.

mark of Lear's madness and the play's cruelty. His rejection of sexuality is stronger even than Iago's.[27] Hughes thinks the 'sulphurous pit' speech is the climax of the drama and of Shakespeare's tragic vision. I am sure Shakespeare made Lear mad in order to say things about human nature and society that would have been unacceptable in a sane character. So much of Shakespeare's social criticism is given throughout his plays to fools, lunatics and villains. But does Lear's madness protect him, or make him more vulnerable? Does Lear find his humanity? The redemptionist school, whether Christian or not, certainly think so. Even Hughes thinks that Lear finally emerges 'corrected, enlightened, transfigured', ready for Cordelia's kiss. But it's also possible that Lear emerges a broken reed, desperate only for female care and the retirement home. I don't know yet.

## THE PLAY'S ENDING

Lear's last three scenes are a series of renunciations. In the *Recognition*, Lear, when he finally realizes where he is, seems bent only on forgetting and forgiving; the analysis of society is quite gone. In *Prison* he renounces any active participation in the world, being happy only to remain in captivity with Cordelia. In the last scene he appears completely at a loss, in a state Felperin describes as 'aporia', radical uncertainty. The *Recognition* appears in many sources. In *Leir* it's a long scene with much potentially comic kneeling and rising by Leir, Cordelia and the King of Gallia, and ending with Leir's cry, 'Come, let's to arms for to redress this wrong'. Shakespeare wrote a short, subtle scene, in which Lear and Cordelia only partially engage. For example, when Lear says Cordelia has cause not to love him, unlike her sisters, most dramatists would have given Cordelia a long speech. Instead she simply says: 'No cause, no cause'. In Q the Doctor says it would be dangerous for Cordelia to prompt Lear to make sense of his past sufferings – and Shakespeare doesn't. By keeping explanations and reconciliation to a minimum, he avoids sentimentality and conventional moralizing. Lear is a changed man, never again to be fully aware of what's going on around him.

In the Russian film Yuri Yarvet smiled and laughed in *Prison*, like a child released from school. It's an image I can't get out of my head.

27  Frank Kermode, *Shakespeare's Language* (London: Allen Lane, 2000), pp. 195-8.

Perhaps if we accept that Lear has discovered his daughter/mother, he has become a child again. If the play had ended here, or with their rescue from prison, then the morality form would still have been intact. Instead Shakespeare makes this extraordinary choice. He could have killed them both offstage, or he could have brought on Cordelia grieving over her father's body, but he chose the most painful option. Lear has witnessed his daughter choking to death, and then carries the body aimlessly about, urging her back to life. The play has become a nightmare fairy tale. Lear/Shakespeare then tantalizes us that Cordelia, like Hermione and Hero, may recover. The audience wills this to be true, for then her and Lear's suffering will be justified. One nineteenth-century rewrite actually made that happen. Lear's trials are often likened to Job's, and this prompts me to read the Bible again. There are clear echoes. 'My kinsfolk have failed, and my familiar friends have forgotten me . . . they whom I loved are turned against me', laments Job (19, vv. 14,19). 'I will be the pattern of all patience', says Lear. The Jacobean audience would have picked up the references, only to be savagely wrong footed. As Kermode says, Lear's story doesn't end like Job's; it ends in the horror and torture of the Last Judgement.

Whether this is a Christian, or a post-Christian, conclusion, there is an apocalyptic, doomsday feel about the end of the play. Shakespeare makes this clear in one of his masterly compressions. 'Is this the promised end?' asks Kent. 'Or image of that horror?' asks Edgar. 'Fall and cease', says Albany. Gobsmacking writing, but Shakespeare offers no answer to these questions. It seems to me there is no resolution at the end of the play. Cordelia's death is random, meaningless. Perhaps Shakespeare felt that to leave her alive, a triumphant queen restored to her realm, would have lessened the tragedy? Her death ensures that there will be no escape into romance: falsehood and suffering will be ruthlessly exposed. My daughter argues that, just as on the heath Lear unbuttons to fling off the lies of human society and become the thing itself, now his soul is throwing off the trappings of the body. Foakes writes that Lear's death is both cruel and gentle, for he has nothing left to live for. But this seems scant consolation, hardly redemptive.

## LEAR AND THE SOLILOQUY

The concept of 'soliloquy' or 'monologue' has to be approached with care. The words themselves don't appear in writing till 1604 and 1668 respectively. John Barton has argued to me that Elizabethan actors were so used to talking to the audience in the course of speeches that they would have found the formalization of a separate 'soliloquy' unnecessary.[28] Nevertheless, as an actor on stage I feel I make a distinction between remarks made 'out front', and those confided directly to the audience. I believe that *Lear* occupies a significant place in Shakespeare's development of the soliloquy. He had already written *Richard II, Hamlet* and *Othello. Antony and Cleopatra, Timon* and *Coriolanus* were to follow. The date of *Macbeth* is uncertain, though it is usually taken to follow *Lear*. Richard II talks a great deal to himself in public, but his only true soliloquy comes in prison, when he at last realizes something of his nature. Hamlet is Shakespeare's most complete study of the self-aware hero, whose capacity for self-analysis and doubt is so great that it leads him to a point of indecision where he becomes the hunted rather than the avenger. Othello's certainties are worked on by the vice figure of Iago, who keeps the audience informed of the workings of his mind at every turn of the plot. Othello himself is allowed two soliloquies, where he reveals his feelings about Desdemona's betrayal and the necessity of killing her. Macbeth is tempted by the witches, urged on by his consort, but falls prey to his own ambition. He is intensely aware of heaven and grace, of how damnable his crime is, but how futile is his attempt to kill his soul, and this he confides to the audience in full.

Lear, in contrast, has no soliloquies. He confides nothing *directly* to the audience. The nearest equivalent is his 'poor naked wretches' speech in 3.4, but even this is cast in the form of a prayer, and Kent is present throughout. Lear reflects little on what is happening to him. He makes sudden announcements – that he did Cordelia wrong, that he's suffering a heart tremor, that he's going mad – but he doesn't analyse or expound on these. When he is finally mad he is eloquent on the subject of society and the human condition, but these remarks seem to be addressed either to those present or to himself, not confided to the audience. Shakespeare's later plays show

28   For a further discussion of this see p. 190.

him turning away from the device he had so fully explored in *Hamlet*, *Othello* and *Macbeth*. Neither Antony nor Cleopatra has soliloquies, there are always soldiers or attendants present, and Coriolanus has only one, before he enters Antium in Act 4.

The portrayal of Lear therefore is an experiment in objectivity. Soliloquies still abound in the play, Edgar and Edmund have several, but Lear is to reveal himself by what he says and does, not by what he tells the audience. This robs the actor of one of his principal tools, but it also gives him greater scope. Hamlet may be a much longer part, but we are in little doubt about his motives and intentions – indeed, about what sort of a person he is. The part of Lear is a field day for speculation – witness the enormous variety of performances over the years – because he himself does not tell us who he is or what he is doing. Had Shakespeare followed his usual path and given Lear soliloquies, we might know why he's dividing up his kingdom, what he thinks of his children, and how he reacts to his growing madness. One reason for this absence of soliloquy must be that Shakespeare conceived his Lear as fatally lacking in self-awareness. Lear doesn't tell us who he is, not because he won't, but because he can't. His discovery of self comes only through madness. Bloom goes further: 'His lack of self-knowledge, blended with his awesome authority, makes him unknowable by us'. Whether *Macbeth* was written immediately before or after, the contrast between Lear and the super-aware Macbeth could not be greater. The two plays show Shakespeare experimenting at the height of his powers.

## WHAT IS THE PLAY ABOUT?

The play may not be *about* anything. Wilson Knight argues that it is 'supreme in that, in this main theme, it faces the very absence of tragic purpose'. Foakes sees a radical instability in the play that permits no confidence in any particular reading. The play offers the paradox that 'we can only learn through suffering', but 'have nothing to learn from it'. Kermode says the play doesn't comment on or tie up its themes; it only presents them. 'The play is not committed; it only shows us humanity at the cliff-edge of its own imaginings.' Kott sees an absurdist, existential universe, where Lear and Gloucester's belief in absolutes is shown to be nonsense, and only the Fool can see that the world is driven by brute force, cruelty and lust. 'All that remains at the end of this gigantic pantomime is the earth – empty and bleeding.'[29] The Elizabethans would have thought this far too extreme, for they believed that it was not given to any individual to understand a complete system of morality. For them Shakespeare was trying to convey some impression of the world's nature, and these last three acts are perhaps his most extreme statement of the reality of the world – and one that chimes greatly with a modern sensibility.

Since the Holocaust and Hiroshima, some critics have argued that the classical notion of 'tragedy', based on individual catastrophe, has lost its meaning. Terry Eagleton has recently asserted that no definition of tragedy more elaborate than 'very sad' has ever worked. Whether 'catastrophe' or 'very sad' is the chosen indicator, *King Lear*, with the destruction of most of its protagonists, would still register highly. Conservative critics argue that tragedy has to depend on either fate or the gods, and that most of us no longer believe in either. The text of *Lear* does not suggest that Shakespeare believed the gods were responsible for Lear's destruction; fate's culpability is more debatable. Left-wing critics hold that tragedy is no longer a desirable form because it is based on self-asserting individuality (of which Lear is certainly guilty). A more centrist view is that modern tragedy can only be based on the hugely inflated degree of liberty that a minority exercise at the expense of the majority's suffering. *King Lear* could meet this definition on the grounds that the deaths of so many are occasioned first by Lear, and then by Goneril and Regan, in their unbridled assertion of supreme power.

We can agree on something: that the play is a ruthless analysis of humanity and society. It shows that our actions have consequences which outrun our best, and worst, intentions. Lear's determination to punish Cordelia results in the deaths of all his daughters, though I would argue this was far from inevitable. The play is also concerned with the platonic shift from appearance to reality: the 'appearance' at the start of the play that the kingdom is secure, Lear is loved by his children, he can retain his kingly authority into retirement; and the 'reality' of the chaos of the second half. It is also, as Wells says, the play of Shakespeare's that is 'most deeply concerned with matters of fundamental human importance – with breakdowns in family relationships, with the effect on the mind of both physical and mental suffering, with what distinguishes man

29   Jan Kott, *Shakespeare Our Contemporary* (London: Methuen, 1964), p. 118.

from the animals, with the need to believe, in the face of all evidence to the contrary, in the existence of unseen benevolent powers'.[30] Perhaps that is enough. Shakespeare comes up with a staggeringly wide selection of questions. It's too much to expect answers.

Yet to me there is a tension in the play between the schematic and the arbitrary that suggests Shakespeare *was* trying to say something. The contradictions are there for a purpose. As Greer puts it, in the play he 'shows us a stripped down version of his mental landscape.' The characters are more clearly divided than in any other of his plays: between old and young, good and bad, an old feudal society based on service and a new self-serving society based on pragmatism. The old have become spiritually blind, the young either reject the dishonesty this blindness breeds or take advantage of it. Lear introduces a spirit of calculation, that love and dowry can be measured. When Goneril, Regan and Edmund come to rule, calculation, rather than imagination, dominates. Does the play then show, as Marxists would have it, a transition from the Middle Ages to a modern world, a feudal economy to a nascent capitalism, an overmighty aristocracy to a new democracy? All this was undoubtedly happening in Jacobean society, and the revolution that was to abolish monarchy and the House of Lords was less than forty years away. But do the young people in the play really exemplify this new order? Aren't Edmund, Goneril and Regan typical fifteenth-century aristocratic predators rather than new seventeenth-century capitalists? Aren't all eleven protagonists members of the ruling class? Is Shakespeare attacking or defending James I's Britain – or sitting on the fence? No morality formula will stick either. The good don't triumph; they mostly suffer along with the bad. The play seems neither Christian, nor even supernatural. There are no ghosts, witches or spirits. The play also explores in a pagan world different interpretations of Nature. Both Lear and Gloucester see it as an organic network of reciprocal obligations; Edmund sees only warring individuals in which the natural state is self-aggrandizement. Both look to Nature for meaning – but the play provides no answer.

Is the play about something more metaphysical, more intangible? One thing that is certain, after four centuries of performance, is that the play's meaning and impact is greater than the sum of its parts. I said on first reading that the word 'suffering' came to mind, and

30    Stanley Wells, RSC programme note (1993).

Kermode takes up the word; 'the consequence of a human tendency to evil, as inflicted on the good by the bad; it can reduce humanity to a bestial condition, under an apparently indifferent heaven'. Maynard Mack argues, 'the victory and the defeat are simultaneous and inseparable. We recoil from suffering, but it is a greater thing to suffer than to lack the feelings and virtues that make it possible to suffer.'[31] Wells thinks the play is finally about love; 'it is love that distinguishes man from the beasts, love that enables Lear to transcend his limitations even as he is defeated by them; love that enables him to die unselfishly'. Richard Eyre told me that he too came to realize in his production that the second half of the play was basically about love. Once all the 'good' characters have been exiled and cast out, love is the power that guides their actions. Lear and Gloucester, essentially loners at the outset, are restored to the love of their lost children and brought to 'an acceptance of the mortality and humanity they have to learn they share with others' (Foakes). When Deborah Warner took her production to Broadmoor, Brian Cox felt the audience instinctively understood that Lear's pain was about expiation and healing, about finding one's own peace, accepting that in my beginning is my end.[32] But does Lear really change? The conventional view of classical tragedy is that the hero attains a kind of knowledge that redeems him, but Shakespeare seems to me consistently to avoid such a comforting moral. Macbeth comes probably the nearest, but even though he may recognize the horror of his actions it leads him neither to expiation or acceptance. Lear in his last scene is hard to fathom. Has he learnt or accepted anything? Can he tell good from evil, true from false? Has madness enveloped him again? Or should we feel that he is in some way representative of humanity, that his anger, rejection, madness, and suffering mirror to an extreme degree our own experience?

The play clearly embraces the two extremes of society: sovereignty, power and authority on the one hand; poor, naked, unaccommodated man on the other. Lear, Gloucester and Edgar, the three longest parts in the play, descend from one state to the other, and gain a new humanity, by exposing themselves 'to feel what wretches feel'. The post-1945 period saw this as a descent into a meaningless chaos;

31   Maynard Mack, quoted in Foakes, *Hamlet versus Lear* (1993), op. cit., p.55.

32   Murray Cox (ed.), *Shakespeare Comes to Broadmoor* (London: Jessica Kingsley, 1992), p. 61.

there is no evidence that they learn anything, they remain deluded about their importance. But you don't have to believe that the play shows either a beneficent supernatural plan, or a meaningless existential universe. Ryan argues that Lear's fate doesn't arise from forces beyond our ken, nor from the ultimate nature of mankind, but from a particular set of circumstances, driven by prevailing modes of thought. Shakespeare's analysis of society urges us to accept another world view, perhaps utopian, which is committed to equality, mutuality and co-operation, rather than division, domination and exploitation.[33] I find this persuasive (though I'm aware I may be reading this into the play because I want to find it there). Edward Bond, as ever, sounds a cautionary note: 'The social moral of Shakespeare's *Lear* is this: endure till in time the world will be made right. That's a dangerous moral for us. We have less time than Shakespeare.' The heart of the play seems to lie in the suffering of Lear, Gloucester, Edgar and Cordelia. The heart of Lear seems to lie on the heath and Dover Beach: that is the centre of the part. I just hope in acting it I shall discover something about this centre.

33  Kiernan Ryan, 'The Subversive Imagination', *New Casebook*, op. cit., pp. 73-82.

# 4

## LEARS IN PERFORMANCE

Lear is one of the four parts we know from contemporary references that Richard Burbage played (the others are Richard III, Hamlet and Othello). Burbage had been in the same company as Shakespeare since the early 1590s, and from 1603 was a shareholder in the 'King's Men'. We know nothing of his performance, except that he would have been about forty-two in 1606 and was noted for restraint rather than bombast. Tradition has it that it was one of his best parts, that Lear 'lived in him'. After the 1660 Restoration it was the least performed of the great tragedies, but Thomas Betterton took it up in 1663, and it is reported to have been 'the greatest efforts of his genius'. Nahum Tate, the poet laureate, found the play 'a heap of jewels unstrung and unpolished, yet so dazzling in their disorder, that I soon perceived I had seized a treasure'. He proceeded to cut the Fool, create a love story between Edgar and Cordelia (who survives), and restore Lear to the throne. Tate has been rightly sneered at, but his new ending was both historically correct and accorded with eighteenth-century susceptibilities of justice and morality, exemplified by Johnson. This 1681 version held the stage for a hundred and fifty years, and was played by Anthony Boheme in the 1720s, followed by James Quin, Barton Booth and Spranger Barry. The most famous eighteenth-century Lear was David Garrick, who played the part between 1742, when he was only twenty-four, and his retirement in 1776. He evidently had doubts about playing it initially, partly because he felt he excelled in comedy, and partly, one would guess, because of his slight stature. He restored some of Shakespeare's text in the first half, but always played Tate's happy end. The general opinion was that he was best in the *Recognition* and *Prison*. The famous Benjamin Wilson painting of 1761 shows how slight and frail he appeared, and it would seem that he was probably the first to conceive Lear as a feeble, well-meaning, ill-used old man. Thomas Davies however witnessed that in the early scenes,

He had, from the most violent rage, descended to sedate
calmness, had seized with unutterable sensibility the various
impressions of terror, and faithfully represented all the turbid
passions of the soul.

In his farewell performances in 1776 Henry Bate recorded that
Garrick could still seize the big moments:

The curse at the close of the first act, his phrenetic appeal to
heaven at the end of the second on Regan's ingratitude were
two such enthusiastic scenes of human exertion that they
caused a kind of momentary petrifaction through the house,
which he soon dissolved as universally into tears.[1]

Spranger Barry became his main rival in the part, and the famous
rhyme,

'A King? Nay, every inch a king'
Such Barry doth appear,
But Garrick's quite a different thing:
He's every inch King Lear.'

suggests that Garrick triumphed mainly as 'Old Man'. John Philip
Kemble reigned supreme at the end of the century, though in 1809
he actually dropped some of Garrick's restorations and reverted to
Tate. Kemble's greatest rival was Edmund Kean. In 1820 *The Times*
reported: 'Nothing could evince greater judgement than the manner
in which he represented the gradual aberration of reason under the
repeated shocks to which he was exposed.' In *Dover Beach* 'the picture of mental alienation was completed, and we believe that a scene
more perfect or pathetic has never been represented on the stage.'
The *Prison* 'was the most masterly of the whole performance. There
was scarcely a dry eye in the theatre.'[2]
    Hazlitt's eyes, however, remained dry:

1  A prime source for reviews of early productions is Stanley Wells (ed),
*Shakespeare in the Theatre* (Oxford and New York: Oxford UP, 1997), pp. 23, 29.
See also Wells, Oxford intro. pp. 62-75.

2  Wells, *Theatre*, ibid., pp. 62-3.

Mr Kean did not appear to us to set his back fairly to the task, or to trust implicitly to the author, but to be trying experiments upon the audience and waiting to see the results. He seemed . . . to be looking out for the effect of what he did, while he was doing it.[3]

Hazlitt puts his finger on one of the great temptations in playing Lear, to invent new and striking ways of playing the 'great moments' – the curse on Goneril, the flight into the storm, the relationship with Poor Tom – without integrating them into a believable whole. Kean had yet another great moment up his sleeve, for in 1823 he restored the tragic ending, declaring that 'no one . . . could know what he was capable of until they had seen him over the dead body of Cordelia.' But the public were not ready for this innovation, whatever the remarkable feats Kean performed over Cordelia, and he reverted to Tate. Nevertheless Kean had injected a degree of naturalistic restraint into the part. Dr Doran wrote, 'his warmest bursts of passion never removed him beyond the weakness of his age; his violence was that of the spirit, not of the frame.' The *Times* only real criticism of the 1820 performance was in the storm scene, that notorious trap for directors and designers, which was

less effective than many others, because the manager, by a strange error, had caused the tempest to be exhibited with so much accuracy that the performer could scarcely be heard amidst the confusion. He should have recollected that it is the bending of Lear's mind under his wrongs that is the object of interest, and not that of a forest beneath the hurricane.

The actor who finally broke with Tate was William Charles Macready who restored the Shakespeare text in a shortened, rearranged version, and put back the Fool, albeit played by an 'impish' nineteen-year-old actress, Priscilla Horton. John Forster, Dickens' friend and biographer, applauded this innovation, arguing that the Fool 'is interwoven with Lear – he is the link that still associates him with Cordelia's love, and the presence of the regal state he has surrendered'. Macready clearly acted Lear in the manner of the mythic Old Testament prophet, 'through all its changes of agony, of anger,

3    Giles Playfair, *Kean* (London: Reinhardt and Evans, 1939), p. 190.

of impatience, of turbulent assertion, of despair, and mighty grief; till on his knees, with arms upraised and head thrown back, the tremendous curse bursts from him amid heaving and reluctant throes of suffering and anguish'. It is said that when Queen Victoria was present he directed the 'poor naked wretches' speech at her, much to her discomfort. 'His representation of the father at the end, broken down to its last despairing struggle, his heart swelling gradually upwards till it bursts in its closing sigh, completed the only perfect picture that we have had of Lear since the age of Betterton.'[4]

The tragic ending was firmly re-established, though the Victorians continued to edit and rearrange the text. Historically inspired pictorialism was also part of Macready's new wave, his setting was suggestive of Druid megaliths, and this was elaborated by Charles Kean, who in 1858 produced an Anglo-Saxon *Lear*, full of boarhunts, spears, skins, antlers, castles and wooden palisades. A reviewer warned:

> There is always danger in scenic illustration, pictorially carried out and archaeologically conducted, that the spectacular will overlay the dramatic, and thus the poetic and histrionic suffer from too violent a contrast with the stage appointments . . .

Stage technology was developing. On the heath 'the clouds and electric fluid travelled rapidly across the sky in the distance, and with a lurid gloom investing the entire landscape, were grandly terrific'. Kean's performance, however, went less for the melodrama, perhaps in reaction to his father, Edmund:

> Mr Kean's delivery of the curse was perfect: the suppressed emotion, the irrepressible exclamatory impulse, and the passionate emphasis, were alike admirable. . .With Lear's madness began a series of new triumphs. 'Reason in madness': that was the poet's problem, that is the actor's test. . . Fanatic frenzy succeeds to fierce madness; and restoration to sanity, preceding a catastrophe that crushes the heart.[5]

Nevertheless once the Romantic frenzy of the 1820s had subsided into Victorian materialism, *Lear* became the least popular of the

4  Wells, *Theatre*, op. cit., pp. 73-6. Alan S. Downer, *The Eminent Tragedian* (Cambridge, Mass.: Harvard UP, 1966), p.238.

5  Wells, *Theatre*, op. cit., pp. 99-102.

great tragedies. Its cosmic scope, its sense of implacable 'otherness' were not to the taste of a trading empire at its wealthiest. Wells quotes the German novelist, Theodor Fontane:

> An English performance lays more emphasis on its pathetic elements. The German performance gives a Lear who is mad and a king, the English above all the old, abused and abandoned man . . . there is always a danger that the high tragic and royal elements will be watered down to the sentimental and petty-bourgeois.[6]

Henry Irving eventually tackled Lear in 1892, and he too opted to emphasize 'old man'. He was influenced by the accounts of Kean's restraint and pathos. His friend, Graham Robertson, recounts how Irving walked the cliffs at Tintagel seeking inspiration and was delighted to find, as he thought, seagull feathers on the ground, which would serve for 'this feather stirs'. He abandoned the idea when Robertson pointed out they were chicken feathers from a nearby farm. Irving cut some fifteen hundred lines, including most of the Gloucester plot, devised new tableaux and generally enhanced his part. On the first night the reception was muted, and Ellen Terry told him she hadn't heard a word he'd said. Henry Arthur Jones, an admirer, wrote that he was 'slow, laboured, mannered, uninspired, screechy, forcibly feeble, failing chiefly where all representations of Lear fail'. Irving modified his performance, but the damage was done and he seldom revived the play.[7] It's a cautionary tale about rewriting the play, and imposing an old man characterization on a text that requires enormous vocal energy.

The play entered the twentieth century with a reputation for being unstageable and a minefield for actors, a view enhanced by Bradley's criticism. The principal rescuer of the play was Harley Granville-Barker in his great Preface of 1927, whose 'chief business', he wrote, was to refute Lamb's opinion that 'Lear is essentially impossible to be represented on a stage'. Important as the Preface is, it does reinforce the view that Lear is a titan, 'more a magnificent portent than

6   Wells, Oxford intro., p. 70.

7   Laurence Irving, *Henry Irving: the Actor and His World* (London: Faber and Faber, 1951), pp. 548, 550-52.

8   Granville-Barker, *Prefaces*, op. cit., p. 261 *passim*.

a man'.[8] Barker finally put his ideas into practice in 1940 with John Gielgud, who had first played the part in 1931 at the age of twenty-seven. Gielgud entered in lavish satin and rich furs, his beard carefully curled, carrying a great staff, every inch a medieval potentate. He himself thought that he didn't have the voice for the storm scenes, and that he was more at home in the resigned wisdom of the second half, where he died joyful in the belief life was returning to Cordelia. He later wrote, 'the part requires considerable staying power and a great variety and strength of voice. You have to decide from the outset whether Lear is a great man who loses his position, or does he acquire greatness and wisdom through suffering'.[9]

Donald Wolfit's Lear is the performance that has most challenged critics. He brought it to London in 1944, when he was forty-two (Burbage's age). James Agate, the most influential critic of his time, wrote that it was 'the greatest piece of Shakespearian acting I have ever seen', and went on:

> What are the things that we demand from any Lear? First, majesty. Second, the quality Blake would have recognized as moral grandeur. Third, mind. Fourth, he must be a man, and what is more, a king, in ruins. There must be enough voice to dominate the thunder, and yet it must be a spent voice . . . Mr Wolfit had and was all the things we demand.

This check-list is highly questionable, but it illustrates a view of the part that continues to this day, and also that many critics and audiences approach the play with a list of preconceptions. Must Lear have moral grandeur, must he have a spent voice? Nobody in the play affirms either. Another critic noted that Wolfit was 'big enough for Lear, but not deep enough', and this reservation is repeated in some form about most Lears. The actor is allowed size or subtlety, he can succeed in either the first or the second half, but not in both. Wolfit certainly had size, I can attest to that. Ronald Harwood describes how, after the curse on Goneril, 'from the air, arms upstretched, Lear clutches the physical parcel, as it were, of his savage imprecation, pulls it down and then, to be rid of it, hurls it at his ingrate daughter'.[10]

9   Morley, *J. G*, pp. 78-9, 169-72. BBC/Renaissance audio cassette intro. (1994).
10   Ronald Harwood, *Sir Donald Wolfit* (London: Secker and Warburg, 1971), pp. 159-67.

Wolfit's peers thought him unsubtle; Gielgud confessed that he regarded him as 'a joke' and never saw his Lear. When Laurence Olivier came to do Lear in 1946 (aged thirty-nine), he had no intention of outbarnstorming Wolfit or outnobling Gielgud. 'Lear is easy', he wrote later, 'he's like all of us, really: he's just a stupid old fart.'[11] Olivier played him as 'an unexpectedly amusing grandfather . . . the performance had an enveloping warmth'. In fact he later told Gielgud that, as natural tenors, they had been lucky to succeed in the part, which he saw as essentially a bass role. The *Times* wrote:

> Mr Olivier knows his Lear well enough to set him in a judicious
> comic light which exposes what is vain and tyrannical in the
> old man's affection for his daughters . . . he is seldom declam-
> atory in the frets and rages lit with flashes of savage irony
> that seize upon Lear . . .but when he lets himself go. . . the
> roof rings. The fear of madness is a recurring motif which
> Mr Olivier casts into grimly comic form which is somehow
> terrifying.

This search for comedy in the role (which is still evident in Olivier's much later 1983 video) tends to make Lear knowing, likeable, and manipulative. Some found this too calculating, too remote. Agate objected, 'Yes, any amount of subtlety and intellectual appeal. But was I moved? Not so much as I ought to have been . . . I have the conviction that Olivier is a comedian by instinct and a tragedian by art.' The demand that the play should be moving seems to apply more to *Lear* than to any other of the tragedies. Tears at the end are a prerequisite – hence Peter Brook's iconoclasm. T.C. Worsley summed up the trio: 'Olivier and Wolfit strike harder, clearer, louder at the note of the majestic or the terrible, but they oversimplify'. Gielgud gives due weight 'to the ironies, the irresolutions, the subtleties of the character'.[12]

A Lear which many thought the most complete they had ever seen was Michael Redgrave's at Stratford in 1953. Redgrave was a huge, bent, Ancient of Days. Kenneth Tynan, who saw most classical parts as bullfights and had his own check-list of requirements, wrote: 'Michael Redgrave has played King Lear and won . . . Lear is

11    Laurence Olivier, *On Acting* (London: Weidenfeld, 1986), p. 90.
12    Quoted in Felix Barker, *The Oliviers* (London: Hamilton, 1953), pp. 248-9.

a labyrinthine citadel, all but impregnable, and it needed a Redgrave to assault it . . . He began finely, conveying grief as well as rage at Cordelia's refusal to flatter him. Physically, already, the whole of Lear was there, a sky scraping oak fit to resist all the lightning in the world. . . The second act decline into madness was perhaps the least impressive stage of Mr Redgrave's campaign – Mr Wolfit effects this transition more eloquently and with less fuss.' *Dover Beach* contained 'the higher mathematics of acting. . . is it a backhanded compliment to say that this actor is best when maddest?'[13]

The next Lear at Stratford was Charles Laughton, directed by Glen Byam Shaw in 1959. Laughton was primarily interested in the second half of the play, what he called 'the terrible journey of Lear to his death'. 'You know why my Lear is the greatest,' he said to a young actor, 'because I'm the first actor to play it on a rising graph after the storm.' He placed the whole emphasis on his gain in humility and understanding, and jettisoned the rage of the first two acts. An admirer wrote, 'he found unity of character in childishness. In the first part he was spoilt, petulant, self-centred; in the second he was innocent, with a sense of wonder, freshness of vision, purity.' Harold Hobson observed, 'that the universe should single out so small a figure for its wrath gives a lurid splendour to the performance; it is as if an ordinary man was called to crucifixion'. One of his many ideas was to create the effect of the storm in his own speaking of the verse. But as Peter Hall said, 'of course in a room it was magic because I was sitting in a room being asked to imagine a storm. But in a theatre it didn't work at all.'[14] The danger of playing on stage a concept conceived in the study is that the actor might be more effective reading the part out. Having seen the production, I rather wish Laughton had.

Three years later, in 1962, Paul Scofield was the complete antithesis to innocence, purity, wonder. Tynan was enraptured by Brook's production: 'Lay to rest the royal Lear with whom generations of star actors have made us reverently familiar; the majestic ancient, wronged and maddened by his vicious daughters; the felled giant, beside whose bulk the other characters crouch like pigmies.' Tynan conveniently forgot that Laughton had already laid the royal Lear to rest, and that he had praised Redgrave for playing the part

13   Kenneth Tynan, *Curtains* (1961), op. cit., pp. 53-4.
14   Callow, *Charles Laughton*, op. cit., pp. 263-71.

and winning as a sky-scraping oak. Brook saw no reason for Lear to be moving or likeable, or on any sort of journey. He saw the role as 'a mountain whose summit has never been reached, the way up strewn with the shattered bodies of earlier visitors – Olivier here, Laughton there: it's frightening'. He saw the play as 'a mighty philosophical farce . . . a world without gods, with no possibility of hopeful resolution'. Tynan characterized Scofield as 'an edgy, capricious old man, intensely difficult to live with'. G.K. Hunter found him an 'overbearing belching boor'. The performance, preserved rather inadequately in the 1971 film, still divides people today. Is it reductive to the point where it becomes an unremitting dirge, or is it the benchmark modern interpretation? Laurence Kitchin took a measured view. He admits:

> I like a touch of baroque excess in my Lears, on the lines of
> Michelangelo's Moses. The verse of the part does invite
> something of the kind, along with self-indulgent acting of a
> self-indulgent old man. . . But if Scofield is not allowed to be
> kingly, he still has immediate authority. . . He does not, like
> the verse at times, aim to rival the storm. He greets it
> ecstatically as a refuge. His best moments are downbeat. . .
> when he wakes in Cordelia's care, Scofield's tone is level,
> subdued, and for the first time patrician. There is a glimpse of
> the royal, tragic hero who gets elbowed out of this rendering
> far too often, from fear of skirting Victorian portentousness,
> no doubt.[15]

Laughton and Scofield redefined the part for the twentieth century. The decade after 1956 was exciting theatrically not just because of the surge of new writers centred on the Royal Court, the influence of Brecht and Beckett, and the rise of the regional actor, but because the classical canon was being reinterpreted at Stratford and the National Theatre. Forty years later there appears some consensus that Scofield was the last great Lear. This must be linked to the apprehension that he is the last of that golden era of classical actors, which included Olivier, Gielgud and Redgrave, and two who never attempted the part, Richardson and Guinness. There is an element of rose-tinted nostalgia here. As we have seen, they in turn all had

15  Wells, *Theatre*, pp. 267-9. Wells, Oxford intro. Foakes, Arden intro.

their detractors; it goes with the part. Who is to say that Anthony Hopkins, Michael Gambon, or Ian Holm are not their equals? What is certain is that since 1945 *King Lear* has been, if not the most performed (that title would still go to *Hamlet*), the most eagerly anticipated and discussed of Shakespeare's tragedies. There is something in the play that accords with modern sensibility in a way that it did not to the Victorians. Seven performances may fairly illustrate the breadth of modern interpretation. There are strong despots like Eric Porter, Anthony Hopkins and Ian Holm, Alzheimer victims like Michael Hordern, manic intellectuals like John Wood, child-like pranksters like Brian Cox, and bemused grandfathers like Robert Stephens.[16] They share common ground only in their efforts to de-romanticize the part, to suggest that Lear is not necessarily a sympathetic figure just because he suffers.

Eric Porter played the part at the RSC for Trevor Nunn in 1968, and again at the Old Vic for Jonathan Miller in 1989. Michael Billington in the *Guardian* proclaimed his check-list when he wrote of the later performance: 'As a portrait of a testy autocrat, it is superb: what it lacks is that gift of self revelation that is the bench mark of great acting'. But John Gross thought 'he is equally convincing in his testiness, his anxiety that nobody should miss the point, his old man's humour, and finally his capacity for suffering'. Paul Taylor noted something more in the *Independent*:

> Eric Porter's magnificent Lear is all the more moving because
> it contains so little self-pity. Madness seems to release in this
> king a wily sense of absurdity and a prankish intellectual
> adventurousness. . . William Empson wrote that we view Lear
> at the end with hushed envy 'not really because he has become
> wise, but because the general human desire for experience has
> been so glutted in him; he has been through everything.'
> Porter's titanic performance convinces you of the truth of this.

Three years earlier Anthony Hopkins appeared at the National Theatre under David Hare. Hopkins himself later said 'he couldn't touch the part' (most Lears would concede this, perhaps not so

---

16  A perceptive summary of recent Lears by Benedict Nightingale can be found in James Ogden and Arthur H. Scouten, *Lear from Study to Stage* (Cranbury: Associated UP, 1997), pp. 226-46. All newspaper reviews are taken from the appropriate *Theatre Record*.

openly). The *Daily Telegraph* thought 'he does his best work of the evening in the scene with the blinded Gloucester (Michael Bryant). . . Here there is a sense of real relationships and depths of inhabited pain'. But Billington thought he had the essential measure of the part:

> Hopkins combines the strength and rage of a bull with an
> extraordinary capacity for pathos. He is a genuine heavyweight
> endowed with emotional finesse. When Cordelia denies him
> the satisfaction of a declared love, he chokes back the tears.
> And Hopkins makes this a key moment in his performance.
> He stops in his tracks when he finds himself later echoing the
> phrase 'nothing can be made out of nothing', and when he
> talks of 'our youngest born' the tears well up in his eyes and in
> our's. Hopkins conveys both Lear's brutishness and his
> emotional vulnerability.

Michael Hordern in 1969, and later on television, could hardly have been more different. He shook, grunted and giggled in an advanced senility that pre-empted any journey towards greater humanity and understanding. Hordern later wrote that his director Jonathan Miller's view was 'that if you didn't approach it as a funny play about people going gaga, you missed a dimension and all you got at the end of the day was a rather depressing tragedy about madness and old age.' Hordern was a great master of the pause, and Martin Esslin noted 'his timing of the silences from which snatches of demented wisdom emerge is masterly and illuminates the subterranean processes of his derangement'.[17] Irving Wardle wrote in the *Times*:

> His Lear is a sharp, peremptory pedant. . . Far from decayed,
> and governed more by thought than by feeling, it takes a long
> time for him to crack. Mr Hordern is not an actor who loses
> himself in surging rhetoric; and it seems that his Lear is
> watching, and calamities fall as if upon some other victim.
> So there is no hysterica passio, no climbing sorrow, and it is a
> huge gap: he scrambles through the thunderous storm speech,
> and even delivers the curse on Goneril in the style of an icy
> legal sentence. But the reading is absolutely consistent. 'Fool,
> I shall go mad' he says, calmly stating it as a fact.

17  Michael Hordern, *A World Elsewhere* (London: Michael O'Mara Books, 1993), pp. 138-40.

In 1990 at Stratford John Wood, under Nicholas Hytner's direction, had some of the same intellectual probity and anti-titanic qualities. He showed the abrupt mood swings between anger and geniality that characterize the manic depressive. As Benedict Nightingale said in the *Times*, 'if someone were to harness this actor's imaginative energy it would create enough electricity to light a dozen homes'. There were some who thought this energy was more a demonstration of virtuosity, always a temptation in the part, but Billington considered by the time it had reached London in 1991 it was the best since Scofield's.

> Wood presents a Lear who has the uncensored capacity of the
> very old to switch in a second from intemperate rage to sweet
> tenderness. Wood conveys superbly Lear's private emotional
> civil war; having forced Goneril to the ground to curse her
> with sterility he then rushes back to clasp her in his arms. But
> Wood also adds an element I have never seen brought out
> before; Lear's insatiable intellectual curiosity. Madness
> produces a heightened awareness so that in the hovel. . . he
> fanatically pursues Poor Tom as if he contained the secret of
> mankind.

Brian Cox also opened in 1990 at the National, under Deborah Warner, determined to concentrate on a human Lear, 'a bit of a curmudgeon, a bit of a silly old boy. . . I do think there are a lot of laughs in *Lear*, it's a play with humour'. This divided critics and audiences, some applauding its humanity, some complaining of a lack of regality and intellectual rigour. Taylor thought it was 'a Lear from whom you never feel remote. There is no distancing grandeur of manner. . . Lear's tragedy is all the more piercing here because Cox so magnificently conveys, before madness, his perplexed, comic humanity.' But Nightingale asked, 'how are we to believe in the spiritual and moral regeneration of someone who seems not just immature, but suffering from near-psychotic infantilism?' Billington gives some idea of Cox's originality when he observed, 'he has a battered shaggy authority and the gift of pathos. . . at the end as Mr Cox bends over Cordelia's inert body popping the Fool's red nose on to hers and smiling seraphically on the reiterated 'Never' he is genuinely moving'. As he played the part on a long world tour Cox made his Lear 'more mercurial and unpredictably dangerous with a strong undercurrent of melancholia. . . I've discovered a lyricism which I had undervalued.'[18]

Robert Stephens in 1993 also divided audiences. He saw him as a 'fond and foolish old man', and was mainly interested in 'his comic potential and his spiritual journey after the storm'.[19] Wardle wrote that he 'is a spoilt old child who had spent his life in a dream of adulation, never angry as nobody had ever crossed him, and finally emerging from his fool's paradise with no more than petulant disbelief'. Nightingale echoed this: 'Stephens sauntered jovially on looking like an over-age Laughing Cavalier and acting like some up-market Barnum. . . rage, vindictiveness and the more superficially forceful emotions are not his forte. . . but how much grief he packs into the lines about 'poor, naked wretches'. With how much simple wonder he discovers 'the barefaced animal' that is unaccommodated man. . . You'll come across tougher, harsher Lears, but none, I think, more vulnerable and tender.'

Ian Holm at the National in 1997, under Richard Eyre, was determined not to short-change the anger of the first two acts, though John Gross thought it 'intense irritability rather than blazing wrath'. Nightingale wrote, 'Holm never slackens in his determination to show us a man whose make-up consists both of seismic anger and of surpassing love'. In his madness he became quiet and awe-struck. John Peter summed him up in the *Sunday Times*:

> Within the brutal, bullet-headed old man with his burly grizzled
> beard, a shrill wounded small boy appears, a boy who has
> grown old but not grown up, crying out indignantly against
> the cruel women from whom he expected warmth, kindness
> and shelter. . . Holm watches people, not so much to find out
> what they think or feel, as to see what effect he is having on
> them . . . Holm's Lear lacks the two most vital qualities of a
> political leader: calculation and patience. His temperament, and
> a lifetime of being obeyed, have deprived him of self-control;
> and like all men who lack this he is fatally oversensitive.

In the twentieth century Lear has been played in an astonishingly wide variety of ways, more so than any other Shakespeare tragic

18   Cox, *Lear Diary*, op. cit., pp. 22, 90.

19   Robert Stephens and Michael Coveney, *Knight Errant* (Bedfordshire: Sceptre Press, 1996), pp. 181-2.

hero. This must stem from the fact that Lear is so old, with no limiting back story, that he tells us so little about himself, and that the play itself is so open to interpretation. The choices therefore appear vast. Is he a child, a dinosaur, an intellectual, a tyrant – or even all four? Does his madness and/or senility allow the actor to take the part in any direction he wants? Just how many of these choices will the text bear? Can one justify a sharp peremptory pedant, or a laughing cavalier, never angry as nobody has ever crossed him? Is he a testy autocrat, or a silly old boy? Does he have perplexed comic humanity or insatiable intellectual curiosity? How many of these are characterizations imposed on the text from outside, or will the play support each and every one?

# 5

## ACTING IN SHAKESPEARE

In acting the only tool you have is your own body. It's an uncertain instrument, and in its unpredictability lies its fascination. The actor may be feeling and expressing one thing, the audience may be experiencing something quite other. There's nothing fair about acting. Intelligent actors come across as dull, dull actors come across as intelligent. A dozen fascinating emotions can pass across the face of one actor, when he's actually thinking about his laundry. Nothing interesting can be communicated by another actor, who has immersed himself in a complexity of thought and emotion. There's a lot of counterfeiting about. Just as no actor is quite sure what they're doing or conveying when they 'act', so they can have no certainty about what their fellow actor is doing. This applies particularly to the rehearsal process. Peter Brook quoted Edith Evans' rehearsal methods as 'Kneading the flour today, darling', 'Putting it back to bake a bit longer', 'Need some yeast now', 'We're basting this morning'.[1] It worked for her, but how were her colleagues to share in the process? This may seem an extreme instance, but I have been amazed at the methods some fellow actors have confessed to. Actors work at different rates, in different ways, with different objectives and different hang-ups. I have been in RSC companies where at the start of the season there seemed no common ground between the principals at all. One was a Celtic romantic, one a Shakespearian traditionalist, one a film naturalist, and the fourth a method maverick. Thankfully, with the British acceptance of compromise, some sort of ensemble was eventually achieved.

Acting is, like any art, a combination of feeling and intellect. Alfred Brendel said recently: 'Feeling and intellect have to go together. Even if the feeling is the origin and the goal, there is the intellect as

1 Peter Brook, *The Empty Space* (London: MacGibbon and Kee, 1968), pp. 29-30.

the controlling and filtering factor, and it is the intellect which makes the work of art possible. Without the intellect what one does is amateurish, it may be full of love and passion, but it's amateurish.'[2] Of course many actors are so terrified of being thought serious that they do anything to mask it – the school of 'I just learn the lines and try not to bump into the furniture.' 'You *think* it, and I'll *do* it, and we'll see who wins,' said a seasoned pro to a university friend of mine. But thought is action, they're not in separate compartments. Another great pianist, Arturo Michelangeli, has a dictum, 'Don't ask whether a musician plays well or accurately, ask them where they stand philosophically in relation to the work'. This the British would put straight into Pseuds' Corner, but it is only another way of asking 'What has the performer got to say?' Do I have anything to say about King Lear? Intellect, however, may make the work of art possible, but it doesn't deliver the performance. If it did, Professor Stanley Wells would be a great Shakespearian actor. I take Brendel to heart. Feeling is the origin, and feeling is also the goal.

## CONVINCING, COMPELLING, ILLUMINATING

Forty years ago in the course of a conversation with the great director Tyrone Guthrie, he offered me this definition of good acting: 'It should be convincing, compelling, and illuminating'. Any three-word definition is reductive, but these adjectives have rattled round in my mind ever since. The bottom line is 'convincing'. Do we suspend our disbelief? The actor claims to be Cleopatra, a postman, Rasputin. Do we, at some level, accept that? It is not simply a matter of appearance. The Cleopatra may be blonde, the Rasputin beardless, yet we may still be willing to suspend our disbelief. It may be to do with circumstance. In the school nativity play we accept that an eight-year-old is the Virgin Mary. At some level she convinces, perhaps by the way she holds the doll baby. On film we are more particular about naturalism. Michael Redgrave convinces as a failed schoolmaster in *The Browning Version*, Laurence Olivier does not in *Term of Trial*. On stage we are more aware of the artificiality of the convention. Will I, at some level, convince as a king who's ruled for fifty years, and who's made men 'skip with his biting falchion'? I've seen Lears who haven't.

2   BBC TV *Omnibus* (2001).

'Compelling' is the icing on the cake. Some might call it 'charisma' or 'star quality'. Is it innate, or can it be acquired? Why can't we take our eyes off certain people even when they're not acting particularly well? Look at Marilyn Monroe in her early films. Of course it's connected with physical attraction, but Hollywood is full of beautiful faces that on screen merge into the wallpaper. Perhaps it's a life force, perhaps it's a suggestion of hidden depths, perhaps it's luck. Some actors strive very hard to be compelling, but only succeed in drawing attention to themselves – not the same thing at all. Things can be done to make a performance appear compelling. It's amazing how charismatic you briefly appear standing centre stage in the brightest light wearing a red costume – but that's not the same thing either. Some believe that you need do nothing, that truth will out, that the audience or camera will be fascinated by the depth and sincerity of your performance alone. Well, sometimes they are and sometimes they aren't. 'Compelling' is unpredictable.

'Illuminating' is where the real hard work comes in. Most worthwhile plays and films take place during the crucial period, often only a few days, of a group of people's lives, whether it's *Hedda Gabler* or *Some Like It Hot*. You have two hours or so to show how and why a person has reached this crisis, and how and why they deal with it in the way they do. What, in short, have you got to say about this character? It's an enormous act of compression. One of the most depressing sights is watching an actor ironing out the contradictions which the author has painstakingly written in. It happens all the time in long running television series: actors complain, 'my character wouldn't say this, do that'. The actor lights on a 'persona' and plays that remorselessly, limiting himself to three moods and four expressions. Film 'stars' have built careers on less. But the art of the actor is to embrace contradiction, choose variety, seek illumination. Shylock may have only five scenes, but he can be a different Shylock in each, depending on whether he's with his daughter, his friend, his debtor, his servant, his superior. 'Play each scene for what it's worth,' David Hare urges me, 'don't try to link them, the author has done that already. The audience never say, 'that's odd, he doesn't seem the same person he was ten minutes ago'.' Every intention, every word, every movement is a potential act of illumination. That's why we rehearse.

## ENERGY, BREATH AND THE ENSEMBLE

Convincing, compelling and illuminating are a fearsome trio to bring together. Few people achieve it. What links the three is, I believe, energy. A choreographer once defined dance as 'the decisions the dancer makes as the energy leaves the body.' It's a good description of acting. We rightly place emphasis on determining the character's intentions, and on accessing our emotions. But thousands of A-level students can work out Lear's dominant and subsidiary intentions. Actors have no monopoly on plumbing feelings of love and hate, sorrow and anger. But neither of these quests are ends in themselves. The actor, once in touch with thoughts and feelings, has to reproduce them. This reproduction has to be energized, and that's where the art lies. The inner impulse is there, how do we express it? Lindsay Anderson may be right when he said, 'the English hate energy', but we're not talking here about forcefulness. Energy, the same word in Greek, Latin and French, literally means to 'put in work'. It may entail a great torrent of work, but audiences are not necessarily convinced by effort. On the contrary, what they most respond to is apparently effortless communication. I say 'apparently', because this is where the art lies: inner energy transformed into effortless empathy. George Burns and Spencer Tracy worked very hard to achieve their results. Tracy used to say, 'I listen, I think, and I speak. And if you think that's easy, try it.' As the energy leaves the body, it has to cope with a welter of tiny problems and it has to shape the decisions that are made. Do I look at him, drop my eyes, raise my hand, shift my position, inflect that word, observe that full stop, run these thoughts together, ironize them, punch them, throw them away? These decisions may be prepared, intuitive or subconscious, but they all have to be 'put in work'. I watched a great actor like Michael Bryant apparently just stand there and say the line, and make the moment achieve an extraordinary clarity and significance, and I marvelled how. I know now that it's because he understood how to control his energy.

Energy is dependent on breathing, and breathing upon oxygen. Together they feed the brain and the voice. Breath in turn needs support from the lower ribcage and the abdomen. If you're not breathing freely from lower enough down you can't sustain the voice and it will lack range and flexibility. Breath is fundamental in giving energy to the thought, the moment, the word, the line. Breathing exercises are the most basic part of an actor's preparation, and fortunately the easiest. If I sound like a fanatic, then I am. Breath is freedom.

Breathing is also the one activity we share with the audience. It has the most obvious returns in comedy. Michael Hordern and Eric Morcambe both understood the importance of getting an audience to breathe with them. Comedy depends greatly on confirming or confounding the audience's expectations, and the size of the laugh can relate to whether one speaks on the breath, or holds or shortens it. In a David Hare play, *The Absence of War*, I had four short sentences. If I spoke them all on one breath, which was very difficult, I got a large laugh. If I broke them up in any way, I halved the laugh. In tragedy the importance of breathing is less obvious, but just as crucial. The thought forms, the impulse to speak arrives, and the way you energize the line depends on the way you breathe it. In tragedy too the audience can be made to breathe with you, indeed at climactic moments they instinctively want to.

## ANTICIPATION AND EGOISM

That other cornerstone of acting, allowing the thought to come into your mind at the right moment, is also largely instinctive. Early in my career I asked Alec McCowen, when we were playing in Peter Luke's *Hadrian VII*, how he knew if he was acting well.

> When I clear my mind, listen to what's said to me, and find myself replying . . . with the lines the author's written for me.
>
> *How often does that happen?*
>
> On a good night, about seventy per cent of the time.
>
> *And on the press night?*
>
> Oh, never on the press night!

Poor critics, condemned to a life of never experiencing actors listening to one another. The great enemy of clearing the mind is anticipation. I later played for a year in *Hadrian VII* with Alec's replacement, the remarkable Canadian actor Douglas Rain. I used to ask him for notes, and he eventually told me I was anticipating him in half a dozen places. I protested that I was not breaking into the ends of his lines. 'No, but I see in your eyes your next thought forming before

I've given you the key words that trigger it.' That's a hard discipline to maintain, especially after three hundred performances, but it's central to the acting process. Acting stays alive, spontaneous and truthful if you can conquer anticipation.

Brecht is reported to have said to an actor in rehearsal:

> This is your moment, don't let it get away. Now it's your turn, and to hell with the play. All those taking part are interested in carrying forward the common cause of the play, yours too. But then there is also your interest, which stands in a certain contradiction to this. Everything lives from this contradiction.[3]

This last sentence is a huge claim, but I believe it says something fundamental about acting. In my experience every young actor naturally falls, however slightly, on one side or other of this divide. He either wants to serve his own interest, or the common cause of the play. He chooses a script either because it has a fat role for him, or because he likes the play. It is, if you like, a paradigm for life. We exist both as individuals, and as social beings. They stand in a certain contradiction to one another, and from this springs our creativity. But where is our primary allegiance? Outsiders might assume that all actors are egoists, hell bent on serving their own interests, or at least the interests of the characters they are playing. But in fact a large number are intent firstly on making the play work. This was certainly my interest when I first came into the theatre. I had to learn a long and bitter lesson; that it was at least as important to stand up for my character as it was for the play. Brecht's company was called the Berliner Ensemble, and the word 'ensemble' has been bandied about for fifty years as a kind of holy grail. We certainly believed in it at the RSC in the '70s. But successful ensembles can't be made up of a group of anonymous players dutifully filling in their bits. It requires passionate discussion as actors fight their corner for the characters they are playing. Anyone may be required to dominate the action.[4] Shakespeare is particularly rich in '2nd servants' and '3rd gentlemen' who briefly take over the play. 'Now it's your turn,'

3   Hubert Witt (ed), *Brecht As They Knew Him* (London: Lawrence and Wishart, 1975), p. 128.

4   Michael Gambon told me a story of Olivier directing O'Casey's *Juno and the Paycock* at the National Theatre, and passionately urging the removal men in the last act: 'This is YOUR forty-five seconds. TAKE IT.'

says Brecht, and provocatively continues, 'and to hell with the play . . .
Everything lives from this contradiction.' I know what he means.
Selflessness in acting is as big a sin as selfishness.


## THE CHALLENGE OF REPETITION

The great problem for the stage actor is reproducing the part night
after night. One of the best descriptions I know of what it's actually
like comes from Ralph Richardson. This may seem odd, since he was
such an idiosyncratic actor who didn't appear to give much thought
to technique. On the contrary, he prepared meticulously. In 1967 he
said in an interview:

'You're really driving four horses, as it were, first going through in
great detail the exact movements which you have decided upon.
You're also listening to the audience, keeping, if you can, very great
control over them. You're also slightly creating the part, in so far as
you're consciously refining the movements, and perhaps inventing
tiny other experiments with new ones. At the same time you are
really living, in one part of your mind, what is happening. Acting is
to some extent a controlled dream. In one part of your consciousness it really and truly is happening. But of course to make it true to
the audience, all the time, the actor must, at any rate some of the
time, believe himself that it is really true . . . The rest is technique,
as I say, of being very careful that the thing is completely accurate,
completely clear, completely as laid down beforehand. In every performance you're trying to find a better way to do it, and what you're
reshaping, the little experiments, may be very small indeed, and
quite unnoticed by your fellow actors; but they are working all the
time. Therefore three or four layers of consciousness are at work.'[5]

I wrote that down the year I became an actor, and I now know it
to be true of a particular kind of British classical actor, of which I
suppose I am one. Many actors, bred in a more improvisatory school
of acting, would consider it essential to reshape the part at every
performance. The climax of any scene can be shifted every night,
sometimes through genuine feeling or need, sometimes quite arbitrarily to achieve spontaneity. It's a technique very suited to film –
'never do two takes the same'. But in film the actor is rarely in charge
of the general shape, that's down to the director and editor. On stage

5   Hal Burton (ed), *Great Acting* (London: BBC Publications, 1967), pp. 71-2.

GONERIL: 'Sir, I do love you more than word can wield the matter.' Lear and Goneril, (Oliver Ford Davies and Suzanne Burden), Act I, Scene i

The FOOL: 'Can you make no use of nothing, nuncle?' The Fool (Anthony O'Donnell) and Lear, Act I, Scene iv

LEAR: 'O, Regan, will you take her by the hand?' Lear, the Fool, Regan (Lizzy McInnerny) and Goneril, Act II, Scene iv

LEAR: 'Blow winds and crack your cheeks!' The set, largely destroyed, Act III, Scene ii

KENT: 'Trouble him not; his wits are gone.' Gloucester (David Ryall), Kent (Paul Jesson), Lear, Edgar (Tom Hollander), Act III, Scene vi

LEAR: 'When we are born we cry that we are come to this great stage of fools.' Edgar, Gloucester and Lear, Act IV, Scene vi

CORDELIA: 'O my dear father, restoration hang thy medicine on my lips.' Cordelia (Nancy Carroll) and Lear, Act IV, Scene vii

LEAR: 'And my poor fool is hanged.' Cordelia and Lear, Act V, Scene iii

the actor is in charge of both detail and shape. The essence of any acting is 'staying in the moment'. Just as a musician can only play one note at a time, so an actor can only move from moment to moment, all the time knowing that every changed detail affects the shape of the whole. The architecture of the part is the business of rehearsal; staying in the moment, without anticipating, the work of performance. 'Every detail must exist', says Brendel, 'and when you have mastered every detail you are free.' How much detail can I master in preparing Lear? Will I ever be free? For, as he says in the storm, 'when the mind's free, the body's delicate'.

## LANGUAGE IN SHAKESPEARE

All the above applies to acting in Shakespeare – only more so.[6] The first special problem is the verse. Fortunately the ten syllable iambic is a natural way to speak in English. Curiously enough, the eight or twelve syllable iambic draws much more attention to the metre. Much of Lear's verse in his first two scenes is very regular, as if to underline his authority and confidence.

> Thŏu hāst hĕr, Frānce; lĕt hēr bĕ thīne, fŏr wē
> Havĕ n̄o sŭch daūghtĕr, nŏr shăll evĕr sēe
> Thăt face ŏf hērs ăgaīn. Thĕrefōre, bĕ gōne,
> Wĭthoūt oŭr grāce, oŭr love, oŭr benīson.

The stresses, however, don't have to follow the iambic beat. In the first line it might be natural to stress 'Thōu hāst hĕr, Frānce', or in the second line 'n̄o sūch daūghtĕr', and the breaking of the rhythm gives added emphasis. This can happen quite naturally, it doesn't necessarily have to be thought out. One of the traps in Shakespeare is to become imprisoned in the metre, and stick with the same tone and tempo throughout a speech. As with any dramatist, you need to look for variety, and the verse should help not hinder you in this. There is often some sort of break, or caesura, in the middle of the line, as there is in each of the four lines above, but this doesn't have to be marked. A more controversial point is whether you should mark the end of each line with an upward inflection and/or a slight breath. These four lines are in fact two rhyming couplets, and it

6   An invaluable guide is John Barton, *Playing Shakespeare* (London and New York: Methuen, 1984).

would be natural to mark 'we' and 'see', even though the sense
carries over. But even where there is no rhyme, Shakespeare's sense
of rhythm usually marks the end of the line in some way. For
example, from 1.4:

> And from her derogate body never spring
> A babe to honour her. If she must teem,
> Create her child of spleen, that it may live
> And be a thwart disnatured torment to her.

You can sense that there is some break, however tiny, after 'spring',
'teem' and 'live'. One of the few set rules is the immediate taking up
of a cue if the speech starts on a half line. Shakespeare sometimes
writes an entire scene in this way, and it's a sure sign that he intended no pauses. On the rare occasions he writes a half line, it usually
indicates a pause. In 2.4. after Lear's half line 'The terrors of the
earth', the Folio adds, as if in explanation, the stage direction 'Storm
and Tempest'.

The Elizabethans had a great ear for antithesis and paradox, and
could evidently spot them many lines apart. Some of my favourite
antitheses are contained in,

> Plate sin with gold,
> And the strong lance of justice hurtles breaks;
> Arm it in rags, a pigmy's straw does pierce it.

'Plate', 'gold' and 'breaks' are perfectly balanced against 'arm', 'rags'
and 'pierce'. 'The strong lance of justice' is contrasted with 'a pigmy's
straw' not just in sense, but in sound. It's difficult to say the first without pompous gravity or the second without diminutive pettiness.

There is a sense in *Lear* that, though Shakespeare started in
regular verse, he cared less and less about strict metre as the play
progresses, and as Lear's mind and his kingdom begin to crumble.
There are many lines of twelve syllables, and lines with anything
from four to seven stresses. One of the main signs of disintegration is
in *Dover Beach*, where it is unclear whether some of Lear's speeches
should be in verse or prose. Sometimes the contrast of verse and
prose is deliberate. In the opening scene Lear's regular verse is pitched
against Gloucester's naturalistic, rambling prose. But which did
Shakespeare intend by,

> I pardon that man's life. What was thy cause?
> Adultery?
> Thou shalt not die; die for adultery? No,
> The wren goes to't and the small gilded fly
> Does lecher in my sight. [End of line]

Does it matter? What it demonstrates is that Shakespeare's prose is often as rhythmic as his verse, and the words have an equal relish. One of the most important things in Shakespeare is for the actor to respond to the language. Lear has his share of grandiloquence:

> All the stored vengeances of heaven fall
> On her ingrateful top! Strike her young bones,
> You taking airs, with lameness!

Lear's feelings about Goneril have to be strong enough to need this size of image. If the actor is not at fever pitch, it can come across as empty bombast. Lines like these need great energy, pace and commitment. So too, in a different way, do Shakespeare's great monosyllabic simplicities:

> O, I have ta'en too little care of this.

> When we are born we cry that we are come
> To this great stage of fools.

> I fear I am not in my perfect mind.

Here the energy and pace have to be contained. It is impossible to rush these lines. Monosyllables have the paradoxical effect of slowing the speaker down. The challenge here is to state, rather than embellish, the line, without losing the emotion that lies behind it. Whether grandiloquent or simple, Shakespeare's language is always in some way 'heightened'. This has to be honoured.

However much we discuss and analyze it, language is not an end in itself. Language is the conveyor of meaning and the key to character. It's a charge often levelled at dramatists that their characters speak in the same language and idiom, but Shakespeare's ear became increasingly acute. In 1.2. Edmund, on best behaviour, speaks with a courtly formality, while Gloucester is naturalistically unbuttoned.

EDMUND    But I have heard him oft maintain it to be fit that, sons at perfect age and fathers declined, the father should be as ward to the son and the son manage his revenue.

GLOUCESTER    O villain, villain! His very opinion in the letter! Abhorred villain! Unnatural, detested, brutish villain – worse than brutish!

A similar contrast is observed in verse when Regan tries to pacify Lear in 2.4.

LEAR                    Beloved Regan,
Thy sister's naught. O, Regan, she hath tied
Sharp-toothed unkindness, like a vulture, here.
I can scarce speak to thee; thou'lt not believe
With how depraved a quality – O, Regan!

REGAN    I pray you, sir, take patience. I have hope
You less know how to value her desert
Than she to scant her duty.

LEAR    Say? How is that?

One of the reasons Edgar's part is so large is that Shakespeare seems drunk on the language he found in Samuel Harsnett's *A Declaration of Egregious Popish Impostures* (1603). To give credence and flavour to Edgar's assumption of a Bedlam beggar, Shakespeare pours out borrowings from Harsnett: 'Peace, Smulkin, peace thou fiend. . . The prince of darkness is a gentleman. Modo he's called, and Mahu'.

But while Shakespeare always needs energy and commitment, he requires coolness as well as passion. It is Hamlet's first instruction to the players.

Speak the speech, I pray you, as I pronounc'd it to you, trippingly on the tongue, but if you mouth it, as many of our players do, I had as lief the town-crier spoke my lines. Nor do not saw the air too much with your hand, thus, but use all gently, for in the very torrent, tempest, and, as I may say, whirlwind of your passion, you must acquire and beget a temperance that may give it smoothness.

I am especially aware of this at the moment, for there is a great temptation in Lear to 'tear a passion to tatters', and to 'out-herod Herod'. The part demands it at times, so all the more reason to look for 'a temperance that may give it smoothness'. Fortunately Shakespeare always helps you in this. Lear's first speech in the storm would seem to be forte, though even John Barton admits, 'I don't quite know how I think this speech should be done. It could be that when you do it [flat out] it's an overlay on Shakespeare rather than a realisation of the text and indeed of the emotions.'[7] Lear's second speech offers some interesting contrasts:

> Rumble thy bellyful! Spit fire, spout rain!
> Nor rain, wind, thunder, fire are my daughters;
> I tax not you, you elements, with unkindness.
> I never gave you kingdom, called you children;
> You owe me no subscription. Why then, let fall
> Your horrible pleasure. Here I stand your slave,
> A poor, infirm, weak and despised old man.
> But yet I call you servile ministers
> That will with two pernicious daughters join
> Your high-engendered battles 'gainst a head
> So old and white as this. O ho! 'tis foul.

The first line still seems to be forte, but the next four and a half introduce a cooling rationality, and the four adjectives linked to old man slow the tempo down further. He seems to rally again on the 'servile ministers', but he is becoming self-pitying rather than challenging. By his next speech he is totally deflated.

> No, I will be the pattern of all patience,
> I will say nothing.

Clues to the emotional and vocal pattern are there if only you respond to the language.

Energy, breath and support are central to the playing of Shakespeare. He himself must have been very aware of this problem, particularly in large open-air theatres and courtyards, and there has been much discussion about whether he intended the actor to

7    Barton, *Playing Shakespeare*, op. cit., p. 143.

breathe on the punctuation marks, or at the end of lines. Most of the decisions about where to take breath are settled naturally and unconsciously, but in a long part there may be a dozen occasions where it has to be consciously resolved. In the second storm speech quoted above, for instance, the actor is running so short of breath that it requires a large and deliberate intake after 'servile ministers' if one is to get through the next two and a half lines on one breath.

## ARCHETYPES AND INDIVIDUALITY

One of the most difficult problems for the modern actor is dealing with Shakespearian archetypes. Elizabethan dramatists were concerned not so much with unique or unusual characters but with presenting convincing renditions of types, viz Jacques' 'seven ages of man' speech. Thus Henry V symbolizes 'national hero' (or even 'scapegrace turned responsible king'), Shylock 'avaricious but oppressed jewry', Macbeth 'vaulting ambition'. This archetypal element can never be entirely discounted. Henry V sees that to win the battle of Agincourt against unlikely odds he has to put on the mantle of 'national hero'. Macbeth's ambition, Othello's jealousy, Shylock's jewishness have to be examined. To present a gentile Shylock, an unkingly Henry V, an unambitious Macbeth may delight those who have seen the play twenty times and long for a revolutionary interpretation, but it is finally reductive. At the same time one of the things we value most in Shakespeare is his ability to humanize his characters. Juliet may speak for universal 'young love', but she is very much an individual. Henry V may strike a kingly pose, but his most telling speech is when he inveighs against the 'idol Ceremony' and the pressures laid 'on the King'. Where the trap lies is to fall into what I call the 'Brutus is noble' syndrome. Because Mark Antony says at the end of *Julius Caesar* 'This was the noblest Roman of them all' and proceeds to eulogize Brutus for another seven lines, the actor can fall into the mode, however subconsciously, of thinking that whatever he does with the part it has to be 'noble'. Brutus in fact makes a catalogue of bad decisions in the play, so that whatever 'nobility' he displays has to be tempered with poor judgement. Macbeth may be an ambitious murderer, but he is the character in the play most aware of his spiritual and metaphysical hinterland. Too much labelling of Shakespeare's characters destroys their precious individuality. It leads critics to declare that Lear has to be a 'titan', and possess 'moral grandeur'. It makes me sympathetic to Brook's question, 'Where on your ticket is it printed that . . . ?' The actor's primary task is to inhabit a human being.

Aligned to the archetype is the 'great moment'. Shakespeare deployed them carefully throughout his plays: Coriolanus's submission to his mother, Lucio's unhooding of the Duke in *Measure for Measure*, the reunion of Viola and Sebastian. They must be given full weight. Judi Dench recalls how on an African tour the audience went wild with delight at the reunion of the twins, thus reminding a British cast, jaded with *Twelfth Night*, that this is the climax the narrative is leading to. A whole host of minor 'moments' have now become identified, forming a kind of check list for aficionados: Hamlet spotting Ophelia is a decoy, Othello noticing Iago is hiding something, Jacques suspecting 'Ganymede' is female. Actors and directors vie with new ways to present these, as if the actor can't be left to play them in the way the text suggests. Some productions also search for new 'moments' to add to the ones Shakespeare has written in. I have watched such 'moments' being manufactured in rehearsal in a deliberate, even cynical, way. 'Let's give this line a new twist, and clearly mark it with a pause and a piece of business: then the audience can't miss it, and it will give the critics something to write about.' It's like the film actor, who knows he only needs six good screen moments, and the rest can be behavourist padding. But acting is more than just coasting from interesting moment to interesting moment. By drawing such attention to themselves they interrupt Shakespeare's essential flow.

## IRONY AND FAITHFULNESS TO THE TEXT

One element in Shakespeare I find difficult is the degree to which he employs irony, 'the conveyance of meaning by words whose literal meaning is the opposite'. The Elizabethans loved it, and once you start looking for it in Shakespeare you begin to suspect it everywhere. Edmund is clearly being ironic when he says,

A credulous father and a brother noble.

but is Lear when he says,

> While we unburdened crawl toward death.

or

> I will be the pattern of all patience?

I once gave a paper on *Coriolanus* at a Shakespeare symposium in Paris, and an earnest French professor floored me with the question, 'Do you think the entire play is an irony?' I now see that there is a sense in which all Shakespeare's plays are ironic. Irony is created by a perception of the disparities between appearance and reality, between what seems, or is acknowledged, to be true, and what is really true. Lear, Goneril and Regan in their first scene set up an appearance of familial and political amity whose reality will be ironically exposed as the play progresses. But how aware are the characters of the ironies they inhabit? Irony nearly always implies the character's ability to stand outside himself, and comment on his own and others' actions. It is a very British characteristic. Actors love it, and audiences respond to it. But it can be a trap. It can be a way of not committing oneself to the thought or emotion of the moment, or of actually declaring oneself superior to it. 'I am declaring myself in love, but wryly acknowledging the stupidity of it.' 'I am expressing anger, but also marking what a useless expense of spirit it is.' It is a way of playing God. This is a temptation to an actor in any play, but in Shakespeare it is red hot. 'I am the most intelligent character in this play, and I am always one step ahead of everyone else.' The actor then begins to hold every line up for inspection – 'this is what my character is saying, but of course it could mean a variety of things'. This tendency to guide an audience through the complexities and contradictions of a part as if it were an illustrated lecture is very beguiling, but finally to be resisted. The audience should be left to do the work for themselves, they don't need ironic footnotes. What they want of the actor is that he inhabits the part and presents a convincing reading.

A final problem, common to all plays but especially to familiar classics: do you play what the text seems to indicate, or do you use the text as a springboard for further interpretation? Or as Hollywood would have it, do you play the script or what the script reminds you of? In a text as contradictory and ambiguous as *Lear*, the script will of course yield multiple interpretations, though some may be more probable than others, but it is still possible to elaborate further. The play might be set in a madhouse, a mortuary or an old people's home. Gloucester might be an astrologer, a butler or a deputy headmaster. The Jonathan Miller thesis is that an author deserves two or three productions faithful to his or her intentions, and after that it is open season. Others argue that if Shakespeare were alive today he would welcome changes/rewrite the plays entirely/be too busy inventing new TV soaps. I don't know quite where I stand on this. We are all unwilling to be thought 'traditionalists', turning the plays into museum pieces. My whole training has been faithfulness to the text, yet my response to it is bound to be post Freud/Hegel/Marx/Brecht/Beckett etc. When you accept to play a part you know you are embarking on an act of re-creation, of re-interpretation. My feeling about Shakespeare is that most of his texts are so rich that it is enough to try and fathom yet again their meaning. No two people will come up with the same answer. I hope not to do anything that is plainly contrary to Shakespeare's intentions. But I wouldn't say this about all plays; some are in urgent need of radical reworking. But not so *King Lear*.

# 6

## PRELIMINARIES

The previous chapter was finished just before 11 September 2001. I heard the news driving a hired Transit van down the Chiswick High Road, a task that unnerves me at the best of times. The news flash ends with the bare sentence, 'Both towers have collapsed'. I can't pull up, I have to drive on. Can she really have said that . . . it could be fifty thousand people . . . last September I was at the top of those towers myself? I couldn't make sense of it, and now, two months and thousands of column inches later, I still can't. Has it radically changed the world? 'Is this the promised end? Or image of that horror? Fall and cease.'

October is unnaturally warm and beautiful. I am filming in Bath Abbey, playing the Archbishop of Canterbury rehearsing the coronation of George VI. Edward VIII has just abdicated. I'm thinking about *King Lear*. Tony Blair is trying to keep the rest of the world on board for the bombing of Afghanistan, raids to which Britain's actually contributing very little. I'm reminded of the thesis about *King Lear's* relevance to the last fifty years: Britain has given away her vast colonies, but clings on to the trappings of imperial power as she slides into second world status. No wonder we do the play so often, and America so seldom.

I am in touch with Jonathan Kent regularly now. We meet, usually for dinner, once a fortnight and discuss the play, the production, the set, cuts and casting. I tell him my ideas for this book and show him what I've written so far. If he's disturbed by the amount of preparation I've done already, he manages to conceal it. He's keen that I should find a publisher. It's an important production for Jonathan, his last for the Almeida after twelve years. I think of the number of artistic directors who have signed off with *Lear*: Glen Byam Shaw at Stratford, Max Stafford-Clark at the Royal Court, Richard Eyre at the National. Opening with *Hamlet*, as Olivier, Hall and Eyre did at the National, and ending with *Lear* seems to have become an English tradition, a passage from youth to age.

The relationship between actor and director is complicated, difficult to describe, sometimes harmonious, sometimes fraught. *Lear* brings out the best and worst in such a relationship, because the part and the play offer such a breadth of choice. Byam Shaw and his Lear, Charles Laughton, had both thought long and hard about the play and clearly didn't agree. As one observer put it, 'What would have been a grand old Shakespearian production was destroyed by Charles, bit by bit – a year's work dismantled. This poor weak producer would say to each of Charles' suggestions, "You're a genius!" We watched with fascination.'[1] Robert Stephens describes the problem and his solution in his autobiography, *Knight Errant*:

> As an actor, I have never played a part without first deciding
> exactly how I was going to play it. I then proceed to make a
> series of adjustments or compromises with the director in
> which I hopefully come out on top. I had a long series of
> meeting with Adrian [Noble]. . . and happily we agreed. Or
> rather he agreed with me. . . Some critics rightly felt that I was
> less interested in the tyranny and rage of the man than in his
> comic potential and his spiritual journey after the storm.[2]

I doubt if the rather benign figure, 'whose only real fault has been to grow too old and too trusting', was really to Adrian's taste. But this is in the tradition of Olivier, who told John Dexter exactly how he was going to play Othello, and Michael Elliott how he wanted to play Lear. Michael Hordern, on the other hand, wrote, 'I had complete confidence in Jonathan Miller and put myself totally in his hands'.[3]

Jonathan and I proceed cautiously but amicably. We have done two Shakespeares, a Chekhov and a Pirandello together, and we know one another's strengths and weaknesses. Jonathan I judge to be good on design concept, text, overall sweep, pace, attack, accessibility and clarity. The Almeida ethic under Jonathan and Ian McDiarmid, is 'high definition acting', very much on the front foot. Jonathan is also

1  Callow, *Laughton*, op. cit., pp. 263-4.
2  Stephens, *Knight Errant*, op. cit., pp. 180, 182.
3  Hordern, *A World Elsewhere*, op. cit., p. 138.

very good at thinking on his feet in rehearsal, in responding to what actors give him. Jonathan would, I think, judge that my strengths are benign humanity, inwardness, detail, irony and clarity. I have played a lot of well-meaning failures. We will need to adjust to one another, and trust that our strengths will be complementary. We share a lot of ground. We agree that Lear abdicates because he fears his mind is going, and that uncontrollable anger is his undoing. We see him as authoritarian, foolish and largely unsympathetic in at least the first two acts. We want to examine how reasonable Goneril and Regan appear until Gloucester's blinding. We see Cordelia's silence as a genuine uncertainty about the nature of love, not as an act of rebellion. We want to emphasize Lear's sense of public humiliation. We swap more detailed ideas. For example, Jonathan likes my suggestion that spending a month each with Goneril and Regan is a stratagem improvised on the spot to replace his plan to live with Cordelia. I like his idea that the map of Britain has already been divided into three folders.

Jonathan has already given a lot of thought to the set. When he first mentioned *Lear* to me in 1998, he said that he had always seen it in a panelled room, and that he hoped to do it in a real Jacobean room in one of the Inns of Court. This worried me initially, as I remembered that in 1994 Max Stafford-Clark had used a panelled set, and this had presented problems when the action moved out of doors. Paul Brown, who has recently designed marvellous sets for Jonathan's *Tempest* and *Platonov*, shows me a model. It is extremely ingenious. Almost every panel in the 'room', which embraces both stage and auditorium, is capable of falling backwards, so that the set can either be destroyed by the actors, or disintegrate of its own accord (via stage management ingenuity). The idea, of course, is that as Lear's mind shatters so does the set, revealing a void beyond. One of Jonathan's further ideas is that Lear will start the destruction himself by smashing a large mirror centre stage. The original stage furniture will all remain on the Act Three heath, and will become part of the chaos of the divided kingdom/Lear's mind. Lear's desk, for example, will become the entrance to the hovel. If the budget will stand it, the audience will return after the interval to find the comforting walls of their auditorium have been breached as well, and that both actor and spectator are now stranded in the former bus garage.[4]

4    The budget did not stand it, alas.

I am very excited by this concept. Past productions have solved the problem of the move from indoors to outdoors by sliding open a back wall. The disintegration of the room, however, adds a further layer of meaning. It bears out all the imagery of 'cracking' and 'splitting' in the storm scene. It allows us to see the collapse of a specific, detailed society. I think this is important. There's a great temptation to put *Lear* in a bare or abstract setting, with neutral timeless costumes. But I don't find Shakespeare works well in the abstract, he's such a very concrete, detailed, social writer. Since he wrote so few contemporary plays, the society he creates is always part Jacobethan, part imagined. Shakespeare knew little more about 800 B.C. than he did about 2002 A.D. But part of his genius was to create worlds that were both well-defined and timeless. In production it's wise to go for the well-defined; timeless should look after itself. Our period is to be twentieth century, but not tied to a particular decade. Costumes may range from 1930s to present day. The advantage of this is the wealth of references the audience will bring to it, whether linking Lear's abdication with Edward VIII's or identifying Regan by the designer clothes she's chosen.

I have two misgivings. First, that the logistics of Paul's set may be too complicated. I envisage a mammoth technical dress rehearsal, cancelled previews, and set machinery not entirely reliable in performance. Second, I worry that the design will signal the production concept. My fear is that the set will tell the audience what to think, not the text and the actors. Jonathan assures me that he is alive to this problem, that he doesn't want the disintegration of the set to be a *coup-de-théâtre*, and that it will be part masked by lighting and sound effects. The set will be Lear's servant, not his master. We shall see. One particular concept gives me great concern. In scene one Jonathan envisages Lear announcing his abdication to the entire nation, and that this is therefore televised. He assures me this won't involve camera crews and P.A.s with clipboards scurrying around, merely a hidden camera, additional lighting and monitors in the auditorium. I fear the literalness of this and that the audience will anticipate that television will continue as a production motif. I had a terrible experience in an RSC *Julius Caesar*, when we had to keep adjusting the forum scene to accommodate onstage cameras and screens (it was dropped after a month of agony). Nothing like that will occur, promises Jonathan . . .

We live in a design-conscious age. The visual has become all important. Naturally it dominates in the cinema, but it increasingly swamps the spoken word on television, where drama is shot like film and scenes with dialogue become ever shorter. Theatre has always embraced spectacle, from medieval mystery plays, to Jacobean masques,eighteenth-century spectaculars, train crashes in Victorian melodrama, Beerbohm Tree's live rabbits in Shakespeare, to the vast technology of the modern musical. It is not what live theatre does best, and there have been periodic returns to simplicity in Gordon Craig's designs, William Poel's Shakespeares, '20s expressionism, settings for Brecht and Beckett, and the RSC's white and black boxes in the '70s, but at the turn of this century audiences have come to expect and revel in visual ingenuity. Perhaps it makes them feel safe, just as young audiences may feel secure if they see that part of their Shakespeare is to be on a television screen. But overdesign in Shakespeare can be a big problem, particularly as the author detailed the setting where he thought necessary in the text. In an RSC *Troilus and Cresssida* I once suggested that I saw the aged Nestor as a tortoise, moving purposefully and very slowly. The director and designer were so taken with this image that I ended up on all fours with a great humped shield on my back. Within thirty seconds of my first appearance the audience spotted that I was a tortoise, and my performance was over. It got me a lot of notices – critics love a clear image to write about – but it didn't serve the development of the play (or my spine).

The production is to run initially for eight weeks from 31 January to 28 March 2002. The money is to be £400 a week, better than the current Equity minimum of £288.50, but not a wage to gladden the heart of a plumber or a policeman. I ask that there should be no mid-week matinees, not even odd extra schools' performances, and Jonathan accedes. This is a great relief. But the Almeida insist we do a Saturday matinee. I approve of this in principle. Many people, particularly those living outside London, can only get to an afternoon performance, and I have always found them an excellent audience. They really want to be there, and their commitment is palpable. Two Edinburgh friends are already planning to get the 7 a.m. train down, and the 6 p.m. back! But seven Lears a week for eight or more weeks could be a killer. Even Wolfit limited his Lears to three a week whenever he could. I have no real idea of how my body and voice will stand up to it. The budget dictates that we have no understudies, so the pressure to be 'on', in whatever state of health, will be enormous. When Alan Howard was doing seven Coriolanuses for two weeks at the Aldwych in 1979, our director Terry Hands brought Peter Hoffman to see it, who was singing in no more than two *Parsifals* a week at Covent Garden. Hoffman greatly admired Alan's vocal power, but was staggered to find he was doing it every night. 'It makes me feel ashamed,' he said.

There is already great interest abroad in the production. Tokyo, Singapore and various cities in Australia would welcome a tour. In Europe, Paris, Zurich, and Düsseldorf seem very positive, and in the U.S.A. Boston and Chicago are particularly interested. I don't know how much I, or my body, relish a world tour, but the European part is very attractive. I twice toured France, Germany and Switzerland with the RSC in the '70s, and found it hugely rewarding. But despite the fact that Paris and Hamburg are closer to London than Glasgow, such tours have become a rarity. Successive governments have shown little interest in funding the national companies or the British Council to tour large-scale productions abroad. This is very short-sighted, as the gains in national prestige, and diplomatic and commercial relations, not to mention cultural exchange, are enormous. I remember in occupied Berlin in 1976 a very non-theatre-going army major telling me that our visit with *Henry V* had done more for British prestige in the city than anything else he could remember. Every summer European companies visit one another's festivals, and they are shocked and disappointed that Britain, whose theatre and actors they hold in such high regard, are invariably absent. The hunger to see Shakespeare in particular in his original language cannot be overestimated.

At our meetings Jonathan and I begin to discuss possible cuts in the text, though I limit my suggestions to Lear's scenes only. This is a difficult area. Many reasons have been put forward for not cutting Shakespeare at all. Major works deserve to be done in their entirety. Nobody cuts *Tristan an Isolde* or Beethoven's Ninth (though personally I think both would benefit). Audiences arrive for a Shakespeare tragedy prepared for a long evening. However obscure, the language communicates at a deep level. In the case of *Lear* we already have the Folio version of about two thousand, nine hundred lines, presumably cut by Shakespeare himself. Why not stick at that? The reasons for further trimming are various, and cumulatively outweigh 'purist' intransigence. First, expedience, the demands of a particular production: since we are doing it modern, certain things don't fit. I can hardly wear a crown on top of a lounge suit, so we have to lose 'This coronet part between you'. Excessive references to pagan gods don't sit well either, so from,

> For by the sacred radiance of the sun,
> The mysteries of Hecate and the night,
> By all the operations of the orbs
> From whom we do exist and cease to be

it seems best to lose the first two lines. If we don't want a herald in the last scene, cut the references to him and give some of the lines to Albany. Second, narrative clarity: Shakespeare was sometimes careless in his story telling, especially in its time sequence. Since in 1.5. Lear can't possibly know Regan is at Gloucester's, 'Go you before to Gloucester with these letters' is confusing. 'Gloucester' is often changed to 'Cornwall', but Jonathan elects to go the whole hog, and change it to 'Regan'. Third, excesses: this is subjective, but I think Shakespeare sometimes overwrote and became repetitious. In 2.4, for example, Lear lays four curses on Goneril. Three seem to me ample, however much Lear is out of control, and we decide to cut,

> You nimble lightnings, dart your blinding flames
> Into her scornful eyes.

Fourth, obscurity: too many unintelligible lines destroy some audience's understanding and concentration.

> I'll able 'em;
> Take that of me, my friend, who have the power
> To seal th' accuser's lips.

seems to me just too difficult. Fifth, length: audiences are resistant to plays that stray too far over three hours. If we start at 7.30 p.m., we need to be down by at least 10.45 p.m. Shakespeare may very well have cut his own plays, either to get them down before dark, or to fit them into the 2 p.m. to 5 p.m. span allotted by the Lord Mayor and the Lord Chamberlain. The final reason is the most questionable, but there is no getting round the claim that we think we can improve on Shakespeare artistically. If he 'never blotted a line' that seems to me a pity. Fortunately in *Lear* he did, because he cut two hundred and eighty-eight Q lines, including, quite rightly, the whole of 4.3. Most directors cut the interminable exchanges between Edgar and Edmund before their duel. More contentiously, I have always found in the *Recognition*,

> for I am mainly ignorant
> What place this is and all the skill I have
> Remembers not these garments; nor I know not
> Where I did lodge last night.

curiously bathetic lines. I realize it reflects Lear's child-like uncertainty and dependence, but it interrupts his main thought flow, which is to drive towards 'I think this lady to be my child Cordelia'. In all Jonathan cuts about 500 lines from the combined Q and F texts. Poor Tom and the Fool probably suffer the most. Lear loses about sixty lines, mostly from Acts 1 and 2. We now have a playing script of about two thousand, seven hundred lines (two hundred less than F). The cuts will remain negotiable (some over Jonathan's dead body). Each of them will prove anathema to somebody.

Every week or so I get an update on casting. Jonathan asks my opinion of various people and I make a few suggestions, but I feel diffident about involving myself too much. Perhaps I've been too long on the other side of the fence, or perhaps, because so many friends and acquaintances have said they'd like to be in it, I want to be able to say that the decision is not finally mine. Fiona Weir, and her senior partner, the great Mary Selway, are both advising, so there is no shortage of input. There's an adage in the theatre that 80% lies in the casting. If the cast is strong and can deliver to their potential, then the play may succeed whether helped or hampered by its production. The best bits of your performance are not going to end up on the cutting room floor. Jonathan quotes two other maxims; one he likes – 'sometimes your twenty-fifth choice should have been your first', and one he doesn't – 'you get the cast you deserve'. Happily, some of the key parts are settled quite early. I am very pleased that Anthony O'Donnell, who has a wonderful Welsh irony and sardonic darkness, is to play the Fool, and David Ryall, whose idiosyncratic naturalism I have always admired, is to be Gloucester. James Frain, so dangerous and unpredictable on film, is Edmund, and Nancy Carroll, a great find, Cordelia. The difficult parts of Goneril, Regan, and Edgar take longer. A surprising number of actresses have already played the elder sisters, and aren't longing to revisit them. Fortunately Jonathan finds Lizzy McInnerny as Regan, and at the last moment Suzanne Burden as Goneril. He auditions many Edgars, and finally decides to go with the Almeida's very successful Tartuffe, Tom Hollander. Paul Jesson is a great bonus as Kent (he has played Prospero and Henry VIII at the RSC), and we're lucky to attract a very strong Albany and Cornwall in Paul Shelley and David Robb. I'm delighted that various old friends such as David Sibley (Oswald), Hugh Simon (the doctor), Paul Benzing (the captain), and eighty-five-year-old Sam Beazley (the Old Man, who else?) are to join the cast. It's a challenging and not altogether predictable group, and I've fortunately worked with most of them before. James Frain should be a good contrast to Tom Hollander, as David Ryall will I think be to me. Some have done very little Shakespeare. David Ryall and Paul Shelley, on the other hand, have already played Lear themselves . . .

October and November I set aside, when I'm not filming, to learning the part. It was David Suchet who first pointed out to me that learning a major part first was the equivalent of two weeks extra rehearsal. Many actors prefer to learn in rehearsal as they interact with other actors and as intentions and moves become apparent. Some fear that by learning it 'cold' they will become trapped into fixed line readings too early on. But with a long and difficult play I find that six, or even eight, weeks is too short a rehearsal period to be starting from scratch. The pressure to make a production cohere and get it to performance pitch can close down choices too early in the process. Widening choices and keeping them open is the key to rehearsal, and the more prepared you are the longer you have. Learning the part first I therefore find a liberating, not a confining, experience, because it's only when you're really sure of the words that you can experiment with playing scenes in totally different ways. I also spend the autumn trying to get my voice and body in trim. I do voice and loosening up exercises most days; very basic work on vowels, consonants and breathing that I have picked up from Cicely Berry and Patsy Rodenburg. I am reluctant to start on a proper exercise regime, not just out of laziness but because every time I've done so in the past I've ended up straining my back. When I was at the RSC my fellow actor Emrys James used to say, 'whenever I feel I ought to take some exercise, I lie down till the feeling goes away', yet few actors used their bodies more eloquently than Emrys. So I steer clear of the gym, and go for long walks instead.

I learn a scene a week. I've read the play so many times that certain speeches come very easily, others prove more intractable. I'm always amazed, given the actor's dread of 'drying', that drama schools pay so little attention to the fundamental skill of memorizing. Actors are left to invent their own methods. Ralph Richardson, when asked, said he wrote the part out in different coloured pencils (Black for exposition? Red for anger? Green for jealousy?). I try not to learn simply by rote (though the rhythm of verse makes this attractive), but to get clear the pegs of the argument, the rungs on the ladder. If I'm certain where my intentions are taking me, if I'm thinking the right thoughts, then the words should come. Often I make 'mental lists'. In 1.1. for example, after Lear has banished Cordelia, he turns to Cornwall and Albany,

> With my two daughters' dowers, digest this third.
> Let pride, which she calls plainness, marry her.
> I do invest you jointly with my power,
> Pre-eminence and all the large effects
> That troop with majesty. Ourself by monthly course,
> With reservation of an hundred knights
> By you to be sustained, shall our abode
> Make with you by due turn; only we shall retain
> The name, and all th' addition to a king: the sway,
> Revenue, execution of the rest
> Beloved son, be yours.

So my 'mental list' would go: one, digest this third; two, invest you with my power; three, 100 knights; four, I retain kingship; five, the rest is yours. One word helps me to another. 'Dowers' gives me the thought about 'marry her'. Alliteration and assonance are rife; three 'd's in the first line, then the two 'p's of 'pride' and 'plainness', and I stay with 'p's for 'power' and 'pre-eminence'. In the last clause the three subjects (like all writers Shakespeare loved threes) start with the elegant word 'sway' and end with the horrible finality of 'execution', so I have a mental picture of both. Shakespeare loved verbal games, and recognizing them helps you both to memorize and to point them. Though the verb is usually the most active word in the sentence, it's harder to visualize and is often more difficult to remember. Fortunately, in extremis, you can usually substitute another verb with less damage to the sense than a different noun might cause.

All this while, I'm naturally thinking about Lear's voice and movement. I feel the text of the first three acts demands a strong voice. Quavery Lears usually become a liability. Luckily, ever since my voice broke at fourteen, I have been able to produce a resonant, bass baritone voice. A Russian conductor, who came to see *Coriolanus* told me, 'You have a voice that can split bricks. You should be singing Alberich in *The Ring*'. The ability to split bricks should be an advantage in the storm that Jonathan is cooking up. The contrast with the 'old and foolish' Lear of the last three scenes will also be the greater. I'm very concerned with how Lear looks, and how his age manifests itself. Jonathan hates anything artificial like wigs and stuck-on beards, he'd be happy for me to play Lear looking like myself. But I think Lear's great age is central to the part. I intend to grow a beard, which I know alas will be pure white, and in some way whiten my hair. Fortunately Paul Brown backs me on this. If Lear's mental and vocal energy is still very active, as it must be to cope with the text, his age would seem to lie in his movement. Jonathan is worried that I will be doddery. I have to reassure him – not doddery, but perhaps stiff, unconfident, a little slow. I don't want to assume a walk on day one of rehearsal, I'm hoping one will emerge.

Friends are beginning to ask me, 'How are you going to play the part?' and I usually reply, 'I don't know'. I've done a great deal of preparation, but I've deliberately skirted round the central problem of what I'm actually going to do. This is not so with all parts. Two years ago in *Coriolanus* I based my Menenius on William Whitelaw, the wily Tory grandee who treated all classes with great bonhomie, but was outmanoeuvred for the leadership by Margaret Thatcher. But there's no one you can *base* Lear on. However 'I don't know' is not strictly true. I know what I'm not going to do, and elimination is one way of arriving at a resolution. He is not in the early stages of senility. He is not a benign grandfather, nor a neurotic intellectual. I simply can't find those in the text. I think he's been a strong king and a patriarchal father. I believe he knows his mind is going, and that uncontrollable anger is its main symptom. What I don't yet know is how he goes mad, how it shows itself, and what it does to him. But, as Frank Auerbach says, 'if the painter knew what the finished picture was going to look like, it would just be handicraft'.

# 7

## REHEARSAL DIARY: FIRST STEPS

*Monday 10 December 2001*

It's arrived at last – Day One. I can't quite believe it (well, I have been waiting three and a half years). I take the familiar journey from Kew Gardens to Highbury and Islington on the North London line, the most interesting railway journey in London. A ten minute walk down Upper St. The restaurants have changed; they say one closes, and a new one opens, every week. Past the Almeida Theatre, which is now a building site, to the Almeida office and its battered old rehearsal room, that holds such good memories for me. I greet the stage management, Rupert Carlile, Maris Sharp, Alex Sims, Helena Lane-Smith and Tracey Clarke. They are old friends, which is lucky because I'm going to be dependent on them for so much. The actors assemble, much hugging and kissing and drinking of coffee. Everyone is nervous. James Frain (Edmund) is still filming in Los Angeles, David Ryall (Gloucester) is, less glamorously, stuck on the tube. The entire staff of the Almeida descend from their offices and introduce themselves. We're shown the model of the set, and the design concept is explained by Jonathan and Paul Brown. No one asks very much. I think they're stunned by its ingenuity. But then it's hardly the moment to express doubts: the set's half built already.

We sit round the table to read the play. Actors have different attitudes to first readings. Some give a performance, some pick their way through the text non-commitally, some read as if they'd first looked at it on the bus that morning. I perform, partly because I can't stop myself, partly because I feel (probably stupidly) that I have something to prove to the company, that I will be a Lear worth following through storm and madness. During the reading I make some face-to-face contact with various actors, particularly the Fool and my daughters, and I feel reassured by that. It's a heartening reading. Most people have made some sort of declaration of what they hope to do with their part. How far will they have moved by opening night? In what's left of the afternoon, Jonathan has some games for us, thankfully undemanding. For example, we take Lear and his three daughters, and state in character the first adjective that comes to mind for each person. Some see Lear as frightening, magnificent, rash; others as frightened, vulnerable, foolish. Interesting. I see my three daughters as (in order) sour, unreliable and a joy.

### Tuesday 11 – Friday 14 December

We slowly work through the play, each actor paraphrasing his or her own part, and we discuss as we go. By the end of Tuesday we have only done the first two scenes. Actors vary in their response to paraphrasing. Some delight in thinking up outrageous synonyms and modernisms, some stay pedantically literal, and some hate it and grasp for vague generalizations. I belong to the first camp. Thus 'Blow winds and crack your cheeks' becomes 'Gust zephyrs and split your dimples like-the-little-cherubs-at-the-corner-of-maps'. It's pure whimsy, but it both gets a laugh and explains the line. Mainly we enjoy the modernisms: 'Some villain hath done me wrong' becomes 'Someone's got it in for me'; 'Go your gait' becomes 'Get lost'. Jonathan is using it both to bring the company together, and to ensure that everyone understands the text; never trust that an actor knows what he's saying. It's obviously helpful to translate archaic words ('fitchew' means 'polecat'), but to an extent it's a fruitless exercise. Shakespeare constantly chose words for their sound and their many-layered ambiguity, and consequently there are no satisfactory synonyms. Lear says in his second line that he will express his 'darker' purpose. Is this inner, deeper, more black, more secret, more troubled, more evil? How can you convey the 'shrouded' sense the word has with a single synonym? But at least you lay bare the problem; how much weight do we give to this adjective? Is he about to announce a little secret, a threatening intent, or a malign bombshell?

This is not a minor textual quirk. In fact it unleashes a long and heated discussion. My argument (already stated) is that the division into three is a bombshell, as Gloucester and Kent think the kingdom is going to be divided between Albany and Cornwall. Rather to my surprise, most of the others argue that the court would always have known that Cordelia was going to get a third of the kingdom as a dowry. I point out that Shakespeare is extremely niggardly about his back story, and therefore we should attach all the more importance to the specific opening lines of the play. The others fall back on 'it's only logical', 'it would be naturally assumed', 'it would be only fair'. Jonathan finally sides with the majority, and of course there's nothing I can do. However much I persist in playing it as a bombshell, unless the court *reacts* accordingly then it won't read as such to the audience. I give in. One favourite theory out the window, and it's only day two. Next day I realize it's not crucial. The audience have so much to take in during scene one that it's probably lost in the detail. Watching *King Lear* I've often had the desire to see a re-run of the first scene, rather as at a film when you wished you'd paid more attention to what was going on under the opening credits.

We spend some time discussing Quarto and Folio variants. In Q Cordelia talks about her love being 'more richer' than her tongue. F has 'more ponderous', which has a heavier ring to it, literally since it once meant simply 'weighty'. Unfortunately today 'ponderous' carries the feeling of 'lumbering' and 'turgid'. 'Richer' is clearer, 'ponderous' a more interesting sound. We leave it open. In Q Lear challenges Cordelia to 'win' a third more opulent than her sisters, in F to 'draw' a third. 'Win' is more on the nail, but once again Shakespeare's second thought, 'draw', is more many-layered. We will try both.

Goneril and Regan's opening speeches are always a problem. Some argue that they are so fluent that they must have been expecting the test. But fluency in Shakespeare is not necessarily a sign of preparedness. Hamlet's soliloquies may be fluent, but they are a lot more interesting if they are being thought through for the first time. Goneril and Regan are courtiers, well versed in telling their father what he wants to hear. We do know they are insincere, because Shakespeare tells us so through their conversation at the end of the scene. Diplomatic insincerity however does not equal monstrousness. Suzanne Burden (Goneril) already knows the speech, as she once did Goneril (or rather the first third of it!) at drama school. Jonathan gets her to stand on the table and say it to everyone. This is difficult for Suzanne, and suddenly the speech sounds hesitant and improvised; a classic instance of releasing a speech through setting up a physical obstacle.

So we continue for the next three days, speeding up slightly as we go. I've worked a great deal on the text, but I still discover things I'd never realized. For example I'd never been quite sure what Lear meant in 3.4. by,

>This tempest will not give me leave to ponder
>On things would hurt me more.

and no edition has a footnote on it. I'd assumed he was saying that the storm was a bad thing, but others in the cast argue that he must mean 'this storm is stopping me dwelling on more painful things' and is therefore a good thing. The most common misreadings usually come from not having properly read what the other characters say in the scene. In 3.6. I didn't understand who 'them' are in the line 'Then let them anatomise Regan'. Tom Hollander (Edgar) points out that it must be the dogs that both Lear and Edgar have just been talking about. I feel suitably stupid.

General discussion throws up a host of interesting ideas. Lizzy McInnerny (Regan) talks about how it is to be the middle daughter in a family, without the power of the eldest or the favoured position of the youngest. Regan is the most devious of the sisters because she has always had to fight her corner the hardest. Paul Shelley, who has played Lear twice himself, makes several interesting comments, for example that Cordelia plays on Lear's mind a great deal of the time. Lear's madness occasions a number of stories from personal experience. The mentally disturbed may state something randomly or start a sentence in mid-thought, and then dare the listener to understand them. 'I am mad, you know', or 'I'm not mad, you know' may similarly probe the visitor. 'Let me have surgeons. I am cut to the brains,' says Lear in *Dover Beach*. How mad is that? To adapt Edgar, 'the maddest is not so long as I can say "I am mad".' Lear runs away at the end of the scene. Mental patients who elude their nurses at the end of the day are known in the trade as 'runners'.

By Friday afternoon we reach the end of the play, and Patsy Rodenburg, head of voice at the National, arrives to give us a session. She's a wonderful teacher and inspiration, and knows the play and its demands very well. The language is going to need a great deal of breath and follow-through to the end of the line. I may need her help.

### Monday 17 December

We move to Sadler's Wells theatre, as we need a larger rehearsal room. It's always difficult adapting to a different space. Sometimes my strongest memories of productions are connected with the rooms in which we rehearsed. From 1975 to 1981 I rehearsed in the shell of the old Victorian Stratford theatre, then called the Conference Hall, and now wonderfully converted into the Swan Theatre. It was an intensely atmospheric room, and some of the run-throughs I watched in there are among the most thrilling theatrical experiences I have ever had. All too often the move to the theatre proper, and the addition of set, costumes and lighting swamped rather than enhanced the pure animal excitement of the run-through. The National Theatre, by contrast, has two huge rehearsal rooms, large enough it seems to house a jumbo jet. But they too have acquired an identity for me: 'serious-work-in-progress-here'.

The Ashton room in the newly rebuilt Sadler's Wells theatre is large, bare, grey-breeze-block utilitarian. But it has windows, a view of a church steeple, mirrors for the dancers (fortunately curtained off for us), and an open pitched roof. It's very unatmospheric, but at least it doesn't feel like a box. At last I can see how large the stage is. It's wider than I thought, eleven and a half metres in fact. I like this, I don't want it to appear too domestic. It's only six and a half metres deep, but beyond the panelling is another seven metres of 'void', which will slowly be revealed as the walls collapse. This is hard to visualize, but fortunately the technical team have already started to build a mock-up of the walls. With curtains that can be quickly ripped off, this will give us a good idea of which panels will collapse. Having an approximation of the set and furniture is an incalculable help.

Monday is mostly taken up by 1.1. We'll probably manage to work through the play six times, so each stage must count. The three daughters are to be on the stage from the start, indeed while the audience are coming in. It's rather as if the ladies had been dispatched to the drawing room to drink and read magazines, while the men talk state business over the port. It's a potentially rich idea. The audience not only meet the daughters first and observe their behaviour, on which so much of the plot hinges, but also get some idea of their frustration and sense of exclusion in a male-dominated society. I just hope they aren't made to go on stage too early. After twenty minutes of silent improvisation you can be exhausted by the time you get to your first scripted line. Gloucester, Kent and Edmund enter and, taking no notice of the women, have their first informal chat, which so economically introduces the meat of the twin plots. Max Stafford-Clark placed this scene in a urinal.

Every production tries to pack a great deal into Lear's first entrance. Lear has been carried in on a throne, a litter, a sedan chair, or even a giant egg. He can enter very slowly on sticks or crutches, in a wheelchair, or leaning on attendants, doctors, or even Cordelia. Two or three minutes of such business can take place between Gloucester's 'The king is coming' and Lear's first line. Jonathan is having none of this. I'm just going to walk on, followed by Albany and Cornwall. Everyone bows to me, and I take note of who is present. It feels very 1930s. I am about to abdicate, though I feel like George V rather than his son Edward VIII. I remember a story that George V's equerry suggested he might be more lenient to his children, and George replied: 'I was afraid of my father, and by God my children are going to be afraid of me'. I sit behind my desk, centre stage. I feel like the chairman of the board. I'm reminded of the Ben Kingsley *Hamlet* at the RSC in 1975, where the brilliant director Buzz Goodbody had a pin-striped Claudius (George Baker) deliver his first speech as if it were a financial report to the AGM. The audience are immediately familiar with the society, the proto-col, and the hierarchy. What is lost is the sense of primitive, pagan, life and death ritual, evident in Kurosawa's *Ran* or the Olivier film. But we must play to our brief. Stonehenge this is not.

I rap out 'The map there'. I've opted for Q, rather than F's 'Give me the map there' (which makes it a pentameter). The peremptory command is another useful indication of Lear's style. Jonathan has long had the idea that 'the map' is three folders. Each contains a map of part of Britain. The division has already been made, and I sign them like a diplomatic agreement. As soon as I start on 'Know that we have divided. . .' the TV lights and monitors are to come on. Jonathan is determined to try this: the abdication is not to be closeted in a Sandringham drawing room, but to be a declaration to the nation. I am yet to be reconciled. I think it over-literal, and that its national importance will read anyway. I also know from past experience that audiences can be confused as to whether they should be looking at the actor or the screen. Where I think it will help is that, 'playing to camera', I can legitimately speak straight out front, treating the audience as part of the action. It also, I think, helps the daughters. They have to come and stand beside me and play to camera, and this formalizes the proceedings and puts them under much greater pressure. They have to persuade the nation they are loving children. Jonathan wants Cordelia to refuse even to move to the table, but to stay in her corner for 'Nothing'. He wants me to move towards her on 'How, how Cordelia, mend your speech a little', thus disrupting the televising of the event. This raises the difficult question of when Lear loses his temper. It could be on 'How, how, Cordelia', even earlier on 'Nothing will come of nothing', or much later on 'Well, let it be so. Thy truth then be thy dower'. It depends on the length of Lear's fuse.

This immediately pitches us into the big question, Lear's anger. Wherever we decide he loses his temper, he seems to remain angry for the rest of the scene, right through the banishing of Kent and the attempt to dissuade Burgundy and France from marrying Cordelia. It's not too difficult to flare up and lose your temper. But why does the anger last so long and how does it manifest itself? I know why Lear's angry – Cordelia's rejection, public humiliation, his plans thwarted – that's not the problem. The difficulty lies in staying angry. Does Lear seethe with uncontrollable rage, become coldly implacable, does the anger come and go, is it mixed with a whole number of different emotions? How much is he still relating to Cordelia? If, as I think, Lear abdicates because he fears his mind is going, where in the scene can I play this? How many contradictions will the scene bear?

I end the day with more questions unresolved than answered, a good state to be in. One thing I hadn't anticipated is how much of the scene I spend hating and attacking Cordelia. There's so little opportunity to establish a loving relationship with her. Usually, when a play concerns a fractured relationship, you look for every opportunity to establish in the opening scenes how close that love once was. I understand why some Lears have cried and expressed obvious regret at Cordelia's 'betrayal', but my reading of the text is that Lear understands very little about his feelings for his daughters, and that regret for his treatment of Cordelia only sets in later in 1.4. If you anticipate this, it makes Lear more sensitive and self-aware than the text indicates.

### Tuesday 18 December

We spend a good deal of this on 1.4. For Lear the scene divides into four: Caius and Oswald, the Fool, the row with Goneril, and his return. This is immediately a help, I may be able to play four different things.

I am struck by the impact of our domestic setting. In 1.3. Goneril has in a fury swept all my favourite photos and ornaments from my desk into a drawer. In their place she puts a bowl of roses. She has taken over my palace (the scene is usually taken to be Goneril's palace, but if that's the case what's happened to Lear's?), and I am being dispossessed. Such actions clarify things for the audience, but they are pushing us towards naturalism and behaviourism; a help and a trap. I enter with my three knights (Paul Benzing, Darren Greer, and Richard Trinder), the other ninety-seven having inexplicably remained in the gun room. How are we going to turn this 'graced palace' into a 'tavern or a brothel' with three knights? Jonathan's solution lies in the rose bowl. I sweep it off the table in disgust, the knights start throwing it around like a rugby ball, tackling one another and crashing to the floor. I like all this (I think it much more interesting to believe Goneril), but I suggest the reason I sweep the bowl off the table is because I want to sit on it to take my boots off. I have a thing about these boots. I'm obviously going to take them off in the storm, and in *Dover Beach* Lear asks Gloucester to pull them off (whether I am actually booted or not). Older men, I've observed, can't wait to get into their slippers.

At this point Kent, now in disguise as Caius, a serving man, usually draws attention to himself, but Jonathan thinks this heavy-handed. He wants Kent to sit in a corner and wait to be noticed. I argue that he can't sit there too long, as Lear would never countenance a roughly clothed servant sitting in his presence. We compromise, and Kent rises quite soon. Paul Jesson suggests that since Kent knows Lear's habits he should take off my boots, and this works well as his reply to 'What services canst do?' The way Kent handles this interview is in fact a guide to Lear's character. He knows Lear likes men who are honest, blunt and trusty, say little and are ready to fight, recognize authority in his countenance, and crack laddish misogynist jokes. I find that very helpful.

The entry of Goneril's steward Oswald (David Sibley) is a further chance for laddish behaviour. After I've slapped Oswald, and Kent has tripped him, Jonathan wants the knights to rough him up. The knights have a further task. In the general fracas Jonathan needs them to harry Oswald by pushing the centre-stage desk to an exact position stage left. The desk is to become the entrance to the hovel in 3.4. and it has to be in front of the trap from which Poor Tom enters. It is an artificial move that has to appear artless and improvised.

The Fool (Anthony O'Donnell) enters. I'm relieved he's not in the first scene. I'm certain the three mentions Lear makes of the Fool early in 1.4. are a deliberate build up to his first grand entrance. The Jacobean audience would have anticipated a turn, and the Fool obliges by dominating the scene for nearly a hundred lines. Lear's happy to take a back seat and be entertained, and I'm certainly happy to let someone else motor the scene for a while. 'Take my coxcomb' is always a problem, and Jonathan has come up with a bold solution. Tony is to wear a large curly wig, pink or green, and whip it off to reveal a close shaved head. We launch into the repartee, which turns out to be jokes and rhymes, interspersed with attacks on Lear for dividing his kingdom, banishing Cordelia and making his 'daughters his mothers'. Why Lear allows him to make these attacks and how he reacts to them is tricky. What is Lear's attitude to retirement? The text will bear various interpretations. He could be feeling morose and bereft, he could already suspect that Goneril doesn't want him, he could be missing Cordelia. But a line I'm keen to pursue is that at this point in the play Lear is basically happy, with Cordelia's absence the only cloud. Wherever possible I want to enjoy the Fool, and even join in the repartee. Lear enjoys being in an all-male world of knights and Fools. He feels secure.

There has been a recent tendency, certainly since Jonathan Miller cast Frank Middlemass in the 1970s, to play the Fool as old as Lear. This has undoubted benefits in terms of wisdom and companionship. Where it goes wrong is when the Fool becomes a superannuated bore who fails to make Lear or anyone laugh at all. It can lead to Lear ignoring and teasing the Fool for his tedious, hackneyed jokes. This seems to me a very unwise choice. Firstly, dispensing with the Fool's role as comic turns him into a heavy-handed Choric Commentator. Secondly, the Fool is the only person in the first two acts that Lear can have a close relationship with, and to cut this off diminishes Lear's humanity and leaves him even more isolated. Tony O'Donnell has played most of Shakespeare's comics (we first acted together at the RSC in 1983 as the Provost and Pompey in *Measure for Measure*), and is very good value as the Fool – witty, inventive, incisive and a good singer. He also excels, like many modern stand-ups, in attacking his audience. The interplay between us is very jagged, as Lear is variously amused, disturbed and angered. It needs a lot of work.

Goneril (Suzanne Burden) enters and Lear immediately makes fun of her – 'What makes that frontlet on?' She has two speeches of indignation and reproof to Lear, and it's important to distinguish between them. The first is fairly mild – 'you protect this course and put it on by your allowance'. Lear's response is apparently sarcastic – 'Are you our daughter. . . Does any here know me?' I'm suddenly reminded of John Cleese in *Fawlty Towers*: 'Sorry, anyone here know me? I'm just the owner of this hotel, the poor idiot who slaves from morning to night. . . etc.' I try this and it seems to work. It certainly bears out Goneril's reference to his 'new pranks'. Her second speech repeats the attacks on his knights but ups the stakes: 'riotous inn. . . epicurism and lust. . . tavern or a brothel'. Then comes her real purpose: 'to disquantity your train' whether he likes it or not. This assumption of ultimate power shakes Lear to the core: 'Darkness and devils. . . degenerate bastard'. His reaction is excessive, but where power is concerned Lear is quick to get the message; Goneril is reneging on 'all th'addition to a king'. What surfaces almost at once is his regret at banishing Cordelia. She has hovered over the scene from its outset. The knight points out the Fool has much pined away since her going into France, and Lear doesn't merely shut him up, he adds, 'I have noted it well'. The Fool constantly refers to her: 'did the third a blessing against his will. . .truth's a dog must to kennel. . .can you make use of nothing, nuncle?' Lear, driven by his anger at Goneril, explicitly condemns himself:

> Beat at this gate that let thy folly in
> And thy dear judgement out.

Jonathan has always wanted the first destruction of the set to be caused by Lear, and that it should be the smashing of a large mirror upstage centre. He suggests that I should do it on 'Detested kite', but I feel that for such a powerful moment there should be some textual warranty. 'Lear, Lear, Lear, beat at this gate' seems the obvious place. Ideally, I'd like to smash the mirror with my forehead, but I'm persuaded this is too dangerous. We shall have to experiment. The curse on Goneril comes straight after. The verse is so regular, so end-stopped, so insistent that it calls out to be done quietly, and this would be a good contrast to anger. Lear, as patriarch and father, can be coldly cruel. He then exits, only to return a minute later. I've always found this odd, it's as if he can't let go of his daughters. Just as in 1.1. he keeps referring back to Cordelia, even though he's disclaimed his paternal care, so now he returns to curse Goneril again. Is he hoping for her to beg forgiveness? His tears start coming. Shakespeare is unusually explicit about these. Every time Lear mentions tears and that he won't weep, it must be a stage direction to the actor that he should be crying. Is his confidence that Regan will be 'kind and comfortable' bravado? It seems better to assume that it's genuine, particularly if Regan is the daughter who's always handled her father diplomatically. His final threat is to take back the crown. The problem is that 'resume the shape' may not be clear to the audience. Is there any further means of communicating this?

That evening my daughter Miranda and I go to see the current Almeida production at King's Cross, Brian Friel's *Faith Healer*. We are also celebrating her birthday. The play has a great reputation, but I've never seen it or read it. It consists of four monologues, by three characters. I'm not normally a lover of the monologue, I keep wanting the character to engage with someone else, but it's a great piece of writing. Jonathan has directed it beautifully, and Ken Stott and Geraldine James are both excellent. Ian McDiarmid invests the character of their manager with a mixture of bonhomie, false optimism, regret and despair that is spellbinding. I am also mesmerized by the huge emptiness of the stage. This is the space that will be revealed when Lear's palace disintegrates, an ugly, haunting, brick void. It's a great setting for *Faith Healer*, but so is it for *King Lear*. I'm afraid my mind kept wandering to its possibilities for the heath, or indeed for the entire play. Perhaps we don't need a set at all, just this anonymous, lowering space? But this is heresy. And the set's already being built.

### Wednesday 19 December

We tackle 1.5. I carry round this image of Scofield sitting on a bench, gazing into the middle distance, scarcely listening to the Fool. But Jonathan doesn't want any of this. The reason I answer the Fool so abruptly is because I'm engaged in furious activity. He wants me to carry on the 'desk story'. I abdicate sitting at it, Goneril throws my possessions into a drawer, I sweep away her rose bowl, now I tip out the drawer and pack my things into a bag. Several of these are photo frames, and I instinctively find myself looking at one when I say 'I did her wrong'. Shakespeare took the risk that the audience would know who the 'her' was, and I'm helping a bit with the photo.

I go along with Jonathan's ideas on the scene, though I'm not totally convinced. A contemplative, internal approach seems to make a better contrast to the anger of 1.4. Never come out of the same trap twice. Jonathan argues Lear's still angry, and this leads to a discussion of how much you have to link scenes and how much they can stand in their own right, almost as separate one-act plays (the David Hare argument). I suspect Jonathan is worried that I too easily fall into contemplative mood, so for the time being I go along with the anger. I think if you trust your director, as I do, then you must try his ideas. If they don't feel right, or you can't make them work, then say so and start again. The advantage of having a lot of power at the top of the scene is that it enables me to switch to something quieter and more internal later on. Lear is going to progress from 'I did her wrong' to 'I will forget my nature', then to 'To take't again perforce', and finally to 'O let me not be mad'. Jonathan suggests that the cue for 'let me not be mad' is seeing myself in the mirror which I have broken. I like that, and say half the speech to the mirror, only turning front for 'Keep me in temper. I would not be mad.' Jonathan wants me to try it all to the mirror, with my back to the audience. That's really cheeky. Far from gazing out front, I'm now facing upstage. I accept this provisionally. We'll need to try it with the mirror in place, and test how loudly I will need to say it in the auditorium. I've always wanted to say the speech very quietly. . . but maybe that's more Scofield baggage.

The British Council are here for a discussion about the projected tour. Various European cities are keen, including now Istanbul, and Chicago are particularly interested as they have a summer Shakespeare festival (which I last played in 1970). But there are problems: the set is so complicated, the financing of the project so huge, and time is beginning to run out. I'm not optimistic the tour will happen. Perhaps just Paris and Zurich? That would be a treat to look forward to.

### Thursday 20 December

I have the day off! David Ryall is back after flu and they have to catch up on the Gloucester scenes. I spend two or three hours on the lines, particularly the cues. I know the words. . .but when do I say them?

*Friday 21 December*

We spend the afternoon on 2.4. It's another scene in sections: finding Kent in the stocks, ordering Gloucester about, the interchange with Regan, the arrival of Goneril, rushing out into the storm.

Shakespeare introduces broad knockabout comedy into 2.2, the stocking of Kent. It seems to me this spills over into Lear's first confrontation with Kent in 2.4.

| | |
|---|---|
| KENT | It is both he and she, |
| | Your son and daughter. |
| LEAR | No. |
| KENT | Yes. |
| LEAR | No, I say. |
| KENT | I say, yea. |
| LEAR | No, no, they would not. |
| KENT | Yes, they have. |
| KENT | By Jupiter, I swear no. |
| KENT | By Juno, I swear ay. |

This is pantomime frontcloth repartee. I'm very keen to find other laughs in Lear, and I'm certain there's one when I exit telling Kent to 'stay here'. Kent, in the stocks, can do little else. At my instigation back in October we've made a large cut in this section. The whole of Kent's explanation of how he came to quarrel with Oswald has gone, since it seems unnecessary information. The problem is there is little to prune in the speech, you either have it or you don't. Paul has fortunately accepted this, though he misses the character line, 'having more man than wit about me'. Since Tony wants to cut the 'Fathers that wear rags' song, this means Lear progresses from '`'`tis worse than murder' almost immediately to 'how this mother swells up toward my heart' and his first tremor. If I can build sufficiently through the Kent cross-talk I should be able to make that consistent.

Lear returns in high rage at Regan and Cornwall's refusal to see him, and this has to come to a violent climax because it leads to his second heart tremor ('O, my heart. My rising heart! But down!'). Fortunately Shakespeare has written some variety into Lear's diatribe, because he tries to calm himself on 'No, but not yet'. This comes after one of my favourite lines, 'Fiery? The fiery duke, tell the hot duke that Lear. . .' (favourite because it too has comic possibilities).

Lear promptly loses his temper again when he sees the stocked
Kent, and I've asked here for a naughty cut in the line:

> Go tell the Duke and 's wife I'd speak with them,
> Now, presently;

The archaic 'presently' gives modern audiences the wrong impression. Cut it – the line scans awkwardly anyway – and I can rap out
a fearsome 'Now', which will link with 'future strife may be prevented Now' in scene one. I'm always looking for repeated words
and actions that illuminate his character. Lear is used to instant
obedience.

Regan (Lizzy McInnerny) and Cornwall (David Robb) enter, and
I think Lear is determined to be nice to his 'last chance' daughter.
The clue is that he uses her name four times in nine lines. As a
father, and actor, I want to touch my daughter, put my arms round
her, even hug her. But is Lear capable of hugging women in a non-
sexual way? I try taking her by the hand, and that feels safe –
desperate but tentative. Lizzy plays Regan as sweetly reasonable, and
this helps me not to understand where she's aiming until she says
'Say you have wronged her, sir'. Then Lear goes into his 'unsightly
tricks' of kneeling and begging Goneril for raiment, bed and food.
Jonathan suggests I scrabble round on my knees like a demented
child. I try it, but I'm not sure. I have to work out very carefully the
gradations of his madness/heart condition. This may be demented
too early (it's also very hard on my knees. . .). On the other hand it
may help me into the cursing of Goneril, which is crazy in its hyper-
bole. The reiteration of 'who put my man in the stocks?' is rather
crazy too.

Goneril arrives, and Regan's taking her by the hand may be the
moment Lear realizes she's lost to him. The third heart tremor ('O
sides, you are too tough! Will you yet hold?') follows immediately.
Regan however persists in the line she's adopted from the start of the
scene – Go back to Goneril, I'm not ready for you yet. 'I prithee,
daughter, do not make me mad' presents me with choices. Is it a real
plea, a reprimand, or a way of exciting sympathy? Is 'But yet thou
art my flesh, my blood, my daughter' a last ditch attempt to assert a
paternal-filial relationship? How self-aware, how analytical is Lear?
When he says Goneril is twice Regan's love because she'll let him have
twice as many followers, is he being ironic, prosaically calculating,

or crazy? The opening of the 'Reason not the need' speech shows a highly perceptive mind at work, quite metaphysical in its depth, but he loses the argument thread after only seven lines. It leads to a sense of disintegration, and what I think is Lear's fourth heart tremor on

> I will have such revenges on you both
> That all the world shall – I will do such things –
> What they are yet I know not . . .

How am I going to differentiate these attacks? I remember having the same problem playing Othello, who has four separate fits/break-downs which are very tricky to differentiate. Though we've only skimmed the surface of the scene, I can see that variety is going to be the big problem. I'm frightened of shouting my way through the arguments. I must find light and shade. I must embrace the contra-dictions.

It's our last rehearsal day before Christmas, and an end-of-term mood creeps into the room. It being the actor-friendly Almeida, we finish the day with champagne and mince pies.


### Christmas 2001

I spend Christmas with Jenny and Miranda at our cottage outside Lyme Regis. It's intensely peaceful, and I do little work on the play. Boxing Day is sunny and beautiful, very little wind, the sea is calm and deep blue. Hundreds of people are walking on the beach, and everyone smiles at one another. It's not very like King's Cross. I drive back that night to London with Miranda. We both have to work next morning – unlike it seems half the rest of the country.


### Thursday 27 December

I read in the paper that Nigel Hawthorne has died, at the compar-atively early age of seventy-two. I feel intensely sad. I didn't know him well, but whenever we talked I felt what an honest, caring, self-effacing man he was. We used to moan together in the National Theatre canteen about doing two shows a day in tiring parts, he in Alan Ben-nett's *The Madness of George III*, and I in David Hare's *Racing Demon*. His last stage performance was as King Lear for the Japanese director Ninagawa at the RSC in 1999. He took the Alzheimer's route and was intensely moving in the later scenes, and audiences loved him. The critics, however, were largely hostile, even cruel, and it left Nigel feeling he lacked the confidence to go back on stage in another part. This adds to my depression.

It's a difficult day because we're blocking Act III. How do you block 'Blow winds and crack your cheeks'? I find myself either saying the lines, which is unreal and rather useless, or shouting away in what seems a hopelessly generalized rant. Jonathan is very helpful in suggesting different ways I might address thunder and lightning, when they seem allies and when enemies. The end of the scene is easier because I am at last relating to the Fool. Likewise in 3.4. I am talking more to Kent. Where does the idea of the 'Poor naked wretches' speech come from? If we're not to do it as a prayer, which is very Christian and seventeenth-century, what triggers it? It anticipates Poor Tom, but it can't be about him as he hasn't entered yet. Shakespeare seems addicted to preparing his audiences for what is to come by making his characters anticipate events. In 2.4. Lear, before he's thought of going out into the storm, says:

> No! Rather I abjure all roofs and choose
> To wage against the enmity o'th' air –
> To be a comrade with the wolf and owl.

The 'naked wretches' speech is wonderful but annoyingly obscure. Will the audience understand 'Take physic, pomp', or even more difficult 'Shake the superflux to them'? Sometimes you yearn to modernize Shakespeare a little to make the meaning crystal clear. The comfort is that a surprising amount of difficult material communicates to an audience, even though they haven't understood it word for word. I have found this particularly so when touring in Europe. In Germany quite complex ideas seem to have been clear to spectators, despite their not necessarily understanding the literal meaning.

The speech is cut short by the appearance of Poor Tom. Just as with 'Reason not the need', Shakespeare seems bent on keeping Lear's moments of self-discovery to a ten-line minimum. Perhaps their brevity will make them more powerful? Tom Hollander, as Poor Tom, has some difficult choices to make. Is he acting a Bedlam beggar very convincingly, has he been totally carried away by the part, or gone temporarily mad himself? I have known excellent actors in despair about making sense of him. Shakespeare announces Edmund to the audience in banner headlines; to Edgar he gives no character at all – except perhaps excessive gullibility and panic. Edgar will discover who he is through Poor Tom and his tortuous relationship with his blind father, but it is a very problematic discovery to make comprehensible. Tom Hollander proceeds very tentatively. While I'm jumping in and flailing about, Tom is standing on the bank, putting the odd toe in. We make very little progress.

3.6. goes a little better. I've always relished the mock trial, dragging the others into my fantasy – I can just see those three little dogs. I'm very aware that I've lost contact with the Fool, and Jonathan suggests that the Fool is the 'false justicer', who's let Regan escape, and that I hit him and this blow confirms to the Fool that he's lost Lear. I prefer to throw the Fool away, discarding him as unwanted. In a few hours Lear has moved from 'Poor fool and knave, I've one part in my heart that's sorry yet for thee' to ignoring and rejecting the Fool. The Fool could help me off to Dover, but Jonathan prefers him to walk out of the story, down into the trap centre-stage, the same trap that will engulf the dead Oswald and the dying Kent. Lear finally falls asleep, lying half naked on the same desk that three weeks before he had used to rule the kingdom.

### Friday 28 December

A much better day. We block *Dover Beach* and I love this scene. There are problems; some parts are so lucid, some so obscure – but which are the crazier? It's very difficult to tell with unbalanced people whether they know what's going on or not, whether chance remarks are random or full of intent. Lear reveals towards the end of the scene that he recognizes Gloucester. Does he know this all along, from 'Goneril with a white beard?', or at least from 'What was thy cause? Adultery?'? Lear enters, chatting happily to imaginary people about pressed soldiers, mice and falconry. As soon as he sees Gloucester and Edgar, he switches to talking about how his courtiers misled him. At some level he recognizes them as courtiers from his past, and soon after he talks about Gloucester's bastard son and his own 'lawful' daughters. This launches him into deep confusion about sex. One moment he is invoking copulation to thrive, the next he is condemning women as centaurs and fiends. This may relate to

Goneril and Regan, but 'Behold yon simpering dame' suggests to me a sexual encounter, or even a marriage, that has embittered Lear for life. In my mind I shall try playing Lear's memories of past sexual humiliations. The audience will understand whatever it chooses.

It is very easy in this scene to hit a particular gabbling vein, and not be able to get out of it. I must find variety. I must distinguish between the cynically flippant and the really tortured. Sex is I think mostly a torture to him, and I want to dig myself in deep by the 'sulphurous pit'. How much does injustice hurt? Is he really distressed by 'Plate sin with gold', or is he largely cynical? Chatting away to Gloucester at the end, two old men sitting in the sun, is glorious. David Ryall is such a real and comforting presence. To my surprise I find the end of the scene, with the two gentlemen, difficult. I can't find an attitude. Is he playing with them, or does he really fear they've come to imprison him? He seems resigned and good-humoured about it, but is he softening them up prior to running away?

### Saturday 29 December

Jonathan wants to get to the end of the play before we break up for the New Year, so we hurry through the last act. For Lear the last three scenes don't require a lot of blocking. For the *Recognition* my throne has now become a wheelchair, and I stay in that till Cordelia helps me to my feet. How weak, how dislocated, how frightened is Lear? I have an impression from past productions of a serene scene, but the text indicates Lear is anything but serene. He's on a wheel of fire, he's mightily abused, he's not sure of his condition, he begs them not to mock and laugh at him, he's prepared to drink their poison, and he declares himself old and foolish. There's also a vocal and physical problem. How weak, how changed is Lear? I want him to have lost both the uprightness and the vocal command of 1.1. The voice is the greater problem, because I don't want to slip into a cod old man's voice. I'm always heartened by a Ralph Richardson story: 'I was playing this old man, and doing my old man voice, and I looked at the text, and it said he was sixty-eight, and I thought, Good heavens I'm seventy-two'. I must keep experimenting.

In *Prison* Jonathan wants Cordelia and myself tied together, with ropes round our wrists. On 'Have I caught thee' it is traditional to embrace one another, but that's now impossible. Again I'm struck by how formal Cordelia is with Lear; she calls him 'oppressed King'.

Lear, by contrast, is informal, happy, even larky. I know how the speech should go, but at the moment I can't see the scene. What's really happening? Who's doing what to whom? It can't just be a pleasant interlude. It's the last time Cordelia speaks, and she's only got four and a half lines, and not very distinguished lines at that. We quickly block through the final scene. I've endured a hundred people telling me to get a light Cordelia. Nancy Carroll is slender, very talented, but nearly six foot. Jonathan has already warned me that he thinks carrying her on in the traditional way is sentimental. He wants me to drag her on. He may be thinking of my dodgy back. In any event, I'm grateful. But where does this 'Get a light Cordelia' come from? It's attributed to both Wolfit and Gielgud, so it seems twentieth-century (remember, for the hundred and fifty years of Tate's version they didn't have to bother), but how has it become such a universal query? Has the carrying on of Cordelia become the most famous piece of stage business in Shakespeare, the ultimate test of an ageing actor's virility? They are going to be disappointed.

We finish about 2 pm, more booze and sandwiches, and I set off for Lyme Regis. Breaks are always welcome, but I'd be happier to keep at it. There's so much to do.

# 8

# REHEARSAL DIARY: MID-PERIOD

*Wednesday 2 January 2002*

I'm getting used to these three day breaks, but it's a false luxury. Now that the final four weeks stretch out unbroken, I'm relieved. We spend the morning going painstakingly through 1.1. I experiment with Lear enjoying his abdication speech. I'm reminded of Margaret Thatcher's final House of Commons question time, after eleven years in power, in which she laid about the opposition and finally declared, to great laughter, 'Oh, I *am* enjoying this!' Lear enjoys ordering everyone about, and then Cordelia spoils it. Jonathan suggests that I rip her portion in half.

> But there's a map inside the folder. Shall I take the map out and tear that?
>
> No, tear the whole thing.
>
> And hand the pieces to Albany and Cornwall?
>
> Don't hand them, throw them. Let them scrabble for them. Lear will enjoy that.
>
> But the pieces of the map could go anywhere?
>
> At this point Paul Shelley interjects: 'You're the king. Do what you like. We'll have to find them.'

I need this reminder. I'm usually so busy looking after everyone else: 'Is this alright, I'm not upstaging you?' Lear is a born upstager.

Kent's first intervention Lear cuts short, but his second is heard out. Why? Are Kent and the Fool the two people Lear will take criticism from? It's a perennial problem for the modern actor in Shakespeare – why does one character allow another to speak at such length? Shakespeare was brilliant at snappy dialogue, so he must have intended it. Was it a dramatic convention, or a convention of the period, that people were allowed to have their say uninterrupted? Did the Elizabethan actor, with only a cue script to go by, wait patiently for the speaker's final line? The listener can appear not to hear, or can insert false interjections, but these are desperate recourses. In Lear's next scene he will echo Kent's criticisms when he regrets letting 'his folly in and his dear judgement out'. But I haven't found a way of listening to Kent. Jonathan doesn't want me to appear to be considering rationally what Kent's saying, but I can't just glare at him or seethe with rage throughout.

Another major problem is Lear's relation to Cordelia. On line 114 he disclaims all his paternal care, but then continues to talk about her, until on line 266 he finally tells her to be gone. Does he refuse to look at her throughout, and address all his remarks to Kent, Burgundy and France? This makes him seem very cold and controlled. I feel that he continues to address her directly because he is hoping for some dialogue with her, hoping above all that she will climb down and apologize. But Cordelia stands her ground, even declaring that she's richer for not having 'a still soliciting eye', or 'such a tongue that I am glad I have not'. Lear counters this with 'Better thou hadst not been born than not to have pleased me better'. Is this a flash of anger, or very deliberate and final? Some Lears have found an opportunity to embrace Cordelia, but I can't find a truthful moment. Am I being too text-bound, or is it Sandringham protocol that's deterring me?

In the afternoon we work on 1.4, and spend an hour or so on the knights making mayhem. Jonathan is extremely good at encouraging men to behave badly (as he did in the drinking scene in *Ivanov*), but will it be too distracting? Jonathan is also pushing me to throw my weight around, and this inevitably leads to my barking orders at them. I am cautious about this, as the convention is that kings don't need to shout (though some did all the time). I know Jonathan is worried about my benign side peeking through, he wants a powerful despot, whose anger flashes at the slightest provocation. Negotiation will have to take place.

We are agreed that Lear is enjoying letting his hair down now he's retired, and this comes out strongly with the Fool. I explore trying to join in with the jokes; thus, 'No lad, teach me' becomes the remark of an inexpert straight man. On 'There's mine; beg another of thy daughters' Tony plonks his wig on my head, and so I play the rest of our double act in a pink wig. Each criticism of the Fool I have to respond to – Lear has a very agile mind – without losing my pleasure at his quips. By the time Goneril arrives, Lear is in a good mood, and this carries him through the 'Are you our daughter?' sequence. Suzanne finds it a help on 'Put away these dispositions' to remove my wig, to Lear's embarrassment, and I think this is fruitful. 'Woe that too late repents' is causing me problems. It doesn't seem a logical reply to Goneril's preceding speech:

> You strike my people, and your disordered rabble
> Make servants of their betters.

Is 'Woe that too late repents' addressed to Albany, who has just entered? Albany has given no indication of repenting anything; indeed he can't get a word in edgeways. Is Lear talking to himself; that it's woefully late to repent dividing his kingdom and disinheriting Cordelia? This is tempting, but terribly difficult to play. Lear scarcely seems in a state of self-doubt, and the remarks about Cordelia are all still to come. Another piece of anticipation? It's very difficult to find a way into the curse on Goneril. Perhaps lines 243-302 (from 'Darkness and devils' to his final exit) should be considered as virtually one speech.

This sense of the end of the scene being a form of soliloquy carries on into 1.5. Shakespeare has given Lear the Fool to talk to, but again he hardly seems to be listening. Yet, though I may be talking out front, it doesn't mean I'm addressing the audience. James Frain has been talking to me about problems he's finding with Edmund's soliloquies. I pass on the best advice I've been given: assume that the audience not only understand your position but are sympathetic to it. In other words, don't defy, or wheedle the audience; talk as if they're on your side. Thus when Edmund says 'A credulous father and a brother noble' (1.2.177), he assumes this should be the judgement of any rational human. By denying Lear soliloquies, Shakespeare is cutting off the character's chance of explanation and empathy.

It's been a long day. I'm exhausted, and my voice has taken a terrible beating. I must be careful.

### Thursday 3 January

I'm not called till 4.30 p.m. I stay in bed till noon, partly out of tiredness, and partly because our central heating has broken down. When

I finally get to the rehearsal room, it's deliciously warm; perhaps I'll live here for the next month. We tackle 2.4. I'm still convinced the opening of the scene is comedic. Even Lear's 'O, how this mother swells up toward my heart' must have struck the Jacobeans as funny, since here's a man talking about having a disease of the womb. Jonathan is doubtful about this. He wants me to be angry from the start, and thinks comedy will diminish Lear's state of mind. He may be right, but Shakespeare has clearly written comedy in. Do we trust him or not? Jonathan breaks up my 'frontcloth' disagreement with Kent by making me move upstage. I stick to my gag on 'Stay here' to Kent in the stocks, and suggest that we at least try it in previews, and see whether the laugh (should there be one) seems valid or not. At Regan and Cornwall's entrance I try to be conciliatory, but again Jonathan wants me to attack on the 'Regan, I think you are' speech, and not soften until 'Beloved Regan, thy sister's naught'. I see his point. Faced by his daughter, Lear's first inclination is to be tough, not gentle. Old habits die hard. Keep him tough, or at any rate maintaining an outer shell of toughness. Directly the audience begin to think he's quite a nice old stick deep down, then we're undermining what I take to be Shakespeare's purpose.

I feel the demented scrabbling round on my knees on 'Dear daughter, I confess that I am old' is beginning to work for me. The conventional parody of cringing suppliant has always seemed to me banal. It also helps me to unleash one of Shakespeare's greatest pieces of irony, 'Age is unnecessary', and to get into the terrible curses on Goneril's bones and beauty. When Goneril enters, Jonathan suggests that I don't play 'Art not ashamed to look upon this beard' as a plea, but as an attack. I accept this, because Regan's taking her sister's hand immediately knocks the wind out of Lear, and leads to 'O sides, you are too tough'. As long as this see-saw of emotions can be made to continue, I don't feel I'm in one unremitting rant. 'I prithee, daughter, do not make me mad' is a retreat. 'Thou art a boil' is a return to the attack. I want to give the bridge passage, 'But yet thou art my flesh, my blood, my daughter', a degree of introspection, of soul-searching, and Jonathan cautiously agrees. How much introspection is there in the Lear of the first two acts? Remember, 'he hath ever but slenderly known himself'. Jonathan warns me not to take the 'O reason not the need' speech too slowly. I argue that I must probe what I'm doing before I gather pace. Speed solves many problems, but not if the detailed work hasn't been done. As Trevor

Nunn's fond of saying, 'Let's stay in the moment, we haven't ex-tracted all the juice yet'.

### Friday 4 January

Act 3 all day. I both relish and dread the *Heath* (as I call these three scenes). I must be clear what I'm raging at. First it's the rain: he wants it to inundate the world. Then it's the lightning: he wants it to singe him in particular. Finally, it's thunder: and he wants it to destroy procreation. Then Lear enters into a discussion with the elements, first approving them – 'Let fall your horrible pleasures' – then attacking them – 'But yet I call you servile ministers'. Exhaus-tion takes over (thank goodness), and he relapses into 'No, I will be the pattern of all patience', which I don't think Lear says ironically. This allows me to sit down – on the sodden throne, an image we want to keep going. I try pointing out towards the audience on 'Tremble thou wretch', in the manner of a Blake prophet. I feel the storm has unlocked something in Lear that will continue through-out his madness and enable him to speak of all his kingdom's evils. Lear believes he is 'a man more sinned against than sinning', but I hope the audience will think it poses them a question. Immediately after this Lear confides in Kent that his wits are on the turn, and this seems to free him to make real, compassionate contact with the Fool. This release of humanity is an enormous relief to me. Jonathan then has the idea that Lear is very taken with the idea of a hovel and straw – the old actor manager being led to terrible digs. I now have two friends to relate to, the Fool and Kent.

3.4, and Tom Hollander has decided to jump in feet first. This is a great relief. The problem with Mad Tom is that however long you spend on the detail, there's really only one way to play the feigned madness – fast and furious. There's little point in pausing, because you can't fill the pause with anything the audience can understand. Once I'm hooked on Tom's every word, the scene gets easier to play. I've now got a third friend to relate to. We next face the undressing problem. I think the Fool and/or Kent should restrain Lear, but how much time does that give me? Enough to get off boots and trousers, but no more?

Sticking with Tom makes 3.6. easier too. I find I'm becoming very manic, leaping about stage managing the trial in a wild and uncontrolled way. The extremity of the storm seems to be pushing towards this, and the text certainly suggests mania – 'To have a thousand with red burning spits come hissing in upon them'. It makes the scene work, but I worry that I may be an actor enjoying being uninhibited. On the other hand the trial on the charge of 'kicking the poor king her father' seems to be a descent into childhood games. Perhaps I should think more about how a child would do it.

### Saturday 5 January

*Dover Beach*, and Jonathan lets me have my head. It's summer, we're in the open air, Lear feels able to say exactly what he likes. I don't know yet how much of the scene is to Gloucester, how much to himself, how much to imaginary people, but I want to keep it very improvisatory. Lear seems to go from happiness to despair to calm and back to happiness. With his guards he is 'jovial'. I find this passage easier now I realize it's almost a continuous speech. Lear is very quick-witted. Shakespeare saw no point in writing slow-witted heroes.

We work through Act Five, again rather too quickly. It's true that the last beat of a play often falls into place once you've made the rest of the action coherent, but Shakespeare's last acts are notoriously difficult. Tyrone Guthrie impressed this on me when I ventured how difficult the last act of *Hamlet* must be to direct. 'Not at all', he said. 'Deciding where the thrones should go is the only tricky bit. That dictates where the duel is and where everyone dies – the rest is straightforward. No, the difficult last acts are the comedies, especially *Twelfth Night*, *Measure for Measure* and *All's Well that Ends Well*.' I've done *Twelfth Night* three times and he's right. New characters keep entering, demanding to be the focus of attention. Where to shunt the others can be a nightmare.

I'm still unresolved about the degree of anguish in the *Recognition*, and *Prison* still doesn't seem to be a scene, but I know we can work these out. We tackle the end of the play with Nancy as a body for the first time. I try grasping her wrist with my left hand and gingerly dragging her across the floor. This works quite easily, though much will depend on what she's wearing, the condition of the stage floor, and whether Nancy's arm stays on. If Lear carries Cordelia on, he naturally places her across the stage and kneels behind her. If I drag her on she naturally ends up with her head towards the audience

and I kneel beside her. If she is on the floor, as opposed to some sort
of catafalque/cart/hillock, then this means Lear has to talk to her
facing down into the stage rather than out into the audience. I'm at
a loss for a moment. I don't want to kneel too long, because my
knees can't take it (bitter experience of other Shakespeare plays), so
I try sitting beside her. Directly I'm sat, I feel like picking her up and
holding her in my arms. As soon as I do this, I feel liberated. Her
head is on my shoulder, my face is clear, I'm facing front, I can talk
to her and I can talk to the audience. It's not so good for talking to
other characters, but then Lear is paying little attention to them. I'm
uncertain how long to hold her, but directly after 'This feather stirs,
she lives' seems a good place to pick her up, and 'No, no, no life' a
good place to put her back down. What seemed to be a problem has
turned into an advantage.

### Monday 7 January

1.1. for the third time. We're already over halfway through our rehearsal time. I make a resolution not to let this scene become a bugbear.
It can never be made to work to everyone's satisfaction, because
Shakespeare short-changed it so much. It's the premise of the fairy
story. Lear's first line has always seemed to me strangely anti-
climactic:

> Attend the lords of France and Burgundy, Gloucester.

It's a detail of business, and it isn't even a pentameter. But now
we're beginning to perform the scene, I realize its importance. The
first thing Lear does is to rap out a peremptory order. The six beats
give it an added weight. And it's an order that concerns two of the
greatest princes of Western Europe, to whom Lear clearly feels equal,
or even superior. The first line says, 'I'm a very great king, totally in
control'.

Then comes the announcement of Lear's darker purpose. The
speech is often taken very slowly, but I try to give it pace. Even so,
Jonathan is continually giving me a note that I'm being too measured. Naturally I don't want to hurry through an announcement of
my abdication and my future plans, so I break the speech down. It
falls into four points. First:

> Know that we have divided
> Into three our kingdom; and 'tis our fast intent
> To shake all cares and business from our age,
> Conferring them on younger strengths, while we
> Unburdened crawl toward death.

This is his most personal announcement, and it has to be given weight. I give a lot of emphasis to the final clause (which is an F addition). 'Unburdened' is I think central to Lear's intention. 'Crawl toward death' is more problematic. My Lear, unlike Laughton's, is not to be a Crawler towards Death. I allow it to be ironic. Lear has not only no intention of crawling, he thinks it unlikely that he will ever die. Some of the court laugh nervously – has he made a joke or not? I like that. I feel it's keeping them on their toes. Second:

> Our son of Cornwall,
> And you, our no less loving son of Albany,
> We have this hour a constant will to publish
> Our daughters' several dowers, that future strife
> May be prevented now.

This was added in F probably to introduce the theme of an incipient civil war between Albany and Cornwall, about which Shakespeare seems to have remained undecided (Kent refers to it in 3.1.19-29, but it's never borne out). Jonathan wants me to rap out the two names, and each to respond in some way. Cornwall is to be in some sort of military garb, Albany in a suit, so that they are immediately contrasted. Again I save my fullest emphasis for the final clause and really hit the concluding 'now'. This thus takes on the air of a military order. Third:

> The two great princes, France and Burgundy,
> Great rivals in our youngest daughter's love,
> Long in our court have made their amorous sojourn,
> And here are to be answered.

The mood lightens. I decide Lear resents giving his favourite daughter up to some other man, and this expresses itself in slight contempt for France and Burgundy. 'Amorous sojourn' is such a heavily pedantic phrase that I give it a lot of comic irony. Fourth:

> Tell me, my daughters,
> Which of you shall we say doth love us most,
> That we our largest bounty may extend
> Where nature doth with merit challenge.

This could be the climax of Lear's speech, the point to which he's driving. I think it's more interesting if it's a kind of whimsical coda, a last minute improvisation. It's for this reason we've agreed to omit the F addition,

> Since now we will divest us both of rule,
> Interest of territory, cares of state,

We've established that it's not a real contest, because the prizes have already been allotted. But Lear decides it might be fun to make them sing for their suppers, on television, in front of the whole nation. It's also a way of bringing them into line, ensuring their future conduct, and in the final analysis humiliating them. I'm aware that this interpretation has much to do with the modernity of our setting. A serious, formal love test sits well in Stonehenge, but less happily in Sandringham. I emphasize the contrast between 'nature' (natural affection) and 'merit'. It makes Lear suitably paternalistic. It's worth noting that each of these four sentences can be done on one breath, and that each drive through to the fullest emphasis on the final clause.

I've broken this speech down at length, to give some idea of how I'm looking for variety in intention, mood, language and emphasis. Once you have this clarity of intention, you can experiment endlessly with how to convey it. I'm in no doubt this opening speech is a test. It announces the kind of king he's been for the last fifty years, and the height from which he's going to fall. If I can give it authority, monomania, humour, and a hint of vulnerability, then the audience may accept me. Humour is important; it relaxes the audience. I laugh at Goneril's protestation that she finds 'speech unable', and Regan's jibe that Goneril 'comes too short', and I hope the audience will laugh with me.

### Tuesday 8 January

1.4, and we work on the knights causing chaos. Are we spending a disproportionate amount of time on something that isn't even in the text? But I remember the space Brook gave to it in 1962, and Kurosawa in *Ran*, and I know that it's central to the Lear-Goneril relationship. The fight director, Terry King, works on my slapping Oswald. Rule number one of stage fights – the person being struck must be in control. With the Fool I realize I'm being too relaxed and jovial, but the switches from laughter to pain are so rapid and abrupt it's hard to make them truthful.

With Goneril I'm beginning to see that I have to maintain a through-line, that my attacks evolve organically and pretty seamlessly. One of the pitfalls of memorizing the part first is that I've learned them as separate speeches, when they're hardly that at all.

I go off to Cosprop, the wonderful period costumiers in Camden Town, where I meet Paul Brown, the designer, and Rachel Dickson, the costume supervisor. We try on a dozen suits, but none seem right for the first scene. I've always imagined that Lear wears something distinctive, like Stalin or Castro, but I can't visualize it. It can't be too strange; Nehru jackets and combat fatigues are out. We try on a black suit. It's not a good fit, but suddenly it seems right. This Lear always wears jet-black double-breasted suits, with wide 40s lapels. Time is short, but Cosprop think they can make one in time. They will also make me a hunting suit for 1.4. and 2.4, or rather two identical suits, as one is going to be rained on a great deal. The second half is easier. I'm mostly in pyjamas. We find a blue striped pair, that is neither hospital nor Noel Coward, and a suitable dressing gown. I leave, elated about the black suit. My reign has an identity.

### Wednesday 9 January

2.4. all morning. Jonathan thinks the successive heart tremors should buckle me up, send my legs to jelly. I know I'm being cautious about this, but I will get braver when we run it (actors tend to put most problems in a huge bin marked 'The Run Will Sort It Out'). We then fall out over the exchange with Gloucester. I don't want to roar at Gloucester too much, especially as David is playing a Gloucester clearly in awe of Lear. But Jonathan doesn't want me to make 'Fiery? What quality?' and 'Informed them?' too ironic. He wants a Lear who's used to crushing people. I understand what he's after, but it's very repetitious to play. It seems to me that Lear, like all Shakespeare's heroes, has a particular relish in words. He enjoys playing linguistic cat and mouse with Gloucester. It remains an area in contention.

After Regan's entrance I have a great desire to clutch her on 'Beloved Regan', so I try this. She is sitting on the arm of the Gloucester armchair, and I wrap her in my arms and kiss the top of her head. I release her on 'Say? How is that?'. Thus emboldened I try seizing her again on 'No, Regan, thou shalt never have my curse', much to her alarm (Regan's, not Lizzy's). She's standing now and Jonathan urges me to hold her from behind, pinioning her arms with mine, and talking into her ear. This I find very releasing, because I can almost whisper to her:

> Tis not in thee
> To grudge my pleasures. Thou better knowst
> The offices of nature, bond of childhood,
> Effects of courtesy, dues of gratitude.
> Thy half o' the kingdom hast thou not forgot,
> Wherein I thee endowed.

This works very well, but it's a risk. How will the audience interpret this physical contact? What I'm playing is that Lear is unused to hugging his daughters and does it very clumsily, but that he is driven by his need to endear himself to his last remaining 'kind and comfortable' daughter. It may well appear, however, that Lear is handling his daughter inappropriately, and that this indicates some sort of past abusive behaviour. This troubles me at first, but then I think I must play what I want to play and the audience must make up their own minds.

I'm still not happy about 'Reason not the need', but I don't know why. I know it, I understand it. Perhaps I'm investing too much in it? Perhaps I must just let it happen – and put it in the bin marked 'Run'. My voice is exhausted after a morning spent on 2.4. . . and after lunch I have to do 'Blow winds'. I'm clear about the rain-lightning-thunder, but I still feel generalized. We have a soundtrack of thunder now, which is a great help, particularly as it gives me respites to draw breath. I'm happier once I get to denouncing my enemies; it's always easier to connect with people, however imaginary. I keep telling myself the rain will help. I once did *The Winter's Tale* at the open-air Ludlow Festival, and one night it rained throughout the three hours. When I started I was mesmerized by the water pouring down the nose of my fellow actor, but as we progressed I realized that the need to communicate through the driving rain with the sodden audience gave the performance a new urgency. I'm hoping piped water will do the same trick for 3.2. and 3.4.

### Thursday 10 January

3.4. and I make a breakthrough on 'unaccommodated man'. The speech is confusing. Lear starts by saying Tom is better off dead, but then moves to 'Thou art the thing itself', which Lear seems to think is an ideal. It's good to be a 'poor, bare, forked animal', and I'm going to join him by stripping, despite the fact that I started by saying naked people in a storm are better off in a grave. In other words it looks a rational speech, but is actually a confused/demented speech containing a possibly sane truth. What Shakespeare illustrates so profoundly is that unbalanced people often say three entirely rational things, and then a fourth that is inappropriate/demented/ mad. What are we going to do when I have my 'private word' with Tom? Mimed speech or mumble, which usually degenerates into 'why are the audience coughing so much?' – and worse – seems pointless. Quite involuntarily I start running my fingers over Tom's face. I feel like an ape grooming its partner, or Miranda in *The Tempest* discovering the wonder of mankind. It seems right, though I've no idea why. And it's *silent*.

In 3.6. I concentrate on relating to Poor Tom. He is both my new best friend and my guru, my philosopher king. I must get him to support me in the trial of Goneril, and when he joins me by 'throwing his head' at the little dogs yelping at my feet, I feel I've made a friend for life – even though I don't like the fashion of his garments. I'm starting to enjoy the scene, mainly because I'm inhabiting a form of invented madness. I say 'invented', because nobody finally knows what it's like to be mad. Those who have recovered from dementia bring a report from the front line, but even that may not be entirely accurate. It's often remarked that actors seem to have no qualms about playing dying and madness, two conditions that they can know nothing about. The audience may recognize a kind of fac- simile of the condition, but the actor has to guess at the feeling that lies behind it.

Going home on the train, I begin to question whether the pattern of my performance is inexorably set, or whether I can still change course. Iris Murdoch puts it wonderfully: 'Any artist knows that the space between the stage where the work is too unformed to have committed itself, and the stage where it is too late to improve it, can be as thin as a needle'. She goes on, forbiddingly: 'Genius perhaps consists in opening out this needle-like area until it covers almost the whole of the working time'.[1] That 'whole' may be unachievable, but the most fruitful period of rehearsal often lies in that state of near-completion which still allows for experiment and change. I seem set on a path of anger descending into mania. It's consistent, it's Jacobean, it's warranted by the text, but is it the most illuminating way of playing the part? The actor's instinct is always towards variety. If it's a comic part, look for the tragedy. If he's an enigma, look for the emotional release. If Lear is angry, look for the quiet stillness. The more shouting you do in the first two acts, the more introspective you can afford to be on the heath. But is this what Shakespeare has written? Lear clearly shouts at the storm. On film you can do this quietly, because you can balance the soundtracks – though it has always struck me as odd: it's as if Lear is thinking, but not articulating, his dialogue with the thunder. But on stage you've got to articulate, and with Jonathan's thunder and rain you've got to articulate loudly. Can 3.4. be quiet? Surely 'Poor naked wretches' can be an introspective prayer? Well, it can, but I think Lear is making a terrible discovery, that for sixty years he's neglected the poor and needy. I don't think his desire to 'show the heavens more just' is a polite prayer. It's a mighty challenge, a fist shaken at the gods.

The search for variety within an architectural whole is one of the performer's most difficult problems. The actor can switch intention, mood, and volume at will, just as the musician can alter tempi and rhythm. With texts as rich as Shakespeare and Beethoven, this variety can yield, from moment to moment, fresh and exciting insights. The problem is keeping a sense of coherent shape, while still observing the contradictions. In the part of Lear it's possible to move from anger to ironic detachment, to soulful revelation, to self-pity, to intellectual curiosity, to childish tantrum, and back to anger in the space of forty lines. It's fascinating to behold, and I've seen Lears who've tried it, but at the end I've usually felt – 'I've no idea who you are or what you're trying to do: very compelling, a rag-bag of illumination, utterly unconvincing'. If Peter Brook is right and a very good production can only reveal two-sevenths of a Shakespeare play, then the urge to illuminate seven-sevenths (the Variorum per-

1    Iris Murdoch, *The Black Prince* (London: Vintage, 1999 ed), p. 189.

formance) may be a false objective. The opposite extreme, staying in the same unvaried state for long scenes, is of course too awful to contemplate.

I come to two conclusions. First, my instinct is towards manic anger and I want to stay with that. I know it's a calculated risk, that some people will find it too intense and unvaried, but I think it will reveal something truthful and interesting. I feel an unexpected freedom in playing Lear. No one in my experience has made the part work totally, so let's continue to explore. This isn't just experiment for experiment's sake. I really believe that the angry/mad approach is the one the text most clearly suggests, and that I have never seen a Lear who has embraced the anger as wholeheartedly as I hope to do. The second is purely practical. From the start Jonathan has been bent on loud thunder, rain with real water, and a collapsing set. I can complement that, top it even, but I can't play under it. If I do it becomes an evening about technology. I've thought it through. But I'm still worried.

### Friday 11 January

We start with *Dover Beach*, and just run it. Following on last night's thoughts about mania, I recognize that Lear's second speech is straight manic-obsessive:

> To say 'ay' and 'no' to everything I said 'ay' and 'no' to was no
> good divinity. When the rain came to wet me once and the
> wind to make me chatter; when the thunder would not peace
> at my bidding, there I found 'em, there I smelt 'em out . . .

I try taking it very fast, almost gabbling, and it feels right. Lear has been rambling away like this for weeks, wearing himself out. Fortunately Gloucester pulls him out of it with 'Is't not the King?', and sets him off on a path that leads to adultery and sex. I've been puzzling how to make the 'sulphurous pit' clear, and I try a piece of mime. For 'Beneath is all the fiend's' I reach down into my own crotch and bring my hands back up, cupped in the shape of a vagina. Being so graphic is a great help, because I can see it 'burning', smell its 'stench', feel it 'consuming' me. Jonathan encourages me on 'Fie, fie, fie! Pah, pah!' to retch and hawk as if I'm really being sick. It certainly helps the plea for an apothecary to 'sweeten his imagination'. As soon as

I sit beside Gloucester I change my mood completely and become quite chatty and merry. I love the 'Plate sin with gold' passage, but again Jonathan urges me not to become ironic. Lear is not detached, above it all, he's bloody angry about the injustices in his kingdom. I think Jonathan's right, but irony is so much easier, so much more 'effective' to play. I'm struck by an unexpected parallel with our own monarch. Queen Elizabeth II, who has reigned for fifty years, must have seen myriad examples of injustice, naked ambition, hypocrisy and double-dealing. She will presumably go to the grave with her secrets undisclosed. So might Lear, but instead he goes mad and out it all tumbles. Lear hasn't 'learned' about injustice, he knew it all the time. It was just repressed, screened off.

I have a breakthrough at the end of the scene. I've already started to play 'Your eyes are in a heavy case, your purse is in a light' as if I was the Fool doing a number. I do the same on the 'man of salt using his eyes for garden water pots', and also on

> I will die bravely, like a smug bridegroom.
> What? I will be jovial. Come, come,
> I am a king, my masters, know you that?

My subtext is: 'I've made a dirty joke, one of the Fool's best, and you've got to laugh because I'm the king'. The two gentlemen start laughing manically, and I play the 'Hamlet trick' on them. I lead them off one way, and then suddenly dart off the other. Well, a good gag's worth repeating (as Shakespeare well knew), and it rounds off the scene with – hopefully – a laugh.

We do Lear's last three scenes. Time for quiet introspection? Well, yes and no. He's nearest to it in *Prison*, happy at life with Cordelia. I love that speech (note to self: don't love it too much). But in the *Recognition* he's recovering from the wheel of fire, begging not to be laughed at, ready to take poison. Who else would have had the courage to write the scene like that? And in the final scene, four howls aren't exactly introspective. What a clever piece of writing it is. Lear tells us right at the top of the scene that he knows Cordelia is dead: not 'I think she's dead', but 'I know when one is dead and when one lives. She's dead as earth'. He couldn't be more categoric. Then for the rest of the scene he plays with the notion that she might be alive. Shakespeare was so taken with this idea, that in his F rewrite he made Lear die still wondering if her lips might not be moving.

I also make another intuitive discovery. I'm rocking Cordelia in my arms, back and forth, back and forth, and I find myself singing the line 'And my poor fool is hanged'. I don't know why, it comes presumably from the rocking. But I immediately see it has a great ambiguity about it. Lear sings a little refrain. Is he aping the Fool singing about Cordelia, or the Fool – or both?

I think I'm beginning to understand Lear's relationship with Cordelia. They love one another but they can't communicate. Whatever Lear's reason for the initial love test and Cordelia's reason for 'Nothing', their communication in scene one is terrible. They don't have an understanding. And Shakespeare is too truthful a writer to pretend that their communication can magically improve in the second half of the play. Cordelia leaves us in no doubt in 4.4. of the 'love, dear love' that she feels for Lear, and her speech and kiss before Lear wakes in 4.7. is full of tenderness, but as soon as they confront one another the communication breaks down. Cordelia may ask for benediction, Lear for forgiveness, but they can't tell one another of their love. Lear does it obliquely in *Prison*, but Cordelia doesn't/can't respond. At first I thought it was Shakespeare avoiding sentimentality, but I now think it's Shakespeare telling the truth about a patriarch-daughter relationship, perhaps of his own relationship with Susanna and/or Judith. They will both die with their love understood but unstated.

It's mid-afternoon and we go back to 1.4. It's extremely hard finishing the play and then returning to an early scene. I want to go home. But I don't. Instead I'm not very inspired. In the evening I'm interviewed by the *Times* over dinner. I talk freely – well, it's hard to shut me up when we get on to the subject of the play. I can tell my interviewer is intrigued, and probably doubtful, as to whether an actor associated with benign ditherers can play Lear. I put forward my ideas about anger as therapy, and how releasing I find it. The usual questions follow: why did I leave academia, how did I come to be in *Star Wars* (I play Queen Amidala's governor, Sio Bibble)? Heaven knows what slant he'll put on it all.

### Saturday 12 January

The end of a long week, and we're back to 1.1. The desk and 'throne' have arrived! I cannot tell you what a help it is, and how rare, to have the actual stage furniture and props for rehearsal. We work on the

row with Kent, because I've never been sure how to listen to his strictures. I've been sitting behind the desk, but I don't think this is helpful. It's the position of power, and once Cordelia's 'Nothing' has unseated him I think it's more interesting if he never regains his throne. The movement of the play is to drive Lear out of home comforts into the open air, rather as Chekhov's three sisters are driven into the attics and finally the garden. If we follow through the line that Lear abdicates for health reasons, mental and physical, then I should explore whether he's suffering in 1.1. Certainly the disproportionate anger at Cordelia is a possible sign of dementia. Is he also suffering heart tremors? There's nothing in the text to justify this, but it's possible he's been concealing them for months. When he finally admits to them in 2.4. they don't seem to come as a surprise. So I try playing that the division of the kingdom has taken a lot out of me, and I lean heavily on the desk, arms splayed, face down. I like the position, it suggests that something's going on which he wishes to conceal. I try being bolder, and I clutch my heart with my hand. Paul Shelley immediately says, 'If it's that bad we'd rush to help you'. Quite right. How often have you seen an over-the-top moment, and wondered why the other characters on stage didn't react to it? I'll have to be less overt.

Lear has to pull himself together and assume a veneer of regal politeness when France and Burgundy enter, but his fury at Cordelia smoulders near the surface. I particularly relish the phrase 'If aught within that little seeming substance': 'seeming', the great cry of Isabella in *Measure*, written perhaps the year before. The irony is so great, because Lear in his anger can't see that Cordelia is the least 'seeming' person in the court. I find a strange high in playing a person who is so catastrophically wrong in his judgements. The scene works especially well as we have such a suave and sophisticated Burgundy (Richard Trinder) and such a young and intense France (Lex Shrapnel).

Jonathan announces that we're heading towards a run-through of the first three acts in the middle of next week. I beg him not to short-change rehearsal of 2.4. and the *Heath*, as they're the scenes I find the hardest. He promises.

## Monday 14 January

We recap 1.4, and do some tidying up. So much of rehearsal is repetition, making precise, increasing familiarity. You can't expect breakthroughs every hour, but there's often a feeling mid-rehearsal that you're bogged down, not making progress, that perhaps you're missing something that should be obvious. I have a long break, and I walk up from Sadler's Wells to the Almeida rehearsal room to do some work on my own, mainly choreographing my movements on the heath. If I'm certain where the thunder and lightning are, then I won't worry about repeating my moves. Time and again on stage you find that movement is a solution even to textual problems.

We rehearse 2.4. at 5 p.m. – a terrible hour of the day to start the most difficult scene in the play. Jonathan says he's finally coming into the open; he hates my joke with the stocked Kent on 'Stay here'. I tell him his hatred was hardly a well-kept secret. I mourn its departure, but it will have to go. Never do gags your director hates (well, not until he's left the production). I'm finding more and more that the scene charts a descent into madness. Jonathan wants me to let fly more at the end of the 'Reason not the need' speech, because it's going to lead almost at once to 'Blow winds' and should be in the same vein. But I'm also aware that he needs me big, as I will be contending with crashing walls. The design concept is at this point dictating how I play the part.

## Tuesday 15 January

The *Heath* all day. My work at the Almeida yesterday has paid off. I'm getting more precise. Lightning gets a sharp response from me, thunder a rumbled one. I've also got a better handle on the 'Tremble thou wretch' speech; it's all you bastards that have got away with it in my kingdom for the last fifty years. I'm seeing more clearly that Lear realizes he's mad to be shouting at the storm, and the intimate contact with the Fool is a way of clinging on to his sanity. I'm enjoying 3.4. more. I relish the passage:

> But where the greater malady is fixed
> The lesser is scarce felt. When the mind's free,
> The body's delicate: this tempest in my mind
> Doth from my senses take all feeling else . . . .

Lear is talking openly about his confusion/madness for the first time and making discoveries about it, and I find that very releasing. The storm both humbles Lear, and puts his much greater difficulties into perspective. I'm frustrated by the word 'delicate'. If only it were, say, 'sensitive', then the audience would understand what I'm saying. But if I appear to know what I'm talking about, hopefully they will too. I try 'unaccommodated man' more as a worship of Poor Tom, but Jonathan thinks I'm making it sound like a famous speech. I'm sure he's right; he has very acute antennae for these things. It's a tricky balance to get: to make a major realization for oneself not sound like a portentous 'speech'. But I don't want to throw the idea away; the moment needs to be marked, but not headlined. I also decide it's time to start stripping on 'Off, off, you lendings'. I take off shoes and trousers, and rush about in shirt and socks. It immediately alters the chemistry of the scene.

3.6, and Tom Hollander has the idea that he should carry me in on his back. We try this, and he manages it. But I'm eight inches taller and probably four stone heavier. I say that I'm worried what weeks of performances will do to his back, and Jonathan suggests that I carry Tom. I like the idea that the disciple Lear is prepared to carry his 'learned Theban', but don't I have enough to worry about? Tom is quite easy to carry, but whether I can do it without shoes on a wet stage remains to be seen. Jonathan wants me to be more sharp and savage in this scene. He doesn't want me to be ironic about Goneril, Lear hates her with a passion. It stops me becoming objective, playing the detached Olympian, the brooding Titan. But it's very exhausting. . .

Tomorrow we have a run of the first three acts. I feel a sore throat coming on.

### Wednesday 16 January

Yes, I have a painful sore throat. It may be bad luck, it may be psychosomatic. In the morning I have a costume fitting. Alan Selzer, the tailor, has made me three suits, beautiful as always, and I feel particularly good in the black suit for 1.1. I go through my costume changes with Paul Brown; I like to have a pattern in my head as we approach run-throughs.

I'm very nervous about the afternoon run. I warn Jonathan that I may have to 'mark' it at half volume because of my throat, but of course I can't. I start fine, and then as I begin the rejection of Cordelia I'm overwhelmed by the familiar feeling that I can't possibly remember such a long part. I talk rubbish for about eight words, and then I'm back on track and the rest of the scene goes fine. It's an interesting business, drying. Actors fear it enormously. Olivier said he had such bad patches during *Othello* that he used to prepare speeches craving the audience's indulgence. I was at that press night in 1964, and I felt the huge tension and expectation in the audience, but I had no intimation of Olivier's demons. He seemed totally in control. In fact audiences don't usually notice 'dries', unless it's a total breakdown or a famous speech is obviously mangled. They just think it's part of the production; a very effective pause, a deliberate stumble, a planned piece of improvisation. But to actors it's a kind of death. Is my memory going? Have I lost my confidence? Am I frightened of the audience? Of course actors laugh and tell jokes about it to relieve their tensions, but the fear is there. It drives some actors off the stage altogether, and into TV and films, sometimes at quite an early age. The important thing is to be able to work out why you dried. As long as you can see the reason – I was distracted, I lost concentration, I never really knew that bit, I don't know what I'm thinking – then it can be put right. The alarming thing is when the words just go, and you have no idea why. Anyway, enough of this, it frightens me just writing it down.

I enjoyed a good deal of the run, an encouraging sign. Playing scenes straight through in succession always gives one a great boost. The emotional and intellectual pattern of the part becomes clearer. Problems are solved along the way, and new ideas intuitively arise – that's the exciting part. Lear has a good rest before 1.4. and 2.4, but the killer is going from 2.4. into the *Heath*. Fortunately by that time you and Lear are both on a roll, and sheer adrenalin carries you along. Jonathan seems very pleased, and the rest of the cast are very encouraging. Rather to my surprise, several say how moving they found it. Since 'being moving' is nowhere in my list of priorities in the first three acts, I'm very relieved. Shakespeare is doing the work for me.

After notes I'm sent off to Mr Joshi, a Harley St. naturopath whom the Almeida swear by. He puts hot cups on me, manipulates and pummels me, and gives me strange potions to drink. Hopefully he can mitigate the problem, or speed the virus on its way. I can't do ten days of run-throughs with a throat like this.

*Thursday 17 January*

I feel worse today. I come in at 12.30 p.m. to do an interview with a nice woman from the *Financial Times*. I could have postponed it, but I'd rather get it over with. I'm short on originality, and I find myself saying the same things that I had to the *Times*. We rehearse *Dover Beach*, and I am not inspired. Jonathan wants a full run-through on Saturday, but I tell him I can't manage it with my throat, and he immediately postpones it. Back to Mr Joshi for acupuncture and massage.

*Friday 18 January*

I've been worrying away about *Prison* not being a scene, and wonder if the key is not Cordelia's distress at losing the battle, failing her father, and now having to face her triumphant sisters. Jonathan and Nancy like this idea, and Nancy's vehemence on 'Shall we not see these daughters and these sisters?' is a great springboard for me to calm her down, and tell her that it's all going to be fine and the gods approve. My speech now has an intention. I'm at last being the parent I should have been, even though my proposed prison idyll is clearly unrealistic. Because our hands are tied behind our backs, we can't embrace, but we've found a way of nuzzling one another, which is I think even more loving. On 'Wipe thine eyes' I kiss her tears away. Past Cordelias have told me of the importance of bonding with their Lears, and I think Nancy and I are beginning to achieve that. But our scenes together are all-too brief.

In the last scene we discuss how the bystanders should react. It's the perennial problem of the last act of tragedies. I've been a courtier at the end of *Hamlet*, when a bewildering series of misfortunes chase one another, all of which affect the court deeply. 'The Queen's been poisoned. . . Hamlet's killed the King. . . now he's dying. . . now Fortinbras has arrived. . .' To find a balance between inert stillness and distracting busy-ness is very difficult, in an odd way an ultimate test of the actor's craft. The end of *King Lear* is easier by comparison, but tricky nonetheless. When Lear calls for a mirror, should everyone start looking for one, or do they realize he's deluded? We decide the latter – much safer.

In the afternoon we run the second half, Acts Four and Five. I am very excited by the scenes I haven't seen before. Even the tying up of the plot in 5.3. is clear and gripping. There isn't a weak link in the cast. Though I'm feeling terrible, I get through my scenes passably. I'm finding it increasingly difficult to write about run-throughs, but I think this is a positive sign. If, as Brendel says, the middle rehearsal period has to be a filtering through the intellect, the end has to be a return to emotion. I just have to hope that the thousand things we have discussed are in place. In a run-through the vital balance is to remember what you've done, but not to give yourself notes as you go along.

Jonathan wants to do 1.1. on Saturday morning, but I tell him I must go to bed. He agrees. I urge him to let everyone have Saturday off, but he says he can't risk it. I don't know whether he's right or not. Six and a half weeks certainly isn't long enough to rehearse *King Lear* (at the RSC or the National you'd get eight to ten), but you may get no good work out of tired or resentful actors. At the RSC in the '70s directors were fond of rehearsing even on Sundays. Actors become like a train set the child/director can't stop playing with.

Saturday and Sunday I spend in bed. Marvellous. But I do go through the part minutely each day – the 'train set' mentality in *me*.

### Monday 21 January

We work rapidly through the first three acts, which I find very tiring as I'm not back to health yet. I mark 'Blow winds'. Jonathan thinks the thunder is a help, but sometimes it gets in the way of the metre (which I'm not such a purist that I can't accept), and rather more importantly with the naturalistic emotional flow. Some thunder rolls I may be able to speak through, others not. We can only work that out at the technical dress rehearsal. Back to Harley St. and more acupuncture.

# 9

## REHEARSAL DIARY: RESOLUTION

*Tuesday 22 January 2002*

Our first complete run-through in the afternoon. There's a forbidding line of new faces out front. The stage management and some of the technical crew have come to see what we're up to. Mark Henderson, our lighting designer, is poised to work out which areas of the stage he has to light. But they're all friends, and will be encouraging, whatever they're thinking deep down. The run goes reasonably well for me. The first scene is still too technical. I can't do the opening of 1.4 with Kent, Oswald and the knights. It's so full of business that I can't yet make it effortless. 2.4. remains my bugbear. It's such a difficult and exhausting scene, and I'm feeling over-directed, that I'm playing notes, not all of which I believe in. On certain passages I'm getting the same note over and over again. I think I'm doing what Jonathan wants, he says 'Do it more'. What I'm really saying is: 'I'm going as far as my taste, sense of character, emotional state will allow'; and he's replying: 'My taste urges you to go further'. The disputed area is of course the anger and aggression of Lear. If I feel I'm manufacturing it artificially, it has to be wrong – or at any rate wrong for me. At the same time if you trust your director, which I do, then you must trust his taste. The good director is the most tasteful audience you'll ever get. I know that Jonathan is trying to pull a performance out of me that nobody thinks I possess. It's a great act of faith on his part.

One thing the run did confirm. I know who I am. On occasions I have reached the late stages of rehearsal and thought: I know why I say and do everything that is laid down for me, but I don't know who this person is, I feel I have no centre. Lear, I thought, might be too difficult, too unknowable. But not so. Perhaps because Lear is not one of Shakespeare's more complicated characters? Anyway, for better or worse I know who *my* Lear is. Now I can make progress.

*Wednesday 23 January*

We work through the first three acts, always the most tiring way for me to spend the day. We speed up the initial row with Cordelia, and this has an interesting effect. As the words tumble out, so the row happens uncontrollably and things are said that can't be unsaid. Cordelia needn't have added fatally, 'Sure I shall never marry like my sisters to love my father all', because she'd already made clear her case. Lear needn't have made his terrible pronouncement, 'Better thou hadst not been born than not to have pleased me better'. I've been saying that with cold implacability, but I realize that it too comes out of anger, triggered by Cordelia's, 'And such a tongue that I am glad I have not'. This 'heat of the moment' reaction extends, I think, to Kent shooting his mouth off about madness, age and rashness, to Lear banishing him, and even to France offering to take Cordelia. Perhaps in retrospect they'd all like to have rethought: Cordelia regrets her outspokenness, Lear his rashness (this we know he feels in 1.4.), even France the absence of dowry. About the only people who keep cool are Burgundy, who knows just what he's after, and Edmund, who watches from his corner and eloquently says nothing. The others have the usual 'courtier problem', and I'm becoming aware that behind my back a whole sub-scene of looks and whispers is being played out between Goneril, Regan, Cornwall and Albany. I just hope they can keep it within limits. . .

It's always galvanizing to speed up a scene, particularly in Shakespeare. Actors should take their cue from Rosalind and speak on the thought. It's hard technically to take any first scene at great pace. It's more comfortable to ease your way in. Playing Lear feels like running a five-thousand-metres race at least. The part starts in a prepared and measured way, and I feel I'm running the first lap at a reasonable pace. Then after four minutes Cordelia says 'Nothing', and suddenly I'm running a hundred-metre sprint, aware that I've another four thousand, eight hundred to go. It's exciting, but unbalanced. But that's what the play is.

I'm finding 1.4. an increasingly rich scene. After the regal pomp of 1.1. we now see Lear as a country squire. It's an illuminating contrast. The scene with the Fool reveals Lear's craving for pleasure and laughter contrasted with his doubts and insecurities. Lear is desperate for the peace of mind he hopes his abdication will bring him, but the Fool reminds him that it can't be bought that easily. His rash misjudgements will force a reckoning. Suzanne is really finding her way into 'disquantity your train'. Many actresses play this speech of Goneril's with implacable composure and authority, but Suzanne's way is different. It's not easy to attack her father, and the speech costs her a good deal. Directly Lear explodes, she flinches. She knows his anger can make him capable of anything; witness the cold, intense destructiveness of the curse. After that, she will be implacable in her need to humble her father. Lear's return after his brief exit, which puzzled me at first, I now understand. Shakespeare didn't want Lear to leave after the curse, a man in control. Lear is only intermittently in control, and when he bursts back in he's rambling and crying almost incoherently. He's realizing his need for loving family, and now suddenly he's only Regan left. He's frightened.

Fear drives him in 1.5. The Fool probes away, but Lear is dismissive, monosyllabic. Out of nowhere comes 'I did her wrong'. It's a very bleak, unequivocal statement. The Fool knows it too. Tony watches me in this scene with a fixed stare that manages to combine concern, despair and irony. I don't know how he does it, but it's an immense help. I love this scene. Beckett or Pinter never wrote a better.

Beckett certainly didn't write 2.4. What is my problem with this scene, why am I finding it so difficult? I try to examine what Shakespeare is doing. We last saw Lear cursing Goneril and fearing that he will go mad. By the end of 2.4. Lear rushes out into the storm, certain that he will go mad. In one scene Shakespeare has to cover a huge amount of ground. I identify another problem. Lear confronts Regan, but she won't declare her hand. She neither comforts him nor fights him. She continually falls back on urging him to return to Goneril; in fact she repeats it four times. Lear, on his part, is so much in need of Regan's love that he is reluctant to attack her. It is not until Regan entreats him 'to bring but five and twenty' that Lear finally acknowledges that Regan is 'more wicked' than Goneril. This is some hundred and thirty lines after Regan's entrance. At last Lear's intention is clear; he wants to take revenge on such 'unnatural hags', and, since he can't think what form this revenge should take, he runs away. For the bulk of the scene therefore Lear is flailing around in a confusion of purposes. He wants to convince Regan of Goneril's wickedness, curse Goneril and refuse to go back to her, impress on Regan her filial duties, find out who stocked Kent, attack Oswald, insist on his hundred knights, and get the gods on his side.

Lear flips from subject to subject, from target to target; the contradictions pile up. His mind is breaking down, and Shakespeare needs a long scene to honour that. It is psychologically acute, but it sets the actor a huge challenge.

My biggest discovery is on 'I prithee, daughter, do not make me mad'. Lear is pleading with Goneril, because he knows that she knows that she has him on the run. The old wild boar is at last so wounded that the sisters know he cannot charge them. I try humbling myself before Goneril, and making for the door on 'We'll no more meet'. But Lear can't leave, because Goneril is 'my flesh, my blood, my daughter', and for the first time I have an overwhelming feeling here of what my own daughter means to me, of how intense is the bond and the mutual dependence, but how difficult total honesty is to achieve. 'I gave you all' I've always done big, because it's something Lear feels very strongly; he repeats it again in the storm, 'whose frank heart gave you all'. 'Those wicked creatures' speech I've been unresolved about. My instinct was that it was a bit crazy, but now that we're running the scene at full tilt I realize that Lear both thinks a fifty-knight daughter really does love him more than a twenty-five-knight daughter, and at some level knows that that's unbalanced. Crazed he must be to lead into the colossal onslaught of 'Reason not the need'. And at last I feel that I can rip into the speech, because it only works at full tilt. I see, now that we're running it, that 'Our basest beggars are in the poorest things superfluous' is exactly the kind of revelation that he will have in the *Heath* and *Dover Beach*. As his mind breaks down so a long suppressed understanding of the roots of the human condition begin to surface. You can argue that adversity is 'teaching' Lear, but I prefer to think it's unlocking his mind.

## Thursday 24 January

In the morning we work quickly through the second half, and then we have our second run-through in the afternoon. My cold is nearly gone and my voice is in a better state. For the first time I feel I'm motoring. 2.4. is the main beneficiary. Thanks to all the work we've done in finding variety, and yet at the same time driving through, I feel unleashed. I can't describe exactly what I did, because I don't know. This is the moment I've been waiting for – the moment when you begin to fly.

The first time I understood this clearly was in the 1984 season at the Barbican. Judi Dench was playing Brecht's *Mother Courage*, a production I wasn't in. Judi's understudy, Leslie Duff, told me that she attended most of Judi's rehearsals and kept thinking, 'That's good, but I could have done that. . . that's an interesting choice, but I might have made that'. Then they came to a run-through, and as Leslie watched she thought, 'I can't have been here for a week, Judi is suddenly playing the part quite differently'. I saw the same thing later that year when I was in Granville-Barker's *Waste* with Judi, directed by John Barton. She and Daniel Massie worked on a scene of impetuous flirtation with enormous detail. One day Judi dropped at least a third of the detail, jettisoning moments I really loved, and just went for the emotional centre. The usual process is to work out a scene's graph in great detail, and hope to retain the detail when you get it up to performance pitch. The high-risk actor is the one who's prepared to throw away the detail in going for the scene's jugular. It doesn't always work. I've seen actors ruin their perform-ance by taking off at the last moment into some generalized limbo. But in *Lear* you have to take risks. No one coming to see this of all plays wants a safe performance.

In some ways this illustrates the difference between stage and screen acting. Many film actors are high-risk, because they will launch into a three-minute take with no clear graph of what they're going to do, physically or emotionally. At the end of the take, they may not remember what they've just done, where they threw the cup, where they started crying. On the next take they may cry in a totally different place. All this the director can accommodate, though it may take some skilful editing to match the shots. The stage actor however may have to reproduce the scene a hundred times. Some actors only feel safe if they meticulously repeat themselves. Indeed however much you want to stay improvisatory, you're bound to repeat yourself. There are few scenes that can be played ten different ways, let alone a hundred. How to keep it fresh, how not to be mech-anical is a major problem. It's easy to fall into the trap of changing things for the sake of it – and usually regretting it. I've known actors change accents (disastrously, if hilariously), enter from unexpected places (causing great confusion to others), or leave the scene early (to general perplexity). The best you can hope for is that if you are deep enough inside the part, changes will occur naturally and truthfully. Let us hope.

Anyway on the Thursday run I began to fly. I knew it, and so did Jonathan and the rest of the cast.

### Friday 25 January

I have the morning off! A lie-in at last! At 8.40 a.m. there's a ring at the bell, a loud knock at the door. I stumble down, and there are the men from British Gas come to install the new boiler. 'No,' I say blearily, 'it's booked for Feb 4th.' 'No, Jan 25th we've got down here,' they claim. I dimly remember they offered us Jan 25th, and Jenny said firmly Feb 4th, as she would be here then. British Gas, as always, have done what suited them. Do I send them away? They've already unloaded mountains of equipment and filled the front garden with pipes and hoses. No, better accept it as a fait accompli: they may never return. At least I shall be here for the next three hours and can answer queries (which mainly turn out to be 'where do you keep your tea bags?'). I also have the crazy hope that they may get it done in one day, and I can triumphantly report to Jenny in the evening that the job is complete. 'Oh yes,' they say, 'no problem, we'll be through by five'.

The afternoon is a third run-through. I'm not sure what to do. Try to fly again, or consolidate the detail? We start, and I dry in the first scene. My concentration is nowhere. Is it British Gas? Is it because Ian McDiarmid, the Almeida's joint artistic director, has come to watch? But that's just an excuse. In my experience actors are greatly generous to one another, particularly in a situation like this. Things improve as the first half gathers pace, and I feel much freer out on the heath. I'm finding the mania solves the problem of how and when does Lear 'go mad'. Lear's 'madness' doesn't bring an abrupt change of character. His mania, which is evident from 1.4. onwards, increases so that he begins to say and do inappropriate/confused/demented things. I remember the psychologist Dorothy Rowe's dictum that 'madness' is just a defence people use when they feel themselves to be under immense threat and have to do something desperate to hold themselves together. The mania dips from time to time, leaving him perfectly lucid, but it most frequently possesses him in 3.4. and 3.6. I feel mania driving me into an alliance with the manic Poor Tom, and into the thousand burning spits and the mock trial. It reaches a climax with the little dogs barking at me, which I had once thought a pathetic line and now see as terrified. But have

I thrown out quiet, pathos, stillness too readily? Garrick and Kean could break hearts with a touch of pathos. But that's not what I'm after. Shakespeare has saved his pathos for acts four and five. Lear on the heath is undoubtedly being exhibitionist, as manic people sometimes are. But is the actor being exhibitionist? It's a narrow distinction, but a vital one to draw. Jonathan gives me a similar note, but on another scene:

> Don't get too at ease in Dover Beach.
>
> But Lear is at last at ease with himself, because he's telling the truth.
>
> Quite, but I felt Oliver was at ease.

True, it's a terrible trap to enjoy a scene too much, though again the actor has a complicated relationship with the audience. I believe that spectators should at some level feel that the performer *is* enjoying himself, even in tragedy. Directly the performer – actor, dancer, musician – seems uncertain, bored, effortful, o'erparted, or even to dislike what he's doing, it communicates straight to the audience.

I also felt in the run that I was getting a through-line on the *Recognition*. Waking up in real turmoil has given me a direction in the scene. Of course if you play bewildered dotage throughout, then the scene is serene and pathetic. But my angry Lear is still bound on a wheel of fire. I love Lear's last two lines. 'You must bear with me' is an expression the old have used down the centuries. 'Pray you now, forget and forgive': Shakespeare has reversed the normal order, Lear can't ask for forgiveness first, he begs instead that they pretend it never happened. 'I am old and foolish': the simpler I can state this, the less sentimental it will be. These runs are also sorting out the voice problem. By the time I've raged through the first three acts, my voice is in a state where broken uncertainty comes naturally. I'm not totally in control of what comes out, but at least it's truthful. I'm not having to put on an old man voice.

Ian McDiarmid is full of praise at the end. 'It's full of sound and fury, signifying *everything*', he says, as neatly a turned compliment as I could have wished for. I choose to believe it.

I get home at 8 p.m. Is the boiler in, the house warm? The house is cold. The boiler is in. . . but they can't make it work. This state-of-the-art 'combi' boiler, which heats the water as it flows through the system, means we have no hot tank, and so no back-up electric immersion heater, and so no hot water. Jenny has been Lear-like in her rage on the phone to British Gas (perhaps she should play the part?). They promise to sort it out tomorrow (Saturday? I think not). So no bath, and off to bed.

### Saturday 26 January

A last run-through. I'm tired, but I manage to galvanize myself into driving the first three acts. Paul Jesson says an interesting thing: 'The way you're playing Lear means I have to do far less work.' I think he means that I'm driving the play where it needs to be driven, and that consequently much of the time he only needs to react; there is a limit to the amount Kent/Caius can push the king. I'm relieved about this. One of the greatest problems for an actor is when the person who should be driving the scene refuses to do so, preferring to react off, or undercut, what others are doing. Paul has also realized something else, that once on the heath he barely needs to keep up the pretence of being Caius. It is Kent trying to help Lear, and Lear is far too deep in to notice. There is a parallel with Edgar. Tom Hollander has been plagued by all the different accents that Edgar should be using, and basically wants none of them. Shakespeare fortunately helps out. Edgar goes so far in Act Four in dropping his Poor Tom accent that Gloucester notices; 'Methinks you're better spoken'. Shakespeare is giving the actor a stage direction that once Gloucester is blind, he can drop the Poor Tom persona, just as when Lear is demented Kent can drop Caius. I see this as some answer to those critics who complain that it's absurd that Kent and Edgar keep up their pretence so long. In a sense they don't.

We have notes, wine, sandwiches. I take the train to Devon for what's left of the weekend. British Gas did come. . . but can't solve the problem. Miranda prefers to stay in London, hot waterless. She writes better when she has the house to herself. Rain and high seas lash the front at Lyme, but it's a good break. I hardly think about Lear. The train journey back takes five hours – South West Trains are preparing for tomorrow's strike.

*Monday 28 January*

We are required to get to the theatre at King's Cross at 9 a.m. This involves standing in a crowded tube for forty minutes, literally unable to move. I think about 'unaccommodated man'. When I arrive, the set is stunning. Or rather the 'room' is stunning. It is far more intimate than I had imagined. Audience and actor share the same space in a large, low-ceilinged panelled room. The only visible lights are wall fittings and chandeliers. The 'set' is a large, somewhat anonymous, mahogany baronial study. The only furniture is Lear's desk and chair centre-stage, three chintzy chairs stage left for the daughters, and Gloucester's armchair and fireplace stage right. It is very economical, every item means something vital. I think it's a wonderful realization of a concept. Anyone who knows the play will understand it immediately. But they will then wonder how the designer is going to do the heath and the great outdoors. The collapse of the set will be a *coup-de-théâtre*, however much Jonathan plays down the idea. Preview audiences should be amazed. Those who read the notices will, alas, come forewarned.

The technical dress rehearsal (the 'tech') is where stage, lights, costume and sound meet the acting, with the acting a poor last. Forty years ago I remember watching an RSC tech at the Edinburgh Festival (for Christopher Fry's *Curtmantle*), which went on all through the night. Now, blessedly, with Equity and E.U. regulations, actors (though rarely technicians) have an eleven-hour break. The last time I did a mammoth tech was at the Barbican, when we went on from Tuesday morning to Friday 6 p.m., and opened Friday 7.30 p.m. without any dress rehearsals at all. At one point I remember blundering about a darkened part of the revolve trying to find the audience so that I could start the scene. Big musical techs can of course go on for weeks, but the normal pattern is two to two and a half days of tech, followed by two dress rehearsals (usually Wednesday evening and Thursday afternoon) and a Thursday night opening. This is the pattern we are attempting to follow.

This *Lear* tech is complicated by various factors. First, the room has to collapse panel by panel through an ingenious system of pulleys operated from under the stage. Occasionally the wire is released, but the panel doesn't fall. Released from its moorings, however, it could fall at any time, and is therefore a potentially lethal hazard. We have to devise routes on to the stage so that actors are never in danger.

Second, we have a lighting problem. To preserve the illusion of the room, the lighting is hidden away in masked panels. This means fewer lamps and a greater need for accuracy. Mark Henderson, whom I have worked with many times, is a brilliant lighting designer and is very partial to side lighting. Lighting from out front tends to be over-generalized and flat, or non-naturalistically pin-point. Side lighting casts swathes of beams right across the stage to fascinating effect, but it presents problems. First you have to find your beam, and second you have to ensure that you're not masking or being masked by others. Move slightly downstage of the actor speaking, as good stage manners prescribe, and you can blot them out. Move far downstage, and you have opened up the channel of light for them, but made life difficult for yourself when it's your turn to speak. It becomes an exercise in negotiation and selflessness, good for the ensemble but bad for the concentration. That said, I can see that as the set disintegrates and the great looming bulk of the bus garage is revealed, Mark's use of light is superb.

Third, in the storm we have not just thunder and lightning, but rain with real water. The five of us out on the heath – Lear, Kent, the Fool, Gloucester and Edgar – have been dreading this. Our dread is justified. Though many jokey references have been made to 'warm rain', the water is of course icy. I am wearing a shirt, which is quickly sodden, and I then take off my boots and trousers. I am now in a shirt, two pairs of underpants and socks. Quite soon the rain, which is supposed to disappear down the cracks between the floorboards, has formed large puddles, though to my relief my sodden socks seem to grip the floor quite well. It becomes clear however that there are dry 'corridors' in between the sprinklers in the ceiling, and if you can manoeuvre yourself into these safe havens you remain relatively dry, while it cascades in front and behind you. Soon I predict the five of us will be strung out in a row across the stage, venturing neither forwards nor backwards. We end Monday in the rain for two hours, but we don't get to the end of 3.4. So Tuesday 10.15 a.m. we are back splashing about for another two hours. Fortunately our expert dresser, Spencer Kitchen, has a range of hot towels and dressing-gowns ready for us. A further consolation is that it's immediately apparent that the rain does a lot of the acting for us. Glorying in the rain and trying to survive in the rain mingle in what I hope is a fruitful combination.

There are other set pieces that take time, particularly the fights and the blinding of Gloucester. We proceed in fits and starts. Some scenes pass surprisingly quickly, others take several hours. There is no music in the first half. Jonathan had first thought of an Elgarish organ accompaniment, but soon scrapped that. Jonathan Dove has arranged a beautiful 'Cordelia theme' for the second half, used very sparingly. I am very relieved: excessive music in plays (and films) is one of my pet hates. All the time Mark is creeping light on to actors' faces and John Leonard is experimenting with sounds, footsteps here, a dog barking there, and of course the thunder. This is John's fifth *Lear*, and he knows his thunder-claps. Once at the Old Vic he had to devise a whole storm sequence overnight on old-fashioned reel-to-reel. Now he can turn a clap into a rumble with two taps on his laptop. Paul Brown is everywhere, making adjustments to the set and suggesting costume alterations. Tentatively he asks me if I would lose my shirt for 3.6. I am now in pants and socks, but by this stage I don't care any longer. My sagging stomach is not a pretty sight, but I think it's authentic. I don't think my Lear has spent his seventies in the gym. I ask:

> What will go next – socks or pants?
>
> The socks make you look vulnerable.
>
> And ridiculous.
>
> Yes.
>
> So it'll be the pants?
>
> No, I think we've all agreed that's too distracting.

So it seems we've gone as far as we're going. But elsewhere the stripping hasn't finished. In the final two scenes I lose first my dressing gown, and then my pyjama top. Paul allows me an old granddad vest. I look like an inmate of a condemned old people's home. Edmund didn't intend Lear to look regal in prison; I like that. But I won't be looking glamorous at the curtain call.

To general surprise we finish the tech Tuesday night. This says volumes for Rupert, Maris, Alex, James, Jason and the technical crew, and for the amount of preparation they have put in. It means we can have dress rehearsals Wednesday afternoon and evening. The afternoon run is officially for the technicians, actors are to take it easy. Of course we don't take it easy, but it does remove some of the pressure. Ivan Kyncl, who photographs all the Almeida productions, arrives and starts snapping away, often about three feet from your face. This is distracting, but I have been through it so many times that I know how to survive. Others don't, and tempers shorten. I start the evening run (acting required) in a reasonable state of mind, and within two lines I know that my voice is damaged. I have gone hoarse, lost range and flexibility. Whether this has been brought on through stress, rain, or using too much voice in the technical, or all three, I don't know, but it will have to be coped with. I ease back a little, and as the scenes progress I settle on a level that is comfortable. I think I know how opera singers feel: I know how to get through this one, but what trouble am I storing up for tomorrow? Except, for singers there's never a tomorrow, they always have at least a day between dress rehearsal and performance.

At the end I ask Jonathan if we can dispense with a third dress rehearsal Thursday afternoon.

> No, the technicians really need it.
>
> I'll have no voice for the evening.
>
> Then you must mark it.

So I use half my voice. This is always an interesting exercise. There's part of me that thinks this is probably how I should be playing the part anyway. The rage is all contained, seething away internally. If I weren't so worried about the evening, I might think I'd learnt a very useful lesson.

The audience start arriving for the first preview that evening. Why have they come? Who, apart from loyal well-wishers, would be so sadistic, or masochistic, to book for a first preview – one that's highly likely to be cancelled? Well, we haven't cancelled, but we're not without last minute hitches. The auditorium seats haven't been properly numbered, and frantic rearrangements have to take place. We finally go up twenty-five minutes late. It hasn't been an easy wait. I'm sharing a small dressing room with Gloucester, Kent, Albany, Cornwall and the Fool. I cannot sit with Olympian calm, meditating my way through the minutes. Temporary 'found' spaces are very exciting, but their backstage facilities rarely rise above the village hall. I think longingly of my bed and shower at the National.

The play finally starts. I negotiate my first speech with apparent authority, the voice is firm if limited, I lose my temper with Cordelia, and then I dry. It's the same thing as before. I'm overwhelmed by the thought of what I have to get through, and my confidence goes. I talk rubbish for two lines: something like 'By all the orbs. . . whose existence we are. . . and cease to be', and then I'm back on track. Curiously, it calms me. It'll never be as bad again. Paul Shelley, my comforter, tells me backstage that no one would have noticed. He may be lying, but Oh, the benefits of sharing a dressing room! I get through the rest of the evening without falter. Everything goes remarkably smoothly, the storm storms on cue, the set falls down in the right places. There is much applause and cheering at the end. There are many tears backstage and quite a few, we are later told, in the audience. So far, so good. I go home to find we have hot water, after six days of ice-cold water at home *and* work.

We have twelve previews before the press night, which is a luxury, though the play is in sufficiently good shape to need only half that number. Waiting nearly two weeks for the 'opening' can become an imposition. The strange thing is that regular theatregoers have come to love previews, irrespective of whether the seats are cheaper, which increasingly they aren't. There must be a few thousand Londoners who want to see a play early on before the critics have pronounced. The previews are thus packed with eager, receptive, intelligent audiences, who mostly want to like the show. They're often the best audiences one ever plays to, and therefore an untrustworthy guide to both the critics and future box-office. Actors seethe with rage when they read poor notices for a play that has palpably gone down well in preview, and are aghast when the box-office immediately falls off. Nursing a play through the first weeks after the critics (unless they have been unanimously benign) is one of the commercial producer's biggest gambles, and some turn tail and close immediately.

Jenny comes on Friday night, and Miranda on Saturday. I put them through this ordeal to ensure that I'm not being so terrible that no-one but family would dare tell me. They are not just supportive, they are extremely enthusiastic. Jenny's notes are on seeking variety, and this becomes my main quest during the following week. Miranda has likes and dislikes, one of which is I should stand up straighter in scene one. This confirms me in a physical pattern that I have been moving towards. While Lear is still on top of things in 1.1. and 1.4. he manages to be his old erect self. A shaking right hand is the only sign of his stress. As he disintegrates in 1.5. and 2.4, the shoulders go, the arms hang in front and he begins to shamble. In other words, forget trying to play eighty at the start of the play, just let it happen. As I think about this, I make a very simple discovery. Shakespeare doesn't tell the audience Lear is over eighty until the *Recognition*, when he is a bedridden shell of his former self. It's as if Shakespeare is saying to Burbage, don't worry about playing very old early on, by the time we get to Act 4 the audience will accept you as eighty plus.

The next week we spend every afternoon working on the play. First we have notes: 'Monday was too general, nothing mattered enough, Tuesday was really jagged and dangerous, Wednesday you've become predictable again' etc. Jonathan keeps reminding me of balance: don't let 1.1. become too domestic, we must really feel you might hit Goneril on 'Ingratitude' in 1.4, make the heart tremors bolder, don't get too cosy with Gloucester in *Dover Beach*, don't lose the joy throughout *Prison*, you can afford to be quieter in the last scene. We make small changes, we fine tune, we make adjustments with set, lighting and sound, we endlessly experiment with mirrors that I can smash without showering my face with glass. At my insistence we spend two hours on 2.4. Playing the scene at night, I find myself swept away. I need to go back and check that I'm being specific at every twist and turn. Audience members speak to us after the show – the bar remains blessedly open – and some write to me. Of course it's nearly all positive, those who hate the show (there must be a few?) have rushed off into the night, but praise is always a stimulus. They remain behind to speak, not so much for what we have done, but because the play has meant so much to them. We are the conduit. Over the weekend I finish off a short rehearsal diary for the *Daily Telegraph*. The interviews in the *Times* and *Financial Times* come out. They are both very fair records of our conversation. In a world where we have come to assume all journalists are out to grind an axe, find an angle, spice things up with a little invention, it's re-assuring to report that in Daniel Rosenthal and Sarah Hemming I met two writers of perfect probity.

The Tuesday press night finally comes. We seem to have been waiting an eternity. Jonathan asks me what I want to do in the after-noon as a preparation. I consult the cast, and we decide on an in-formal word run of the first three acts. However petrified we may be in the evening, that afternoon we really talked and listened to one another. That night I'm nervous about the first scene, as I always am. My voice is still somewhat hoarse, and lacking flexibility. Audience reaction is more muted than usual, as I knew it would be. But we're confident in what we're doing, and tension gives the performance an extra edge. I feel it's work in progress, and tonight is probably the best we've done it so far. We'll get better. The critics stampede for the exit as soon as we finish, their editors having decreed it's to be an 'overnighter'. By the time the cheering starts they're well out in the King's Cross night. Jenny and Miranda come round. I think they've been more nervous than me. The Almeida throws a great party as usual (though the music's too loud for conversation), and I meet up with a lot of friends. I'm just very, very relieved.

And the notices? Well, I don't read them till the run's over [but I discuss them at the end of Chapter 11]. I find them too disturbing. Bad notices are upsetting, naturally, and rarely constructive. Good notices have a habit of highlighting certain moments, certain lines, which makes me self-conscious. It puts a label of approval on things which I want to be part of a seamless whole. It upsets my rhythm. But of course I soon pick up their gist. *Times* and *Telegraph* very good, *Guardian* good, *Mail* mediocre, *Independent* poor. I endure the usual dressing room jokes about 'You obviously wrote some of them yourself'. But there are worse things to have to endure.

## *10*

# A CONVERSATION WITH THE DIRECTOR

*I talked to Jonathan Kent in June 2002,*
*two months after the end of the run.*

OFD   Let's start with some obvious questions. Why did you want to do *King Lear*? When had you first thought of doing it?

JK   I wanted to do *Lear* particularly because of you. Of course, if you're a director of Shakespeare it's a play which at some point you envisage doing. But, just as with Hamlet, you don't say I'm going to do *Hamlet*, who shall we get to play him? That would be a fruitless exercise. It's got to be embodied by the man playing the part.

OFD   What gave you the idea that I could play Lear?

JK   Well, it's just having worked with you four times before. It really began during *Ivanov*.

OFD   Because Shabielsky [Ivanov's penniless uncle] is a Lear-like figure?

JK   No, not really. Qualities of you actually, getting to know you, and then particularly in *Naked*, where your vulnerability and, for a very big man, your . . . I'm searching for a polite word . . . your shambling figure: you have a child-like quality too, which interested me for the second half of Lear. I also knew you were a presence, though for the first half I was worried about your benign aspect. But for the second half what interested me was the loss of self in the progress of the play, and that was something I felt you could embody.

OFD   You didn't see this as a farewell production? Many artistic directors have made it so.

JK    No. In a way my farewell to the Almeida itself was *The Tempest* [December 2000], though we never admitted it, because that would have been grotesquely sentimental, and fortunately nobody knew we were leaving at that point. I suppose a lot of people leave on a *Lear*, because it is in some way a summation, the greatest expression of Shakespeare's genius there is, an unimaginable play, and directors probably feel that's something they have to work towards.

OFD    Tell me about the set. You talked early on to me about this panelled room – where did that come from?

JK    I first pictured doing it in a Lincoln's Inn panelled Elizabethan hall, because I was interested in the whole notion of it happening to a degree within his own head. The image I had was of a panelled room with the rain falling through the roof on to a sofa. I drove our graphic designers mad because that's the poster I always imagined – a sodden sofa in a room.

OFD    Do you know where that came from?

JK    It's the invasion of the quotidian by external forces. It's about the thin buttress of our acquired surroundings keeping chaos at bay, and panelled rooms seem to me an apt metaphor for that.

OFD    Having got a panelled room, had you always seen it modern?

JK    Yes. Because, as I said to you, one of the reasons I'm interested in the play is because of my grandmother's Alzheimer's and her loss of self, and being in exile from the land of her own intelligence. The terrifying notion of losing the land of your mind is frightening for me, and that's why I wanted it to be recognizably contemporary, so that everyday objects became frightening in themselves. For instance, my initial idea was that Poor Tom would burst out of the sofa, that would be the hovel. That wasn't practical in the end, and the desk was another solution.

OFD    What are the pros and cons of doing Shakespeare modern?

JK    I was always rather resolutely against it, because I thought it begged more questions than it answered. What one wants to do is create a world that is credible for the play. It wasn't really present-day – you wore a suit, but people fought with swords. The point was to create a world where neither jarred. It was, dread word for any actor to hear, an eclectic world. I have moved towards that kind of world for Shakespeare. For instance in *Richard II* [which was done in a simplified fourteenth-century costume] I thought that would be inappropriate, but actually watching it later on I was sorry that we hadn't moved it. For instance, the deposition scene would have been wonderful if it had been in front of men in suits, and I regretted that I hadn't been bolder with it. Part of the process of *Richard II* is the great shift in Britain: and with the coming of Bolingbroke you get the beginning of modern Britain. It's the tarmacking over of Arthurian, chivalric Britain. I'm not very good at watching my own productions, because all I can see is where I have failed it, and not where something works.

OFD    Some people had doubts about the setting of the first scene of *Lear*, but as the play progressed they seemed happy with the eclecticism of it.

JK    What you and I were concerned about was not the *coup-de-théâtre* – 'O my God, the set's falling down' – but that it should be the splintering of a place and also a mind: that it should not happen in a way that stopped the breath and so fractured the play. What I hoped happened was a graduated disintegration, and in the second half, when the tempest was over, that it was all gone. It is a play so clearly of two halves, broken by the storm. The play lifts out of the structure of the everyday into something more abstract and more mysterious.

OFD    What led you into thinking that anger was the key to Lear in the first two acts?

JK    It's the anger of a person who has no real communication with the people he supposedly loves, and that anger is a kind of buttress. Lear's only mode is one of imposition of power and the demands that power makes. These are all the male qualities, and anybody who inhabits the male, without the mitigating force of the feminine, I think resides in a sort of anger. It's the animus in excelsis. Just as if you reside entirely in the anima, that in the end destroys you too.

Because Lear dealt entirely in the male qualities, he could only exist in a form of anger, which is then turned against himself and destroys him. But in the second half of the play he learns compassion, he learns the feminine qualities, when it's partially, but I don't think entirely, too late.

OFD   Is that something that interests you particularly, people that reside in their maleness?

JK   I was briefly in analysis, and very fruitfully too, to a Jungian analyst. I'm interested in the animus and the anima. For instance I did *Medea*, which is the reverse of this, a person who exists in the anima with terribly destructive results. These are the extremes of emotions, because we're dealing with great art, with kings and great figures of imagination, with archetypes, and of course they're taken to extremes, and that's where theatre is for me the most interesting. I think that's what classical theatre can do for us, it can illustrate in magnified form our own psychological and emotional components.

OFD   You and Ian [McDiarmid] have talked about the Almeida's belief in high-definition acting. Is this linked?

JK   Anybody who loves theatre is interested in great performance. In British theatre there is a danger, as with all the arts, of it being polite and restrained in a way that moves it towards the middle of the road, rather than accommodating and allowing the extremes of our existence. I don't think this is just about acting, I think that it's about the way we truly are. I believe that some of the time we present these extremes of our existence on stage in a more modified form than they actually exist in our own heads. I believe in a theatre that embraces the extremes of our existence – not I hope, though it's a charge sometimes levelled against me, that actors are pushed to extremes that exclude the possibilities of reality or truth or recognition. I simply don't believe people behaving extremely rules out truth, though we have in England a certain ethic of 'keeping things within bounds'.

OFD   Yes, probably the thing I think most often watching British theatre is 'the stakes are not high enough'.

JK   Exactly. It's what's happened to our classical acting through the training of television and film. You have to accommodate the emotional and technical demands of Shakespeare. You need to be able to go to extremes. I think it's limiting just to find the middle ground.

OFD   One of the conundrums of Lear is how much it's a process of self-discovery, a journey towards enlightenment. This is greatly complicated by his madness. What do you think Shakespeare is trying to do?

JK   He acquires compassion, and empathy. His madness is an odd mixture of delusion and piercing sanity. He has empathy for Gloucester, he recognizes his daughter, and these are signs of mental health. Psychotic or mad behaviour is a retreat from being able to empathize with your fellow man. But he is not an evolved man at the end.

OFD   There is no sense that at the end of his life he's discovered the error of his ways and seen the moral light, which was clearly an idea the nineteenth century liked about their Lears.

JK   But he's forced into a situation, through his own doing, where he has to confront himself. And he has to confront a life that he has, through power, been buttressed against. He's also full of self-loathing. He does think we're all guilty. So in a sense there is an evolution, but it's not willed nor is it arrived at – it's somehow given to him. Tell me, do you see him as a truly tragic figure?

OFD   That's difficult to answer. He's arrived at the end of his life with so little understanding of human nature, such poor communication with the people around him, and a sense that he's losing his mind. It seems to me tragic that he brings so much upon himself.

JK   I think he isn't a tragic figure, but that he earns tragic status through suffering, and that makes him a curious and interesting figure in Shakespeare. His trajectory isn't one of a fall from grace and then a redemption. He's someone whom it's hard to sympathize with, but inevitably by the end one recognizes one's own frailty and humanity writ large.

OFD   A problem all productions struggle with is how much Goneril and Regan want to destroy their father, or whether they merely want to cut him down to size.

JK   They're trying to deal with an impossible situation, with a man who has abdicated all responsibility yet at the same time wants all the privileges of position, and this makes their assumption of responsibility impossible. I don't think it's a desire to revenge themselves on someone who's clearly been a ghastly father, it's people fighting for their political lives.

OFD   Watching *Lear* after it had opened, how different was it from the way you'd first imagined it?

JK   I'm sure in many ways. Let me give you one small example, though it's a scenic one – the disintegration of the room. I wanted the chaos of the outside world to bleed through. Inevitably when you drop walls, these are large punctuations, and what I had imagined in my head was the splintering of wood, and the synapses of the brain and the room starting to pull apart, and the small fissures to appear as the blood vessels begin to burst in the brain. In practice the falling of heavy panels of wood and steel were larger punctuations than the film I had in my head. I was always nervous that they would fracture you, your performances, but I don't think they did.

OFD   *Lear* is often called the most ensemble of the great tragedies.

JK   And some of the parts, particularly Edgar, are fiendishly difficult to play, and to make a decision about. And we were lucky that we had a very good group of actors. The story lines and strands of the play are so complex and demanding in six or seven of the leading parts, in a way they are in no other Shakespeare play.

OFD   People generally commented on the clarity of the production, and this must owe a lot to you.

JK   Well, I'm pleased about that, but I do feel, 'Christ, of course it's clear, that's the whole point!' It's a compliment to all your performances. I think I do have a clear view of the progress of the play. I believe I have a fairly strong architectural view of any play I direct, which is both a virtue and a vice. One of my virtues is I have a strong sense of rhythm. Directing lies in rhythm, and I think it's a great aid to understanding and clarity. By rhythm I don't just mean verse and metre, I mean the way scenes abut one another, the way they move the action on. Where you rein in and where you drive on is a very valuable tool in communicating a play.

OFD   One problem is the degree of irony in the play, and particularly in the part of Lear. You would often warn me against becoming ironic, especially in *Dover Beach*.

JK   Irony argues a kind of sanity, an overview that Lear doesn't have. Irony can be incredibly useful, it's one of the things in which our genius in acting lies, but it's also a danger. It's a trap for actors, but also for audiences – they long to ironize because it lets them off the hook. Years ago I did a production of Corneille's *Le Cid*, and the one thing about Corneille is that, like Racine, he's a complete stranger to irony. But there was a great gravitational pull during the run to ironize the situation, and the danger was that the actors played that, and the audience could therefore remain removed from it, and think that 'Corneille's not nearly as painful as I thought he was going to be', but actually the savagery was blunted. Irony cossets you.

OFD   And critics love it.

JK   Love it. Critics don't like the full frontal approach. They would say it was cruder, but I think it gives them less to write about. Critics are by nature dispassionate, they have to be, and they love to salute it in others. The other danger is that actors start becoming their own critics, and comment on what they're doing as they go along.

The difficulty is that so many people have seen *Lear* twenty-five times, and it all becomes a checklist of how's he going to do the madness or *Dover Beach*, rather than approaching it with a proper naivety. That's why I like American audiences. In our patronizing Anglo-Saxon way we think they won't get the ironies, but they are much more alive, much more attentive, because they're not watching the way you're doing it, they're watching the play. We tend to compare and contrast, and it's a way of evading the play. I'm glad we did three of our Shakespeares in new spaces. To find your way to a place you've never heard of, to sit in a strange environment, and to be shocked and provoked, means you approach the whole experience of theatre differently. It's important for an audience not just to slip into their seats in familiar surroundings and think 'O goodness me, it's 7.25 p.m. on Tuesday, it must be *Lear*'.

# AFTERMATH

From the very first preview I was struck by how closely the audience listened. I have never felt so much concentration in the theatre. I could feel it in Lear's first speech, particularly at the point where I say, 'Tell me, my daughters.' I left a slight pause, as if searching how exactly to phrase the love test, and the audience seemed to hold their collective breath. It's the power of myth. Lear is about to ask the fatal question. We need him to, for the ritual to be played out, but we don't want him to. It's the power and property of live theatre. Of course every night there must have been bored and inattentive people, but at certain points in the play even the odd wrigglers and coughers were stilled: the curse on Goneril, 'I did her wrong', 'O let me not be mad', 'Reason not the need', 'the thing itself', 'You do me wrong to take me out of the grave', and much of the final scene. Best silence of all was after 'I know thee well enough. Thy name is Gloucester' in *Dover Beach*. Even sometimes a slight gasp. It was a pause that I felt could hang in the air indefinitely (I was very disciplined about moving on. . . well, fairly disciplined).

Why this unusual attention? I think it was partly the nature of the set, and the way it encompassed the whole auditorium, so that we had a shared intimacy. Partly the speed, and I think the clarity, with which we played, that both enabled and demanded attentiveness. Partly, the kind of audience that the Almeida attracts; loyal regulars, those excited by the originality and accessibility of Jonathan's productions, those intrigued by what might be achieved in a bus garage in seamy King's Cross. We were comfortably full the entire run. But finally, of course, it is the play. Stanley Wells may be right that '*King Lear* is so widely regarded as the most intensely serious and profoundly moving of Shakespeare's plays. . . that going to see a performance is in danger of seeming like participating in a religious ritual'. I know people who will go to see *Lear* in much the same spirit that they go to see the Rembrandts at the National Gallery or attend a performance of the *St Matthew Passion*. This iconization of *Lear* may not be a good thing. It may have turned it into a sacred cow, a World Heritage site. This however is not my experience. I have found people only too ready to say they find the play incomprehensible, too bleak, too improbable, yet at the same time concede that it is an extraordinary experience. The National Gallery recently had an exhibition of Rembrandt self-portraits. One critic said that after a time the portraits seemed to be reviewing him, rather than the reverse. I have had a similar experience watching *King Lear*.

Audiences were not just attentive, they often seemed on the verge of laughter. Of course Shakespeare has built in some laughs. There's one very early on:

> GLOUCESTER   I have so often blushed to acknowledge him that now I am brazed to 't.
>
> KENT   I cannot conceive you.
>
> GLOUCESTER   Sir, this young fellow's mother could.

Waiting to enter, we would judge the audience's disposition by the size of the laugh (as hundreds have before us). If none came, David Ryall would expertly coax them with knowing looks on 'yet was his mother fair, there was good sport at his making'. On the rare occasions when this got no return, we knew we were in for a tough evening. Gloucester, Edmund, Edgar, Goneril, Kent, Oswald and of course the Fool all have comic moments. Lear has his share: 'I do not like the fashion of your garments' to the near naked Tom, 'Goneril with a white beard' to Gloucester. But what affected me more were not so much the outright laughs, rewarding as they were, but the uncertain smiles. In *Lear* there is so much that borders on the edge of laughter. 'I will forget my nature; so kind a father!' says Lear in 1.5, and the audience don't know whether to laugh or hiss. 'But I'll not chide thee', says Lear to Goneril in 2.4, when he has just cursed her with lameness and infected beauty. 'I remember thine eyes well enough', says Lear to the blind Gloucester, and the casual cruelty makes the audience stifle their laughter. Time and again the absurdity, the grotesqueness of the moment leaves the audience floundering. When Gloucester attempts suicide, and merely collapses in a heap, should they laugh or not? Children would.

This sense of the absurd is part of a general discovery about the shape of the play. I feel that Lear is beginning to break down in 1.1, this becomes explicit in 1.4. and 1.5, and is played out to the full in 2.4. Orwell said that in his sane moments Lear hardly ever makes an intelligent remark. There's some truth in that, and it's what makes playing the first two acts so difficult. No wonder so many actors have decided to stroll through them. In 1.1. Lear shows himself to be an able if despotic ruler, but the rest of his behaviour is that of a solipsistic child. He remains a child in 1.4, apart from his first moment of self-discovery about Cordelia:

> O most small fault,
> How ugly didst thou in Cordelia show,
> Which like an engine wrenched my frame of nature
> From the fixed place, drew from my heart all love
> And added to the gall.

In 2.4. his repeated heart tremors bring on some glimpses of understanding about the human condition:

> We are not ourselves
> When nature, being oppressed, commands the mind
> To suffer with the body.

But it is not until 'Reason not the need' that we reach any intelligent philosophising, and by this time Lear has spoken some 350 lines, nearly half his part. Of course you can invest any lines with an aura of Olympian wisdom if you have the voice and charisma of a Gielgud, but I don't think it's being true to Shakespeare. Until Lear breaks down, he's a spoilt child with little understanding of himself, and none of other people. It's a brave piece of writing, but it's not easy to play. It confounds all the actor's craving for sympathy, variety, comedy, ironic detachment, and intelligent overview. I could never have achieved so blinkered a figure without Jonathan's watchful eye urging me not to stray into more congenial areas. But it's not a portrait of an old man/tragic hero that is comfortable for either actor or audience.

In his first ten writing years Shakespeare explored largely sympathetic tragic heroes: Henry VI, Romeo, Richard 11, Brutus, culminating in Hamlet. From Macbeth onwards Shakespeare experiments with less sympathetic figures, that alienate us in some way through their destructive passions: Antony, Cleopatra, Timon, Coriolanus, even Leontes and Prospero. Othello and Lear, which I have both now played, seem to me his transitional experiments. Othello, initially 'noble', loses much of our sympathy through his gullibility, jealousy, and desire for revenge. *King Lear* is the experiment in reverse. Lear, an unattractive despot at the outset, finally wins some sympathy through his suffering and madness. Both parts are very much in two halves. The part of Lear is extremely difficult in its first three acts, the part of Othello in its last three. Acts Four and Five are easier for Lear, not because they are shorter, or even because of madness, but because his perspective has changed. In the first two acts he's not just angry, he doesn't know what to make of the world. With his daughters' rejection of him his world has gone awry, he is floundering, completely at a loss. But on the heath he starts to denounce social injustice and show concern for others. He begins to understand the world, to make sense of it, and he feels liberated. His suffering doesn't stop, his insights and altruism are gained at a cost, but his grasp of reality, demented though he may be in patches, asserts itself. Physically he may be the victim, at the mercy of others, but mentally and spiritually he is freed. I found it a huge relief to play this liberation.

What I found in performance is that from Act Three onwards a form of dementia, or at any rate unbalance, enters not just Lear but the rest of the cast. Cornwall and Regan, egged on by Goneril, pluck out Gloucester's eyes and send him to smell his way to Dover, when killing him would be a much more sensible option. Cornwall's servant rises up against his master, when he knows it must doom him. Gloucester travels all the way to Dover to commit suicide, accepts Edgar's constant changes of accent with little demur, and believes that he has fallen over a cliff with not a scratch upon him. Both Edgar and Kent preserve their incognitos for no very good reason. Edmund thinks he can enjoy both sisters, and that he can execute Lear and Cordelia without blame. Goneril's solution to a hopeless love triangle is to poison her sister. All of this is Shakespeare's invention. It might be argued that the reason Shakespeare was wise to borrow other people's plots is that his own were ludicrously implausible. Certainly Tolstoy and Bradley would endorse this, and argue that *Othello* and *Macbeth* are therefore far superior plays. But I think Shakespeare knew what he was doing, and that these absurdities are the stuff of the play. From Lear's reckless exit into the storm, the world of the play goes topsy-turvy. It is difficult to argue that the play takes place in Lear's head, as one can, say, of Prospero in *The Tempest*, but the unbalance that Lear's abdication brings about seems to me to infect all the characters. No wonder the rest of the play takes place in the open air, on an unspecified 'heath', and then near Dover, a place that takes on an almost Alice-in-Wonderland aura. No wonder the battle takes place offstage in an atmosphere of unreality. No wonder Goneril and Regan exit for their brief double death. It's a world gone mad. Only Albany's dogged good sense and Edgar's last minute acceptance of responsibility wrench the play back on to some sort of even keel.

I knew from the start that we had to choose a path and follow it through. Even if it revealed only Brook's two-sevenths of the play, it was still better than a compromise that yielded nothing clear at all. We decided on an anger that turns manic. It's justified by the text, but then so are other routes. It's psychologically consistent, and clear for the audience to follow. It's extremely tiring to play, and it's difficult to find variety and, perhaps more important, surprise. It means forsaking reflection, inwardness, and a good deal of ironic detachment, but then I don't find that is Shakespeare's intention. In real life a manic Lear would be immensely repetitive and tiring – that is the nature of the affliction. On stage those are qualities that have to be tempered for easier consumption. I would love to play Lear again, perhaps at seventy. If I did, I would experiment in certain other directions. I could never forsake the anger, but I think I would look harder for curiosity, doubt, humour, self-revelation, self-understanding. I might make him older and more feeble. I might lurch more markedly between lucidity and confusion. I might fight the storm less, and use it to bring healing and understanding. I don't know if I could achieve any of these and still keep a coherent shape, but it would be worth a try.

When I get into performance I always look for the moment in the play when I feel relaxed, when the nerves are finally gone. I always hope that it will be after a scene or two, but in *Lear* I find that it was later than usual. From the moment I strip off my clothes in 3.4. I feel free of care, that I can do the rest of the play without problem. It can't be coincidence that from the moment I unbutton, literally and metaphorically, I feel freed. In so much of the first two acts Lear is hiding his real self, cocooned in a web of status and pretence. He thinks he can give away his kingdom and maintain his personal authority. He thinks his daughters love him, because that is the nature of filial gratitude. He thinks if Cordelia disagrees with him that she doesn't love him. He thinks he's still a dragon, when he is patently not. The Lear of the first two acts is Shakespeare's most complete study of the intolerant patriarch, a figure who had intrigued him from Capulet through to Duke Frederick and Polonius. He is the antithesis of that other great study of old age, Falstaff. But as I play the part, I feel the Lear of the heath onwards is the author unbuttoning himself. I know how derided such claims invariably are, but I sense it in my bones. Shakespeare is not unknowable.

Diana Rigg, Scofield's Cordelia, had warned me not to lose energy in the second half. There's a great danger of coasting through *Dover Beach*. It's summer, the sun is shining, the stage is open, you've had a 45-minute break, the horrors of the *Heath* lie behind you. But the scene needs the maximum of concentration. Lear switches from topic to topic, from hypocritical courtiers, to adultery, to the horrors of sex, to the injustices of the law, to the great stage of fools. He has taken on the free association of the Fool, of the modern stand-up comedian, and like them he needs the utmost energy and discipline. In the *Recognition* you need to fight the comforts of bed. Lear is on a wheel of fire, and even when he recognizes Cordelia his first thought is to drink the poison she must be offering him. Bradley and others talk of the 'ecstasy' of this meeting, and I wonder if we have read the same scene. A lesser dramatist would have written ecstasy; Shakespeare has written fear, bewilderment and guilt. It is such a short scene, and there are so many different things to play in it. *Prison* is even shorter, and Edmund is anxious to have them hustled away. As soon as Lear falls into the elegiac, there is no scene. Lear is desperate to make up for lost time, to reassure Cordelia that there is still a future for their love. And the last scene, where Lear is close to death? He enters carrying/dragging a body, shouting at all present to 'howl'. Is he at peace with his courtiers? No, they're 'men of stone. . . murderers, traitors all'. With his last gasp of energy he tries to will Cordelia back to life. Lear does not intend to go gentle into that good night, he will rage to the end. Lear's last four scenes are some of the best writing Shakespeare ever achieved. No wonder some actors decide to concentrate on the second half of the play; the writing is so grateful. But it's not easy.

Lamb's dictum that '*Lear* is essentially impossible to be represented on a stage' has permeated so much later criticism. There is a natural academic tendency to think the play can be better appreciated in the study, that its real power lies in its language. A radio performance might seem to be the ideal. Yet listening to an excellent radio production in autumn 2001, I was struck by how many of my memories of the play were visual. I'm not talking so much about settings, though designers usually respond to the breadth and difficulties of the play with sets of considerable imagination. I'm thinking more about what the characters look like, and the visual impact of what they do to one another. I can remember vividly how Lear, the Fool, the daughters, Poor Tom appeared in past productions. There are so many striking visual moments: the division of the kingdom, Lear and the Fool, Edmund wounding himself, Kent in the stocks, Lear in the storm, Poor Tom's entrance, Gloucester's eyes being put out, his 'suicide', Lear garlanded with flowers, the *Recognition*, Goneril and the poisoned Regan squabbling over Edmund, the duel, Lear carrying on Cordelia. Jonathan and Paul Brown paid great attention to the visual. One example lay in the gradual stripping of Lear. By the press night we had perfected a complicated process. In 1.4. I wore a three piece suit with tie, by my entrance into 2.4. I had lost my waistcoat and tie (in the vain journey to Cornwall's), during the scene I threw off my jacket (on the 'age is unnecessary' parody) and went out into the storm in shirt and braces. In 3.4. I shed trousers and boots, and I entered 3.6 in underpants and socks. This gradual stripping of the symbols of status, and reduction towards 'the thing itself', was much commented on by audiences. It would be odd in a play so much about sight and seeing, if its impact was not appreciated most fully on a stage. I find it as full of striking visual images as *Macbeth*, and more so than *Hamlet* or *Othello*.

Another of Bradley's strictures was that the play has too many characters, that 'Shakespeare has too vast a material to use with complete dramatic effectiveness'. No one would want to claim that the resolution of the double plot in Act Five is a masterpiece of construction. There is indeed too much material to cram into too little space. But what struck me most, playing the 'leading' part, was what a strong element of ensemble the play has. There are eleven leading parts in the play, twelve if you include Oswald. The parallel plot has in Gloucester, Edmund and Edgar parts of enormous richness. There is a case to be made that the true centre of the play is the 'education of Edgar'. The skill with which Shakespeare intertwines the two plots through Gloucester, Edmund, Goneril and Regan is enormous. All twelve protagonists have a journey through the play, the attribute an actor most looks for when playing a part. Compare this with the three other great tragedies, where Hamlet and Claudius, Othello and Iago, Macbeth and Lady Macbeth hog half the lines between them. What is also remarkable is how many of the characters think they have succeeded in their ambitions, only to have their triumph torn from them at the last moment. Oswald is a prime example. A lesser dramatist would have made him just a necessary go-between. But Shakespeare gives Oswald his own agenda. When he chances upon Gloucester he realizes,

> That eyeless head of thine was first framed flesh
> To raise my fortunes!

The 'bold peasant', Edgar, will clearly be no barrier to killing Gloucester and claiming the prize and preferment that follows. But just as success seems assured, it's snatched away from him. 'O untimely death, death!' exclaims Oswald, and it could be the death knell of so many others in the play.

As the run progresses the actor discovers how much the general *mis-en-scène* is working with him. I felt very happy with my clothes, with the descent from beautifully cut black suit to vest and pyjama trousers. They said so much about status and old age. I never fully came to terms with the set. I think the concept was brilliant, but I found myself having to force certain things to accommodate it, mainly in 2.4. and the *Heath*. At times I felt I was playing my cello, and the orchestra, far from accompanying me, were drowning me out. The thunder, lightning and rain were all legitimate, but I sometimes thought they belonged on a larger stage. This question of scale is very difficult to judge. It is a great mistake, particularly in Shakespeare, to think you give small, cinematic performances in studio spaces and large, grandiose ones in huge theatres. I have been in a production that transferred from the comparatively intimate Cottesloe at the National to the vast space of the Olivier. The amount of energy you need does not alter greatly, it's the way you use the energy, the degree to which you contain it or expand it that counts.

Nevertheless at times in *Lear* I felt both the set and my performance belonged in a larger space. On the heath I could scarcely have used more voice if I'd been in Drury Lane. After the press night the Old Vic were keen that we should transfer the production there, and it would have been interesting to see how comfortably it sat in a nine-hundred-seat theatre. But the set and auditorium concept proved too difficult and expensive to travel, and both the Old Vic transfer and the projected tour were eventually abandoned. Instead we ran the play for a further two and a half weeks, seventy-five perform-ances in all.

Lear proved an extremely emotional part, and I was often reminded of the thin line between technical control and emotional indulgence. Once, at the end of 1.4, I became so choked with rage and tears on:

> Life and death, I am ashamed
> That thou hast power to shake my manhood thus,
> That these hot tears, which break from me perforce,
> Should make thee worth them.

that I became quite incoherent, 'manhood' came out mysteriously as 'forehead' (much to Paul Shelley's amusement), and for a moment I had no idea what followed. Crying can be a great problem on stage, either because it won't happen to order or because it over-whelms you. This had happened to me unexpectedly three years before when I was playing the poet Philip Larkin in a new play by Ben Brown, *Larkin With Women*. Larkin, in hospital and near to death, recounted how Wordsworth had nearly been the death of him. He was driving down the M.1. at 70 mph, someone had read Words-worth's *Immortality Ode* on the radio, and Larkin found himself so blinded with tears that he nearly killed himself. It so happens that I perform a Wordsworth recital containing the ode, which *I* am quite unable to get through without crying. Twice during the Larkin run I found myself crying so helplessly that I thought I couldn't continue. Only the reminder that audiences have paid to cry themselves, not watch actors indulging, pulled me round. So I was determined not to cry in the last scene as I rocked Cordelia's body. Halfway through the run the tears came one night. Why should that have happened after forty performances? I had no idea, but I tried to replicate it the next night. No tears came, and I remembered a cautionary example. In 1992 I was playing Mazzini Dunn to Paul Scofield's Captain Shotover in a production of Shaw's *Heartbreak House*. Shotover pretends to mistake Mazzini for Bosun Dunn, 'a thief, a pirate, and a murderer'. When the real Bosun Dunn appears, Shotover turns on Mazzini crying, 'Why have you imposed upon me?' One night he attacked me with the full force of Lear to Goneril. It was shattering. I asked Paul later where it came from. He said he had no idea. He tried it again the next night, but it only rang ninety per cent true. He never attempted it again.

I said that by the time I came to run-throughs I thought I knew who I was, that I'd found a centre to my Lear. That feeling I never lost, and I think the key to it was language. I couldn't really know what it was to be eighty plus, to have been a king most of my life, or to feel I was losing my wits. All that was an imaginative leap. But I did come to think that I owned the words I spoke. As Peggy Ashcroft said, 'You can appreciate a line, but it's no good thinking you know how to say it until you've found the character.' But when you have found the character you then need the language. The two are complementary, vital partners. It's not enough to be thinking or feeling extreme, language and action are the only ways you can express them. I found myself responding to the verse more and more.

> Thou think'st 'tis much that this contentious storm
> Invades us to the skin: so 'tis to thee,
> But where the greater malady is fixed,
> The lesser is scarce felt. When the mind's free,
> The body's delicate: this tempest in my mind
> Doth from my senses take all feeling else,
> Save what beats there, filial ingratitude.
> Is it not as this mouth should tear this hand
> For lifting food to't? But I will punish home.

Lear is trying to cope with the tempest, his disintegrating mind, and his daughters' betrayal. He *needs* phrases as large as 'invades us to the skin', 'the greater malady is fixed', 'this tempest in my mind', and 'tear this hand' to express the size of his experience. I also began to feel certain recurring words like hammer blows; 'nature' in 2.4. and 'sight' in *Dover Beach*. This might seem like a conscious intellectual exercise, but in fact the words forced themselves upon me. The most profound was 'nothing'.

Nothing. I have sworn. (1.1.)
Nothing can be made out of nothing. (1.4.)
I will say nothing. (3.2.)
Coulds't thou save nothing? (3.4.)

Nothing may have a positive side, but nothing is what we shall all come to.

The reason why one acts particularly well on certain nights remains a riddle. It has nothing necessarily to do with preparation. I like Artur Rubinstein's account: 'Some nights you prepare perfectly, practise for three hours, eat the right things, lie down for an hour, and you start playing and within minutes you wonder: why am I playing so boringly? Another night you arrive late, don't practise, don't rest, wolf down a sandwich, start playing and wonder: why am I playing so well?' Of course you may fool yourself about the quality of what you're doing, but I think with experience you recognize when inspiration has struck. My best analogy is sporting. Batsmen, tennis players, footballers talk about having that extra half-second to think. I find it the same with acting. On occasions everything seems clear and possible. You have time to make decisions, to change direction, to try something new, to go further than ever before. You attack one line with a new ferocity, another you throw away and double the laugh. It's immensely exhilarating. It gives you a freedom and power you never thought possible. Both audience and cast recognize it. On the few occasions when I thought I was really playing the part, fellow actors always commented on it. But I have no idea why it happened.

As the run progressed I had the familiar feeling that our company had begun to own the play, or rather the version of the play that we had re-created. In 2001 Neil LaBute wrote and directed *The Shape of Things* at the Almeida. In the programme he wrote:

'It meant something to me when I wrote it, yes, but it means something else now, or many different things. I used to be the authority here but now I'm just a casual observer. The actors are the ones who own the piece. . . they know it better than anyone else. They should, anyway, or they've got no business being out there.'

John Whiting said much the same to us in 1961 about a university production of his play *Saint's Day*, and I think most playwrights would agree. I see no reason why Shakespeare, who wrote so many plays, had them performed so infrequently by our standards, and seemed so uninterested in their individual publication, should have felt any different. In my experience playwrights veer towards the simple, rather than the complex, explanation. Arthur Miller, challenged about a difficult page of his text at the RSC, answered: 'It's just a bridge passage. I should say it as fast as you can.' Sometimes in rehearsal, when we were bogged down in a particularly complex moment, I fancied I could hear Shakespeare saying the same. But just because Shakespeare may have seen no problems in a scene doesn't mean that the actors are off the hook. If actors have to 'own the piece', 'know it better than anyone else', a hundred and one contradictory thoughts may pass through their minds in a speech that their author had dashed off rapidly and intuitively. Actors only have 'business being out there' if they take the responsibility for an act of re-creation. It's what makes acting worthwhile.

As the run progressed, I got more and more feedback from audiences. Fortunately no one stood up at the end, as happened once at Stratford, and shouted, 'Perfidious interpretation!' From audience letters, certain threads emerged. One was clarity. 'The opening scenes has a searing inhabited clarity.' 'Line after line bounced up in fresh and thought provoking ways.' 'My daughter is studying the play for A level and by the end was pink with pleasure – so much had become clear.' It was a Lear that many found accessible. 'You let us find a rationale for his irrationality, reason for his unreason.' 'I've been watching Lears since Wolfit and I've admired quite a few for a variety of reasons. I think that yours may be the first which I have fully *understood*. Thank you.' Being an understandable Lear may not be the answer to the play, but it shows the merit of choosing a consistent path. One writer understood exactly what I was trying to do. 'It was a Lear not so much changed by his experiences it seemed to me, as *revealed* by them, with the end crowning the work as a whole.'

The set and the storm brought a variety of reactions. Some liked it: 'The storm scene was one of the most astonishing and effective things I've ever seen done on any stage. . . all too often one has to make do with some loud rumbles, a few flashes and such imagination as one possesses.' Some were concerned: 'My only criticism would be that the unrelenting storm had me worried about the actors risking vocal strain, so I was thinking about actors not characters.' Some took the line: 'You did very well, considering what you were up against.' Some could not accept the design concept: 'I couldn't square the literal and very real world of the Edwardian court at the beginning with having to emblematically represent a heath. . . the desk always looked like a blinking desk, not the entrance to a cave or shelter.' But some thought Paul and Jonathan had pulled it off: 'The storm looked and sounded amazing – there's something about the real sound of water on wood that strikes a chill into one's bourgeois heart. I would defend its taking up attention . . . it was very cunning the way it was very loud but didn't interfere with the words at all.' My fear about the television in 1.1. proved exaggerated: most people thought it helped rather than hindered.

My attempts to vie with the storm were not all in vain. 'You had an animal physicality which made him dangerous from first to last.' Timothy West wrote: 'A wonderful performance and of such ENERGY – what do you eat/drink/practise/do to keep your voice in shape after six such powerful storms per week. I'd love to know.' The last scenes of the play are nothing if not moving. 'I taught the play from 1962 – 98 and have seen many productions but never one that moved me so much.' 'For me it was the complex humanity of the man that was so interesting.' And one we might have written ourselves: 'For the first time I left a performance of *Lear* having travelled the emotional, physical and spiritual journey that Shakespeare so brilliantly captured.'

So much for people who'd paid for their seats. Now for the press. London is exceptional, perhaps unique, in having so many newspapers and journals that carry theatre reviews. They flourish by disagreement. In my experience it's impossible to present a production so good that it doesn't get one stinker, or so bad that it doesn't get one rave. But I think, in the case of a great tragedy, the range of their reactions are very illuminating about the play.

THE PRODUCTION    James Inverne (*Sunday Telegraph*): 'A production that, often brilliantly, blends symbolism with realism.' Michael Billington (*The Guardian*): 'As an evening it makes up in vigour what it lacks in subtlety.' Charles Spencer (*Daily Telegraph*): 'Jonathan Kent is bowing out of the Almeida with a flash of inspiration. . . a breathtakingly fine staging.' Katherine Duncan-Jones (*New Statesman*): 'Despite all its excesses (too many gimmicks and gadgets, too much noise, water and furniture moving) this is an important production. Don't miss the Almeida's last bus.' John Peter (*Sunday Times*): 'It bears all the hallmarks of [Jonathan Kent's] great gifts: theatricality combined with intelligence, a willingness to take risks and re-assess masterpieces, a fierce concentration on the text and what it tells you about the characters, and a rare and blessed ability to work for as well as with his actors, to liberate as well as direct them and make them glow in their own light.'

THE SET    Words like 'riveting', 'spectacular', 'intelligent', and 'exciting' were much bandied about. Spencer: [Its collapse is] 'a thrilling metaphor for both the transience of power and the fragility of human sanity.' Susannah Clapp (*The Observer*): 'It can't be a good sign when the climactic moment in a Shakespeare play is a magnificent, synchronized collapse of the set.' Peter: 'The set as symbol. Fine, but there is something self-conscious, almost programmatic about all this.' Nicholas de Jongh (*Evening Standard*): 'It seems as if the action is staged in the solitude of Lear's mind, that we're watching a right royal nightmare, spurred by dementia. Then, in a thrilling *coup-de-théâtre*, the huge set begins to split, break and fall as the storm starts. Rain pelts down upon the collapsed palace study, which becomes the blasted heath. . . a nightmare tempest in the monarch's mind.'

DOES THE LEAR CONVINCE?    Benedict Nightingale (*The Times*): (Preview) 'Has a performer with a gift for portraying gentle people the power to tackle Shakespeare's raving king? . . . The mountain awaits.' (Review) 'I shouldn't have worried. Davies produces stronger and more plentiful emotions than I had assumed to be within his range.' Kate Bassett (*Independent on Sunday*): 'Indeed Ford Davies – the cuddliest old softie in British theatre [the things you discover!] – proves a Lear of startling authority and snarling ferocity.' Rhoda Koenig (*The Independent*): 'He might do for the director of a branch office, but as Lear he lacks a certain variety. Lear arrogant, Lear affronted, Lear compassionate, Lear demented, all speak in the same curmudgeonly rant.' Billington: 'He has a commanding presence, a resonant voice and is every inch the patriarchal bully confronting his own moral blindness.'

DOES THE ANGER INTO MADNESS WORK?    De Jongh: 'We have rarely seen a more dangerous and angry Lear. . . the violent unpredictability of this frosty king signals something which the text accommodates. This Lear's behaviour is symptomatic of early-stage senile dementia.' Duncan-Jones: 'Davies's Lear is mad almost from the outset, in the Elizabethan or the modern American sense of 'mad': he is furiously angry, sometimes comically so.' Clapp: 'It's hard for anyone to look other than quaintly dotty tiptoeing through puddles in pants and socks.' Alistair Macaulay (*Financial Times*): 'I have never heard a louder Lear. . . he bellows at the elements in a kind of gargantuan gargle.' Billington: 'If his performance is too fortissimo and lacking in internal contradictions it is because the production itself demands a raging Lear.' Inverne: 'The grizzled, hulking figure hurls himself around the stage, bellowing with frustration – but he also knows when not to shout. His most impressive moment is the cursing of Goneril.' Nightingale: [His voice is] 'apt to develop a rough, grinding sound at climaxes. . .but that doesn't finally matter, for what's inside it is nothing less than the emotional truth. . . its prime strength is the subtle yet forceful lesson in feeling that Davies gives us as he moves from raging self-pity to compassion and calm.'

WERE THEY MOVED?    Bassett: 'The tenderness of the death scene is heartrending. A great performance.' Michael Coveney (*Daily Mail*): 'He does not move you, or rather me, to tears.' Billington: 'When they come, Ford Davies's moments of calm are stunning.' Clapp: 'His address over the body of Cordelia is a series of musing, plangent, rhetorical questions.' Spencer: 'It is the beautifully rapt reconciliation with Cordelia and his abstracted grief as he tenderly cradles her dead body in his arms that nudge the performance into greatness.'

DOES LEAR CHANGE?    Nightingale: 'He's a man slowly but genuinely transformed. . . from a ferocious Old Testament prophet' to a 'demented scrounger from Cardboard City.' Spencer: 'His transition from snarling tyranny to loving tenderness is played with such truth, and such clarity, that one feels like cheering.' Inverne: 'And if he misses the ability shared by the great Lears to catch the transformation of a soul, he convincingly depicts the humbling and healing of a man.' Peter: 'His Lear learns something by the end, but. . . he does not fundamentally change. It is the rather desperate idealism from nineteenth-century Germany, overlaid with crass Marxist optimism, that has conditioned us to expect grown-up people to 'change', i.e. improve, by experience. Ford Davies's Lear is much the same difficult, ratty old man at the end as he has been at the beginning. He has learnt that he has made a catastrophic mistake.

He is penitent but not humble, and you watch him in judgmental compassion. . . Like King Ixion of mythology, he is bound upon a wheel of fire, and Ford Davies never lets you forget that, like Ixion, Lear has created his own monsters.'

I think you can see why I don't read the notices immediately. One question I have left to last. Having played it seventy-five times, what did I come to feel the part of Lear was about? The first two acts felt like a terrifying exposure of a family's inability to communicate. An aged patriarch sheds his power. His two heirs can only feel secure in this sudden rush of responsibility by cutting him down to size. His communication with the daughter he loves reveals they have no common language. He goes out into the wilderness, and this condemns him to an early death. But he is afforded a curse and a blessing. He goes mad, and he is liberated. He lives for a time in a dream/nightmare, where truths about himself and society are exposed. Things that he had always known, but buried, about sex, power, and injustice are revealed to him. He wakes from the dream, and all that he remembers is the primacy of love. This knowledge won't stave off disaster and death, but it brings him some understanding and healing. The play seems to me to say that life is crippled by a failure of understanding, that inequality and injustice corrode our existence, but that human nature can – even in the most extreme circumstances – rise above this. It feels, despite everything, a hopeful play.

# APPENDIX

# A CONVERSATION WITH JOHN BARTON

*John and I talked in September 2002,*
*five months after the production.*

JB  I have co-directed *Lear* but never directed it in full, though it moves me in the study perhaps more than any other Shakespeare play. This is perhaps because it is not only the most emotionally charged, but also the most demanding verbally, and I don't think I would know how to help actors achieve both. Perhaps Shakespeare demands too much from the actors here, at least in places. And though you certainly brought it off heroically, I felt you had to keep forcing it along in the first half, perhaps more than felt right for you. At the beginning Lear seems all-masterful, but very soon the part becomes essentially reactive: he grows emotionally violent, but in spite of his fulminations he remains passive. Perhaps that's why he needs to talk so much: when he loses power, words are all he has.

Lear, like Timon and Leontes, confronts an audience with a kind of verbal overkill which is very hard for an actor to sustain. Cutting is needed but is not the answer; the actor playing Lear needs more help from a director than I am confident of providing. The trap in rehearsal seems to me to lie in trying to find a logical or psychological through-line in the part. Shakespeare does not always bother to provide that. It is we today who require it of him and impose a logic which was not his.

OFD  Are you saying that *Hamlet, Macbeth* and *Othello* are leading inexorably to a conclusion that you can partly anticipate, but not so with *Lear*?

JB  Well, in *Lear* it's less certain, and at the end it's less certain whether it's worked out well anyway. Lear dies and the survivors go on. We don't know who's going to live happily ever after; Kent just signs off, and the rest disappear.

OFD    Were you very influenced by Peter Brook's 1962 production?

JB    No, I wasn't. I admired it terrifically, but I didn't like one or two key things. I understand the difference between the Quarto and the Folio, which leads to cutting the joint-stool scene [3.6.], but I don't agree with cutting the servants after the blinding of Gloucester or the cutting down of Albany. Albany seems to me very important; the quiet man takes over and retains a certain integrity. I like that very much.

OFD    Brook also cut Edmund's death-bed repentance.

JB    Yes, I regret that. Such changes are typical of Shakespeare. He is often accused of inconsistency and contradiction. Yet 'contradiction' seems the key word for me in Shakespeare: the actor should always embrace that. Human beings contradict themselves all the time. Perhaps Shakespeare started with how his sources ended the story, then felt it wasn't the way he was going, and so began to ring the changes and even turn the plot on its head.

OFD    We've often talked of the Elizabethan's notion – or lack of notion – of 'character'.

JB    I think it's very significant that they didn't have the word 'character'; it came in with the novel in 1750. They had the word 'part'. This didn't mean that they lacked a deep sense of complex and ambiguous character, but no Elizabethan actor turned up to Shakespeare's rehearsals and said 'I don't understand my character', or 'I don't think my character would do this' – that wasn't in their currency or culture. If the first thing an actor asks is, 'How does my character work?', he is prejudging what are the clues in the text that reveal and define character. I prefer the word 'temperament'. If you find a contradiction in a speech you have to first ask 'why', what clues does it give you; but don't dodge the challenge by cutting it.

OFD    Do you find the part of Lear full of contradictions?

JB    Oh yes. One problem of Lear is that there is so much text, so much raging. How does an actor sustain it without boring the audience? The audience picks up quickly that a person is very angry, very unhappy, suicidal, deeply emotional or whatever. That can be expressed in a few lines, but I've always thought Shakespeare's long emotional speeches are about trying to *deal* with emotion, not just expressing them. There are many places where a speech goes in different directions. If you play rage and anger consistently in the first half it leads to vocal forcing, and the text itself can become muddled. I'm not sure an actor can sustain a text at full blast for very long. But I don't know the answer to this. You had to rage and you found the vocal power to sustain it. So you solved it, but I wasn't sure that you should have been pushed so hard to do so.

A key question I remember asking Trevor Nunn, when we did the play in 1976, was, 'At what point can we say with assurance that Lear actually goes mad?' I still don't know the answer. He's frightened of going mad, therefore he's trying not to go mad – that's obvious enough – but I'm not sure that he ever goes *utterly* mad. He says too many wise things in the course of undergoing a massive mental crisis and breakdown. I think the second half is easier for an actor to play because it's more human, and Lear achieves glimpses of wisdom. He says some perfectly rational things, then goes wild for a while, and then has moments that are completely sane. I think when he cries, 'Howl, howl, howl', it is not madness, it's about grief.

So what is madness? It can be about guilt, shame, dread – you name it. For whatever reason, what his daughters do to him breaks down and destroys what Lear is. When he goes out into a storm he gets a certain release. He asks the heavens to descend, but that is not exactly madness. He then gets involved with Edgar, a seeming madman, and takes him perfectly seriously. That's pretty neurotic and strange, but is it mad? Like Edgar, doesn't he take on a new role to deal with a new situation?

I don't think the medical vocabulary of today, certainly not that of Shakespeare's day, gives us the answer. The word 'mad' itself, its origin and meaning, is about rage: 'mad with rage', 'mad with grief'. It means an excess of emotion triggered by something that's happened to you, or something you've done. So I question the madness.

OFD   What about *Dover Beach*, when he's talking about press-money, archers and mice?

JB   I would argue: 'Don't decide whether you're mad or not, try the scene. Start by being playful'. He's obsessed by his daughters and what's happened to him, and he comes on and plays games. Is that madness? To watch an actor having to act mad for a long period leads to diminishing returns. Ask yourself rather when the text is not mad, and explore the variety of his raging moods and pains. 'What is he actually *doing*?' – that is always a key question.

OFD   What about the soliloquy? Is there a distinction between the Elizabethan actor routinely addressing the audience and a speech where he is left alone on stage?

JB   We can't be certain about that, and I don't think anyone has given their mind fully to it, though I've tried to. It's perfectly clear when the text says 'aside', and when you're left solo on a stage – that's straightforward. But as a basic need for an Elizabethan actor was to communicate verbally with the audience, I think there's a lot of text where one should boldly address the audience *within* speeches, switching back and forth from listener to audience. I've come to believe that more and more strongly, and in practice I've found it works. I think today we don't dare really to explore that. If an actor is playing a major part, his relationship with the audience matters just as much as his relationship with the other characters. Henry V is a good example: his key speech, 'Upon the King', doesn't work unless he speaks directly to the audience.

OFD   Who is the most satisfying Lear that you've seen?

JB   I honestly don't know. I remember some great productions, but I don't remember a great Lear, only many Lears with great moments.

OFD   What does this say about the part? Is it too contradictory, or not well enough written?

JB   I think in time some director or actor will solve it, will thrash out the problems and reach a solution that works. I thought you went very far towards solving it, but you were confronted with pressures and problems, which you loyally and triumphantly worked on, but you couldn't finally go further than your brief. You can't play an interpretation, you can only enact one.

OFD    I wonder if Shakespeare made it such an ensemble play because he realized he couldn't put Lear right at the centre of the play?

JB    It's normal for Shakespeare to have a double plot going, and I think in *Lear* the second plot is in story-telling terms easier to handle. This is often so. In *Twelfth Night* Orsino and Viola is I suppose the main plot, but the main story is played out in Olivia's household. Lear is a loose cannon: if he supposedly going mad early in the play, he hasn't got a plot of action. He is within plots pursued by others.

OFD    The last decision he makes is going out into the storm.

JB    Exactly, and then he starts to enjoy himself. Don't you think?

OFD    He does enjoy quite a lot of Acts Three and Four.

JB    Yes, I knew you'd do the second half well. I think the crux in actually rehearsing a play is to do with the relationship and chemistry between director and actors. Not just whether they agree or not: they may be in complete harmony, but they may not spark the right thing off in one another.

OFD    Why do you think you've never seen a way of doing the play?

JB    It's possibly sheer cowardice or ineptness. At school I got into Shakespeare through *King Lear.* I remember reading Lear's awakening, and how the scene moved me very much. I never planned to be a director, and now I've done most of the plays I find myself as passionate about *Lear* as ever, but I still don't know how to do it.

OFD    With Lear do you think the strong patriarch is a better path to go down than the ailing old man?

JB    I think it depends on how each actor decides to launch the start of the play. You have to set up a lot of skittles in the first scene, and there are no absolutes about how Lear himself is, because he very soon begins to fall apart. Whether he is a monomaniac in the first scene doesn't matter for long, because as soon as you get to Goneril and the knights we're in a different world anyway. How one does the first scene simply helps to launch an actor into orbit and make him feel right, but it may not greatly affect what then happens immediately afterwards. Consistently cosmic Lears don't work. I completely accepted your way of doing 1.1, because I knew you would change so rapidly.

OFD   Do you think Goneril and Regan are out to get Lear? Actresses have found them so difficult, even Judi Dench escaped the 1976 production as soon as she could.

JB   It's the one part that defeated her. She said, 'Can't I kick him in the foot with a poisoned boot?' Goneril and Regan are the most difficult women's parts in Shakespeare without a doubt. Lear asks to be destroyed because of what he does, but it's part of the needful *mechanism* of the plot that they must smash him. I think playing them as rationally as possible at the beginning is the right way, however much they soon develop into monsters. Lear's problem is that he can't cope with their attack, and instead of counter-attacking with his hundred knights he loses his temper and becomes vulnerable by a quite understandable self-pity. He should have restored his own authority, but he doesn't because he can't. Something internal is triggered in him, and he blows it. Goneril is the demon, and Regan is the weaker one. Goneril must not play 'I am evil', but 'I am a politician', which she is. Power corrupts, and both sisters are corrupted from the beginning, though they hide it.

OFD   How do you see the Fool?

JB   Michael Williams was the greatest Fool I've seen. He had all the skills of the music-hall clown, but he also had great humanity and a sort of cosmic wisdom. He could do them all, because he was an unusual mixture as an actor. He had great range in Shakespeare; he could do the straight parts and romantic parts and every conceivable kind of clown.

OFD   And Gloucester?

JB   I've seen a lot of good Gloucesters; your David Ryall was very good. I think the part can always work, it's not a problem. But he's not as big a person as Lear; the important thing is always to cast the two actors the right way round.

OFD    And Edgar?

JB    Ah, nobody's ever solved that one. He's as difficult as Lear. I have never met a happy Edgar in mid-rehearsal. You give it to a young, eager actor, who doesn't know how hard it's going to be, and hope for the best. Edgar takes over at the end and becomes more and more important and rational. No one understands really why he goes so far over the top with his madman act in Act Three, or why he never reveals himself to his father, though one can or has to invent a reason and play it. All one can say is 'Trust it, go for it' and it will work. But if an actor thinks too nicely about insoluble complexities he too is in danger of going mad himself.

# PROGRAMME NOTE

BY GAIL MCCRACKEN PRICE (HARVARD UNIVERSITY, U.S.A.)

*An actor doesn't usually see the programme until the night of the first preview. Does the main article have any connection with what we're doing on stage? Sometimes you read an interpretation, commissioned months beforehand, that bears no relation to the production as it has evolved. Sometimes it contains material of such insight that you wished you'd had it available in rehearsal – too late to change everything on the night of the first performance. Happily Gail McCracken Price has written something of great relevance to what we were attempting.*

In the psychology of the sixteenth century as expressed by the French moral philosopher, Peter de La Primaudaye and read by Shakespeare, the soul and the spirit were believed to animate human life. The *soul* was defined as the energy of life in the material body and brain. The *spirit* was understood to enliven the immaterial mind in its primary function of seeking wisdom and truth. The soul gains knowledge through perception of the senses and cognising data. The spirit understands through discernment. Historically the soul and spirit of the divinely appointed monarch are under the protection of God. The sovereign is to retain the title, power and prerogative of king until his mortal body dies. Should he renounce his kingship, he then becomes vulnerable to the vicissitudes of ordinary men. In *The Tragedy of King Lear* the eponymous king is engaged in a cataclysmic struggle for the survival of his soul and spirit, a struggle driven by his decision to divide and dispose of his kingdom.

Lear convenes his court to enact his darker purpose. Made fearful by the deterioration of age and threat of internecine conflict, he announces his intent to surrender his powers while seeking to retain the name of King and the company of one hundred knights. Lear has not engaged his spirit in a discerning search for wisdom, nor has he sought to understand the consequences of his actions for the safety of his kingdom or himself. Rather his concern is to avoid future conflict by surrendering the material reality of his kingdom in the form of generous gifts of land and wealth to his daughters and their husbands.

Lear has made Cordelia's devotion the focal point of his remaining life. He begs her tenderness of heart and her loving nurturance of his royal spirit and human soul; Cordelia proffers dutiful and generous devotion to him as her father. In her response, Cordelia dissolves his royal identity into his role as parent, indicating she 'shall never marry like my sisters to love my father all'. The result is a cataclysm of tectonic proportions, deforming the mind and spirit of the King and threatening the existence of his youngest daughter. She has in effect condemned him to hell, and he responds in kind, placing her value beneath the barbarity of the Scythian. Kent confronts Lear with his madness and inability to 'see clearly'. Lear banishes his loyal and zealous servant from the country, a country he no longer rules.

Primaudaye would explain Lear's reaction as one of corrupted judgment. Lear's reason and judgment have become infected with an intense concern for personal safety and gratification of his aging soul and body. Primaudaye observes 'the more evil and carnal are the affection [emotions and passions], the more in number and the more violent: yea such as do not only trouble and pervert the internal senses of the soul, but the external senses also of the body.' Lear cannot see clearly. Without Cordelia, Lear's life begins to shatter with grief as he attempts to negotiate the retirement he has created in his mind with the plans of those who must live it day to day.

A sixteenth-century understanding of grief is not confined to a sense of loss, but includes a sorrow related to malevolence. In Primaudaye's explanation of grief, the heart is under the pressure of a 'present evil' from a 'grievous wound'. Without life-preserving joy inherent in hope, the body and mind will slowly die from the 'dolour and torment' arising from fearful anticipation of further evil. Tom McAlindon has observed that grief can transmute love into a hunger for revenge that knows no bounds. This hunger for revenge emerges when an individual senses the personality is threatened with collapse, and the vitality begins to depart from the soul and spirit. Lear is threatened with this terrifying dissolution of his mind and body. The terror will give way to vengeful violence when reasons for self-restraint are removed.

After the banishment of Cordelia and Kent, Goneril and Regan speak of their father's radical changes with age, changes embedded in his poor judgment and made worse by their withdrawal from him. They move away from fear of becoming victims of the deteriorating reason that caused him to cast out the sister he has always loved most. After the abdication, if we were to enter their quiet corner without preconception, we would see two well-gowned women, without a mother to guide them or mollify their father, and perhaps recently married as they are without children. They have witnessed in silence and shock their father's favourite child and his devoted Earl banished. They anticipate further manifestations of his impulsive rage if their father retains his kingly authority and the support of his knights. Regan suggests time to think, Goneril responds with something of her father's impulsiveness.

Once in her castle, Lear's knights appear disorderly to Goneril, as does his all-licensed Fool, who regularly inveighs against her. The debate about the behaviour of the knights is a function of who owns the eyes being turned on them. To Lear they are his companions and now his single source of pleasure. In his eyes they are the healing balm, returning to him some sense of prowess, freedom and even the joyful moments he remembers as King. To Goneril they are a source of disruptive power that could threaten her position within her household. To Albany's particular brand of morality and social engagement, they are inconsequential, and he calls for patience as the well-respected sixteenth century antidote to intemperance. Goneril initially attempts reason and flattery by speaking to his good wisdom, hoping to gain her father's understanding of her resistance to the behaviour of his entourage. He responds with an expression of threat as his identity begins to destabilize: 'Who is it that can tell me who I am?' The Fool replies: 'Lear's shadow', provoking an outburst of grief from the beleaguered man. Lear's cognition begins to deteriorate as his sense of being and substance fades.

Embedded in her own real and imagined fears, Goneril seems unaware of the effect of her request that he disquantity his train. She is treating him now as guest and father, giving the request the same magnitude of consequence as Cordelia's response in the love test. To surrender his knights is to surrender the name of King and what remains of his royal identity. He in turn calls forth the goddess of

Nature to curse her identity as the future mother of heirs, calling for no child to emerge from her derogate body. Her reaction suggests that she still believes that his curse will be fulfilled with the same effect as those issued when he was in charge of his kingdom. Any remaining wish for reconciliation in Goneril's heart turns from fear into malevolence as she seeks power over Lear's mind in the way he has claimed it over her reproductive life. Her father now openly becomes her adversary and she strives to empower herself against him. R.A. Foakes, in footnotes to the Arden text, observes that Shakespeare's conception of Goneril seems to change. From this point, after Lear's call for the destruction of her capacity for mothering and with it the milk of human kindness, it is difficult to find traces of human kindness in her.

Goneril seeks an alliance with Gloucester's illegitimate son, Edmund, who has turned against everyone who cannot help him gain a place in a culture offering little opportunity to those who are illegitimate, regardless of merit. According to Roy Baumeister, had Edmund agreed to the diminished appraisal he received from society, he would have become morose and self-absorbed. By rejecting society's valuation of him as illegitimate, he is energized to seek redress. He desires to restructure society with the base (himself) transferred to the pinnacle by whatever means possible. He eschews all human bonds beyond those enabling him to make the climb, turning his malevolence on a father who loves him as he loves his proper son and a brother who by nature does not suspect harm because he is so far from initiating any to others. Discarding all love, Edmund is able to release himself from any internalised guilt that would place restraints on his actions and motivate reparation and responsibility. He is testimony to the influence of cultural practice on human violence. Goneril is drawn to his virility. In times of terror, when the personality as well as the body is threatened with dissolution, the virility of aggressive men heightens their attraction to women, keeping both in sufficient connection with the body to know they are still alive and reasonably intact. This is the need-filled love primarily of the soul.

The love of the spirit between Kent and Lear, and the Fool and his master has a different effect. As Kent (in the disguise of Caius) and the Fool come close to Lear in his need, his mind begins to revive. In the midst of hope that Regan will rescue him, and hearing the familiar prattling of his Fool, Lear's spirit recovers the capacity for compassion and confession. 'I did her wrong.' The referent of his confession is unclear in this moment, and becomes evident only in reunion with Cordelia. When he arrives at the castle of Regan and Cornwall, he is again betrayed and reduced in spirit, mind and body to an outcast. In the storm raging without, he opens the gates to the vehemence within, a response understood in the sixteenth century as anger overtaking the will:

> . . .after that anger has once got the bridle at will, the whole
> mind and judgment is so blinded and carried headlong, that
> an angry man thinks of nothing but revenge, in so much that
> he forgets himself and cares not what he does, or what harm
> will light upon himself in so doing, so that he may be avenged.
> And many times he will murmur against heaven and earth. . .
>                                   (Primaudaye, 1594, 11:55, 497)

Lear's friends attempt to shelter him from the tempest within and without. In the hovel where he is taken to rest and recover, he comes upon the disguised Edgar, now a wandering Bedlam beggar uttering words heard by priests exorcizing devils. Lear's ability to cognize the world has sufficiently narrowed to the point that he imagines Poor Tom exists in his present state because of treatment by his daughters. In his own outcast state, Lear experiences the elements as Poor Tom knows them, and responds with a profound compassion.

On the heath, wisdom and madness merge in the old King, whose vehemence is all but spent. Now removed from virtually all human connectedness, Lear creates a fantasy world that echoes the fantasy landscape Edgar designs to preserve the life of his blind father, Gloucester. Newly empowered in his crown of flowers, Lear reclaims his kingship, providing himself with money, commenting on the technique of an archer, throwing a gauntlet to challenge a giant. Shakespeare understands that all human madness contains elements of personal history, of truth, and even of compassion. When the blind Gloucester appears in his presence, Lear constructs a judgment scene in which he forgives adultery and from some deep inner recess recreates a brothel scene, setting off a cacophony of vile images. Like a child fearful of acquiring the same malady, Lear cruelly mocks Gloucester's blindness, pours venom on deceit, mixes 'matter and impertinency' by infusing Biblical texts with images having pornographic elements. When Gloucester notes his madness,

Lear proves his sanity as he bemoans this world that begins and ends in grief: 'We came crying hither. . . to this great stage of fools.'

In reunion with Cordelia's gentle soul, Lear surrenders his great rage to her love and again finds himself in her eyes. In Jonathan Kent's words, the play is a 'flight toward love' as Lear moves from transactional relatedness, through madness into compassionate love for the daughter who returns his devotion.

# PRODUCTION CREDITS

*Cast in order of speaking*

| | |
|---|---|
| EARL OF KENT | Paul Jesson |
| EARL OF GLOUCESTER | David Ryall |
| EDMUND | James Frain |
| KING LEAR | Oliver Ford Davies |
| GONERIL | Suzanne Burden |
| CORDELIA | Nancy Carroll |
| REGAN | Lizzy McInnerny |
| DUKE OF ALBANY | Paul Shelley |
| DUKE OF CORNWALL | David Robb |
| DUKE OF BURGUNDY | Richard Trinder |
| KING OF FRANCE | Lex Shrapnel |
| EDGAR | Tom Hollander |
| OSWALD | David Sibley |
| FOOL | Anthony O'Donnell |
| KNIGHT | Darren Greer |
| CURAN | Hugh Simon |
| OLD MAN | Sam Beazley |
| GENTLEMAN | Paul Benzing |

*Other parts played by members of the Company*

| | |
|---|---|
| *Direction* | Jonathan Kent |
| *Design* | Paul Brown |
| *Lighting* | Mark Henderson |
| *Music* | Jonathan Dove |
| *Sound* | John A Leonard |

|                           |                                      |
|--------------------------:|--------------------------------------|
| *Casting*                 | Fiona Weir, Mary Selway              |
| *Assistant Director*      | Owen Lewis                           |
| *Fight Director*          | Terry King                           |
| *Voice Coach*             | Patsy Rodenburg                      |
| *Production Manager*      | James Crout                          |
| *Production Photographer* | Ivan Kyncl                           |
| *Company Manager*         | Rupert Carlile                       |
| *Stage Manager*           | Maris Sharp                          |
| *Deputy Stage Manager*    | Alex Sims                            |
| *Assistant Stage Managers*| Patrick Birch, Helena Lane-Smith     |
| *Head of Wardrobe*        | Edward Gibbon                        |
| *Wardrobe Supervisor*     | Spencer Kitchen                      |
| *Hair and Make-up*        | Rick Strickland                      |
| *Costume Supervisor*      | Rachel Dickson                       |
| *Chief Technician*        | Jason Wescombe                       |
| *Master Carpenter*        | Craig Emerson                        |

# FURTHER READING

John Barton, *Playing Shakespeare*, London and New York: Methuen, 1984

Jonathan Bate, *The Genius of Shakespeare*, London: Picador, 1997

Harold Bloom, *Shakespeare: the Invention of the Human*, London: Fourth Estate, 1999

A.C. Bradley, *Shakespearean Tragedy*, London: Macmillan, 1905

Simon Callow, *Charles Laughton: a Difficult Actor*, London: Methuen, 1987

Brian Cox, *The Lear Diaries*, London: Methuen, 1992

Stephen A. Diamond, *Anger, Madness, and the Daimonic*, New York: State University of New York, 1996

R.A. Foakes, *King Lear*, Arden ed., 1997

R.A. Foakes, *Hamlet versus Lear*, Cambridge and New York: Cambridge University Press, 1993

H. Granville-Barker, *Prefaces to Shakespeare, Vol I*, London: B.T. Batsford, 1930

Germaine Greer, *Shakespeare*, Oxford: Oxford Paperbacks, 1986

Jay L. Halio (ed.), *Critical Essays on Shakespeare's King Lear*, New York: Simon and Schuster, 1996

Ronald Harwood, *Sir Donald Wolfit*, London: Secker and Warburg, 1971

Park Honan, *Shakespeare: a Life*, Oxford: Oxford Paperbacks, 1998

Ted Hughes, *Shakespeare and the Goddess of Complete Being*, London and New York: Faber and Faber, 1992

Frank Kermode, *Shakespeare's Language*, London: Allen Lane Press, 2000

Frank Kermode (ed.), *King Lear Casebook,* Basingstoke: Macmillan, 1992

James Ogden and Arthur H. Scouten (eds.), *Lear from Study to Stage,* Cranbury: Associated University Press, 1997

Kiernan Ryan (ed.), *King Lear New Casebook,* Houndsmill: Macmillan, 1997

Kenneth Tynan, *Curtains,* London: Longman, 1961

Rene Weiss (ed.), *King Lear: a Parallel Text Edition,* London: Longman Annotated Texts, 1993

Stanley Wells (ed.), *The History of King Lear: the Oxford Shakespeare,* Oxford and New York: Oxford University Press, 2000

Stanley Wells (ed.), *Shakespeare in the Theatre,* Oxford and New York: Oxford Paperbacks, 1997

# INDEX